Hands-On Machine Learning with TensorFlow.js

A guide to building ML applications integrated with web technology using the TensorFlow.js library

Kai Sasaki

BIRMINGHAM - MUMBAI

Hands-On Machine Learning with TensorFlow.js

Commissioning Editor: Sunith Shetty
Acquisition Editor: Devika Battike
Content Development Editor: Athikho Sapuni Rishana
Senior Editor: Sofi Rogers
Technical Editor: Joseph Sunil
Copy Editor: Safis Editing
Project Coordinator: Aishwarya Mohan
Proofreader: Safis Editing
Indexer: Priyanka Dhadke
Production Designer: Aparna Bhagat

First published: November 2019

Production reference: 1261119

Published by Packt Publishing Ltd.
Livery Place
35 Livery Street
Birmingham
B3 2PB, UK.

ISBN 978-1-83882-173-9

www.packt.com

Packt.com

Subscribe to our online digital library for full access to over 7,000 books and videos, as well as industry-leading tools to help you plan your personal development and advance your career. For more information, please visit our website.

Why subscribe?

- Spend less time learning and more time coding with practical eBooks and videos from over 4,000 industry professionals

- Improve your learning with skill plans built especially for you

- Get a free eBook or video every month

- Fully searchable for easy access to vital information

- Copy and paste, print, and bookmark content

Did you know that Packt offers eBook versions of every book published, with PDF and ePub files available? You can upgrade to the eBook version at www.packt.com and, as a print book customer, you are entitled to a discount on the eBook copy. Get in touch with us at customercare@packtpub.com for more details.

At www.packt.com, you can also read a collection of free technical articles, sign up for a range of free newsletters, and receive exclusive discounts and offers on Packt books and eBooks.

Contributors

About the author

Kai Sasaki works as a software engineer at Treasure Data. He engages in developing large-scale distributed systems to make data valuable. His passion for creating artificial intelligence by processing large-scale data led him to the field of machine learning. He is one of the initial contributors to TensorFlow.js and keeps working to add new operators that are required for new types of machine learning models. Because of his work, he received the Google Open Source Peer Bonus in 2018.

About the reviewers

Edoh Kodjo graduated twice as an engineer in networking and in computer science, and is a software developer/data scientist. He started developing an interest in machine learning and artificial intelligence soon after graduating. Since then, his interest in the field has kept on growing. He currently works as a software engineer on a project for computer vision. As a frontend and JavaScript fanatic, he is a **machine learning for the web** advocate. Here is his motto—*Life is an endless road, coding is an endless loop for a while!*, which sums up how much he loves coding.

Nick Bourdakos is a developer advocate at IBM in NYC and the creator of Cloud Annotations, a collaborative open source image annotation tool for training computer vision models. His expertise is in machine learning, mainly deep learning applied to computer vision problems. He is passionate when it comes to teaching people about machine learning and has a course on YouTube regarding TensorFlow.js.

Packt is searching for authors like you

If you're interested in becoming an author for Packt, please visit `authors.packtpub.com` and apply today. We have worked with thousands of developers and tech professionals, just like you, to help them share their insight with the global tech community. You can make a general application, apply for a specific hot topic that we are recruiting an author for, or submit your own idea.

Table of Contents

Preface

TensorFlow.js is a framework that enables you to create performant **machine learning** (**ML**) applications that run smoothly in a web browser. With this book, you will learn how to use TensorFlow.js to implement various ML models through an example-based approach.

In this book, you'll understand how ML models can be built on the web. Moving on, you will get to grips with using the TensorFlow.js ecosystem to develop applications more efficiently. The book will then guide you through implementing ML techniques and algorithms such as regression, clustering, **fast Fourier transform** (**FFT**), and dimensionality reduction. You will later use the Bellman equation to solve **Markov decision process** (**MDP**) problems and understand how it is related to reinforcement learning. Finally, you will explore techniques for deploying ML-based web applications and training models with TensorFlow Core. Throughout this ML book, you'll discover useful tips and tricks that will build on your knowledge.

By the end of this book, you will be equipped with the skills you need to create your own web-based ML applications and fine-tune models to achieve high performance.

Who this book is for

This book is for web developers who want to learn how to integrate ML techniques with web-based applications from scratch. This book will also appeal to data scientists, ML practitioners, and deep learning enthusiasts who are looking to perform accelerated, browser-based ML on the web using TensorFlow.js. Working knowledge of the JavaScript programming language is all you need to get started.

What this book covers

Chapter 1, *Machine Learning for the Web*, will show you the importance of ML on the web platform. Fundamentally, ML applications should provide some value to the users through a user-facing interface such as a web platform. In this chapter, we will leverage ML on the web platform to remove the fences between the user-facing environment and the environment where traditional server-side ML runs. You will learn how to install TensorFlow.js and set up the environment around it.

Chapter 2, *Importing Pretrained Models into TensorFlow.js*, explains how to import Keras pretrained models into TensorFlow.js. Since TensorFlow Core can train such a model efficiently, we can easily reuse the model in a client-side application.

Chapter 3, *TensorFlow.js Ecosystem*, shows you how to use some frameworks and libraries running with TensorFlow.js that are used to construct ML models, so that you can develop your own application more efficiently.

Chapter 4, *Polynomial Regression*, shows you how TensorFlow.js APIs are used with the simplest models. The application we look at predicts the y value of a sine curve with a given x value by using a polynomial regression model, implemented with a neural network.

Chapter 5, *Classification with Logistic Regression*, teaches you how to implement a classification model such as a logistic regression model. With the help of a practical example, we will teach you how to write a logistic regression application to classify flower types with the Iris dataset.

Chapter 6, *Unsupervised Learning*, demonstrates the potential of TensorFlow as an ML framework by implementing a clustering algorithm such as k-means and demonstrating unsupervised learning. We will be implementing the k-means algorithm using the Iris dataset.

Chapter 7, *Sequential Data Analysis*, explains how the FFT algorithm is implemented in TensorFlow and how to use it in an ML application. You will also learn how complex numerical types are implemented in TensorFlow.js.

Chapter 8, *Dimensionality Reduction*, introduces t-SNE and how it can be implemented in TensorFlow.js.

Chapter 9, *Solving Markov Decision Problems*, introduces the implementation of the Bellman equation for solving MDP problems and explains how it is related to reinforcement learning.

Chapter 10, *Deploying Machine Learning Applications*, shows you the general ways to create a package from a TensorFlow.js application.

Chapter 11, *Tuning Applications to Achieve High Performance*, shows you how to make use of certain backend implementations to pursue high performance as well as giving you tips for tuning an application written in TensorFlow.js.

Chapter 12, *Future Works around TensorFlow.js*, covers more advanced features and optimizations implemented in TensorFlow.js so that you can learn about what is going on in TensorFlow.js projects.

To get the most out of this book

Working knowledge of JavaScript will be handy.

Download the example code files

You can download the example code files for this book from your account at
`www.packt.com`. If you purchased this book elsewhere, you can visit
`www.packtpub.com/support` and register to have the files emailed directly to you.

You can download the code files by following these steps:

1. Log in or register at `www.packt.com`.
2. Select the **Support** tab.
3. Click on **Code Downloads**.
4. Enter the name of the book in the **Search** box and follow the onscreen instructions.

Once the file is downloaded, please make sure that you unzip or extract the folder using the latest version of:

- WinRAR/7-Zip for Windows
- Zipeg/iZip/UnRarX for Mac
- 7-Zip/PeaZip for Linux

The code bundle for the book is also hosted on GitHub at `https://github.com/
PacktPublishing/Hands-On-Machine-Learning-with-TensorFlow.js`. In case there's an
update to the code, it will be updated on the existing GitHub repository.

We also have other code bundles from our rich catalog of books and videos available
at `https://github.com/PacktPublishing/`. Check them out!

Download the color images

We also provide a PDF file that has color images of the screenshots/diagrams used in this
book. You can download it here: `http://www.packtpub.com/sites/default/files/
downloads/9781838821739_ColorImages.pdf`.

Conventions used

There are a number of text conventions used throughout this book.

CodeInText: Indicates code words in text, database table names, folder names, filenames, file extensions, pathnames, dummy URLs, user input, and Twitter handles. Here is an example: "GraphDef is a definition to describe the graph structure in the protocol buffer."

A block of code is set as follows:

```
message GraphDef {
  repeated NodeDef node = 1;
  VersionDef versions = 4;
  FunctionDefLibrary library = 2;
}
```

Any command-line input or output is written as follows:

```
$ ls my_tfjs_model
```

Bold: Indicates a new term, an important word, or words that you see on screen. For example, words in menus or dialog boxes appear in the text like this. Here is an example: "For example, **ResNet-50**, which is one of the major deep learning models for image classification, takes up 100 MB."

Warnings or important notes appear like this.

Tips and tricks appear like this.

Get in touch

Feedback from our readers is always welcome.

General feedback: If you have questions about any aspect of this book, mention the book title in the subject of your message and email us at customercare@packtpub.com.

Errata: Although we have taken every care to ensure the accuracy of our content, mistakes do happen. If you have found a mistake in this book, we would be grateful if you would report this to us. Please visit www.packtpub.com/support/errata, selecting your book, clicking on the Errata Submission Form link, and entering the details.

Piracy: If you come across any illegal copies of our works in any form on the internet, we would be grateful if you would provide us with the location address or website name. Please contact us at copyright@packt.com with a link to the material.

If you are interested in becoming an author: If there is a topic that you have expertise in and you are interested in either writing or contributing to a book, please visit authors.packtpub.com.

Reviews

Please leave a review. Once you have read and used this book, why not leave a review on the site that you purchased it from? Potential readers can then see and use your unbiased opinion to make purchase decisions, we at Packt can understand what you think about our products, and our authors can see your feedback on their book. Thank you!

For more information about Packt, please visit packt.com.

Section 1: The Rationale of Machine Learning and the Usage of TensorFlow.js

In this section, readers will explore how machine learning applications work on the web platform. They will also learn how to set up an environment to run TensorFlow.js. Furthermore, readers will learn how to import pretrained models from Keras into TensorFlow.js. This section will also cover the ecosystem around TensorFlow.js.

This section contains the following chapters:

- Chapter 1, *Machine Learning for the Web*
- Chapter 2, *Importing Pretrained Models into TensorFlow.js*
- Chapter 3, *TensorFlow.js Ecosystem*

Machine Learning for the Web 1

In this book, we will learn how to use TensorFlow.js to create machine learning applications. You'll need to be familiar with the following in order to get started:

- Web-based programming languages, such as JavaScript and TypeScript
- Web platform technology stacks (only a basic knowledge is required)
- The fundamentals of machine learning algorithms

In this chapter, we are going to clarify why machine learning on the web is crucial in modern machine learning use cases and when to use web technology so that you can run your applications. You will also be introduced to the basic APIs of TensorFlow.js so that you can construct machine learning models. These topics act as the basis for the chapters that follow.

In this chapter, we will cover the following topics:

- Why machine learning on the web?
- Operation graphs
- What is TensorFlow.js?
- Installing TensorFlow.js
- The low-level API
- The Layers API

Technical requirements

In this chapter, as a prerequisite, you need to prepare the following libraries or frameworks in your environment:

- **A web browser (Chrome is recommended)**: TensorFlow.js primarily runs on web browsers.

- **The Node.js environment, which contains a node package manager (npm)**: Node.js is necessary since it resolves dependencies so that we can run TensorFlow.js.
- **TypeScript compiler**: TensorFlow.js and its application are often written in TypeScript.
- **Python (3.x is recommended)**: We need this so that we can run Python-dependent tools such as `tfjs-converter` and the TensorFlow Python API.

If you are unsure about how to build the environment, please look at the *Further reading* section, which can be found at the end of this chapter. You will find these resources useful while you set up these prerequisites.

 The code we'll be using in this book can be found in this book's GitHub repository: `https://github.com/PacktPublishing/Hands-On-Machine-Learning-with-TensorFlow.js`.

Why machine learning on the web?

Machine learning technology was invented in the 1950s. Back then, there was no such period where machine learning was the exciting field in computer science that it currently is. However, thanks to breakthroughs in areas of deep learning and artificial intelligence, a huge amount of resources in terms of money and manpower have been devoted to help research it. For example, it isn't unusual to use an extensive amount of computing power that's leveraged by GPUs in laboratories in universities. Nowadays, industries and academics are cooperating to make progress in the computer science field. We are living in an era that's creating and facing large-scale data like never before. The importance of machine learning mainly comes from the demand for providing value by making use of this large-scale data. Machine learning technology gives us a chance to find innovative insights in a scalable and reproducible manner more than ever. For the last decade, intensive research has been done in the machine learning field. Deep learning is one such technology that has achieved accuracy that competes with human intelligence in relation to problems such as image recognition, audio generation, and machine translation. Many machine learning frameworks are emerging and being developed by both academics and industries in order to follow this trend. These technologies can contribute to making such use cases more abundant so that more research can take place.

However, creating a user-friendly application using machine learning is still a challenge. Most machine learning frameworks are designed and optimized to run in an environment that uses distributed systems that are running on thousands of machines and accelerators, such as GPUs. Generally, a machine learning model is used to predict something that's unknown to us after we've trained a model with a known dataset. Environments that contain GPUs and accelerators are exclusively used for the training phase. Although this allows us to train the machine learning model efficiently, it builds a wall between training the model and the inference of the model because it is necessary to make the trained model work on real data. We may need to fine-tune the model with a custom user dataset or convert the model into an executable format in the user's environment. This means that we need to deal with new challenges in terms of integrating between the machine learning model and the user-facing environment when we try to create applications that leverage machine learning technology. Porting machine learning models to platforms that users use often requires intensive work and skill because they're not compatible with the environment. It is common for data scientists who usually use Python as their primary language to struggle with building web applications with JavaScript.

In that sense, the web is the environment that's used the most by the end users of any kind of application. Machine learning applications are not an exception. More and more users are expected to use machine learning applications while they're on the web. Therefore, the web can be seen as the next frontier for machine learning applications because of its potential in terms of how many users use it. The technology that makes machine learning runnable on the web expands the possible use cases for machine learning in the real world. In this book, we are going to learn how to run machine learning on the web by using a modern framework known as TensorFlow.js. TensorFlow.js is a framework that is compatible with TensorFlow APIs so that users can create machine learning applications on the web. Apart from providing the flexibility of web-based machine learning applications, it also provides satisfactory performance since it uses an acceleration mechanism that's provided by modern web browsers.

This book is a practical guide to applying machine learning technologies to the web so that our users can quickly benefit and get value from our applications. It's assumed that you are a developer who wants to create a machine learning application with a rich user interface swiftly and efficiently.

Operation graphs

Before diving into TensorFlow.js itself, we need to be familiar with the idea of operation graphs, or calculation graphs, which are common constructs that we'll use to build machine learning models alongside modern frameworks such as TensorFlow. In these frameworks, the data is represented as a tensor. A tensor is a data structure that represents an arbitrary dimensional array. Those of you who have used the NumPy library in Python may already be familiar with this concept. In NumPy, ndarray is commonly used to display various kinds of data in machine learning, such as images and audio, regardless of whether it's structured or unstructured.

Modern machine learning frameworks, including TensorFlow, illustrates the fact that machine learning models are operation graphs of tensors. An operation graph is defined as a chain that's used for the manipulation or transformation of tensors.

Visualizing an operation graph

Operation graphs are at the core of modern machine learning frameworks, including TensorFlow. They are powerful and flexible constructs that allow us to build any kind of mathematical structure technically. Let's take a look at this important structure in more detail.

The following diagram is an example of an operation graph that represents a simple classification neural network. As you can see, the operation graph illustrates the flow of the data. The squared nodes represent the tensors for the input, output, and intermediate nodes. Each tensor transformation is represented by oval nodes. These are responsible for changing the shape of the tensor, the values inside it, and their control flow. This indicates that you can construct any kind of data flow while you're writing code with certain programming languages:

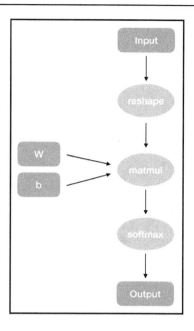

But does this mean that operation graphs are the best choice when we're constructing a machine learning model? Let's take a look at another factor that demonstrates the advantages of using an operation graph to represent a machine learning model.

Automatic differentiation

Machine learning models, especially deep learning models, can optimize their own parameters based on the error rate that's calculated by the value of the derivative function. However, generally, it is impossible to derive the derivative function of any function. This means that there's no practical way of calculating the error rates of each parameter for any machine learning model. Around the 1960s, an algorithm was invented to solve this problem, known as **backpropagation**. Backpropagation is an algorithm that allows us to derive the value to be optimized for each operation node in the graph. This algorithm implements the following steps:

1. It finds the error rate between the prediction result of the model and the target value in a supervised learning context.
2. It propagates the error rate so that it's proportional to what the predicted result contributes. We do this for each operation node.
3. It updates the model's parameters based on the propagated error rate.

In *Step 2*, the backpropagation algorithm calculates the error rate without knowing the derivative function of the whole model. All it needs to know is the derivative function of each operation node. Let's say we have an operation node that calculates the logarithm of the input:

$$f(x) = log(x)$$

The derivative function of the logarithm is as follows:

$$\frac{df}{dx} = \frac{1}{x}$$

Then, we can simply illustrate how the value is calculated by using the logarithm operation node. The path that's used to calculate the result of the function is called the **forward path**, while the path that's used for the derivative function of the node is called the **backward path**. The forward path is used to predict the target that contains the incoming input. The output of the operation is passed to the next node to generate the final prediction result. On the other hand, the backward path is necessary to train the model based on its error rate. The value that needs to be optimized for each operation node is calculated by the error rate that's propagated by the backward path. Instead of needing to know what the derivative function of the whole model is, all we need to do is pass the error rate by using the derivative function of each operation node. The following diagram shows the flow of the forward and backward paths:

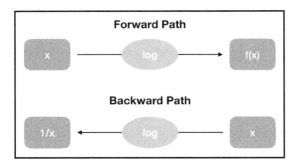

As you may already know, the graph's structure can be used for backpropagation. Combining the operation nodes that already have forward and backward paths means that we can create a trainable machine learning model. If there are various kinds of operation nodes with forward and backward paths, this makes it easy for us to implement a new type of model and experiment with the data we have.

As shown in the following diagram, the error that's calculated by using the difference between the predicted result and the target value is propagated through the layers, which are multiplied by the derivatives that are defined by each layer. Each error (Δy_n) that needs to be propagated is decided on by the derivative function and the structure of the layer. This means that a layer can only calculate the error with the error value from the upstream layer. For example, the `matmul` operator can calculate the updated values for W and b just by using the propagated error, that is, Δy_2. α and β are the coefficients that are obtained by the calculation when it uses the output value in the forward path:

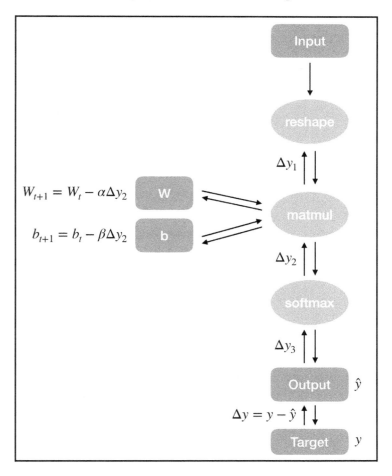

As you can see, each layer in the phase of the backpropagation algorithm only depends on the upstream layer that gives the error value to the layer. As we can see, each operator in the layer only needs to recognize the error value from the upper layer and its own value, which is used in the forward path. This makes implementation much simpler. Each operator can be agnostic to the neighboring operators in the operation graph. All we need to care about is the error value that's passed to the operator. Let's take a look at an example of a log operator in TensorFlow.js:

```
function log_<T extends Tensor>(x: T|TensorLike): T {
  const $x = convertToTensor(x, 'x', 'log');

  // dy is the error value from the upper operator.
  const grad = (dy: T, saved: Tensor[]) => {
    const [$x] = saved;
    return {$x: () => dy.div($x.toFloat()) as T};
  };

  // ENGINE is the actual backend implementation depending on the platform
(e.g. WebGL)
  return ENGINE.runKernel((backend, save) => {
    const res = backend.log($x);
    save([$x]);
    return res;
  }, {$x}, grad);
```

You don't need to fully understand what the preceding code does here, but please be aware that `grad` is defined as the function that's used to calculate the error value of this operator and that it is propagated to any low-level operators. Here, it is necessary to implement the forward path (`backend.log($x)`) and the backward path (`grad`), but we don't need to know what kind of operators are being used in the upper and lower layers. This provides us with the flexibility to construct the machine learning model just by combining predefined operators so that they act like Lego blocks.

In most cases, we can use the eager style to construct the operation graph, which allows us to build the graph intuitively. The dependencies between operations are clearer when we use the eager style. We will cover the eager style in more detail later in this chapter.

This is exactly what TensorFlow.js does for us. TensorFlow.js is a library that allows programmers to construct operation graphs by combining existing operations so that they can try out any kind of model without caring about the model's optimization. This is one of the beneficial and amusing things about using TensorFlow.js as a machine learning platform.

Now that we've looked at the code of TensorFlow.js, we need to talk about what TensorFlow.js is. In the next section, we'll talk about TensorFlow.js in more detail.

What is TensorFlow.js?

TensorFlow.js is a framework that we can use to construct machine learning models that are compatible with TensorFlow Python APIs. Unlike TensorFlow Python APIs, TensorFlow.js can be seamlessly integrated with the web so that we can quickly run machine learning algorithms on any platform. It was originally invented by Google and published as a piece of open source software known initially as **deeplearn.js**. Thanks to the contributions of developers, it is one of the most actively developed projects in the TensorFlow family.

 You can view many of the interesting demo applications by going to the TensorFlow.js demo page: https://www.tensorflow.org/js/demos/. This collection demonstrates the richness and potential of TensorFlow.js as a machine learning framework.

But why is TensorFlow.js so important to developers who are trying to create machine learning applications? There are several characteristics that illustrate the significance of this framework. We'll go over some of these now.

Seamless integration with web technologies

Since TensorFlow.js is written in TypeScript, it can be naturally integrated with existing web technologies. This means that a machine learning model that's been written with TensorFlow.js can be run in a web browser without any modifications having to be made. This ensures that we can make use of the rich user interface that the web browser provides. Actually, TensorFlow.js itself has its own set of utilities so that we can import the **Document Object Model (DOM)** element of an image as a tensor, such as a canvas. This makes it easy for us to run the application with the data that's available on the internet. The **teachable machine** is a good example of the power of integrating with the web. It uses input from webcams by using the browser API.

The following is a screenshot of the teachable machine (`https://teachablemachine.withgoogle.com/`):

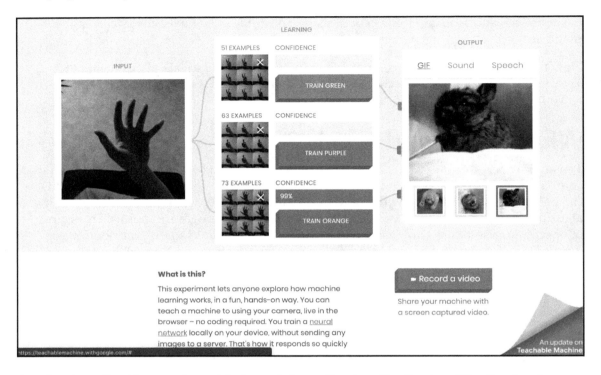

Another benefit of integrating with the web is application distribution. Distributing the application is a common challenge that many developers face. We need to find a way of distributing the package and making sure that it works as expected in the user environment. The web platform was originally developed to distribute such resources globally. Due to the nature of the platform, package distribution can be done scalably and efficiently, and web browsers hide the complexity of accessing local resources securely. Therefore, we can easily make our model available to the entire world as we publish our website or web application.

Hardware acceleration using web browser APIs

One possible drawback of using a web browser as a machine learning platform is performance. Web browsers are usually single-process applications. Typically, they don't work with CPU-intensive use cases such as machine learning. However, there are some ways we can achieve high performance in web browsers. Modern web browsers provide standard APIs that use local hardware accelerators, such as GPUs. For example, WebGL is a standardized specification that allows us to use GPUs from web browsers with ease. By making use of such APIs, TensorFlow.js can achieve competitive performance, even in web browsers.

Although WebGL was originally developed for graphical processing, TensorFlow.js has its own wrapper that hides the implementation details of each platform. This is known as the **backend**. In TensorFlow.js, the backend provides a standard interface for application developers so that they don't need to care about the details of the implementation. Since TensorFlow.js supports CPU, WebGL, WebGPU, and Node.js as backends, we can use these acceleration mechanisms through the same interface. The Node.js backend illustrates the possibility of running TensorFlow.js on the server side so that we can reuse the same code on the client side and the server side. Even today, new platforms are being supported; for example, Electron, WebAssembly, and OpenGL ES may be supported in the near future. Their performance characteristics are all different. We will look at this in more detail later in this book.

Compatibility with TensorFlow

TensorFlow is definitely one of the most popular machine learning frameworks out there. Quite a few libraries and ecosystems have been designed to cooperate with TensorFlow so that we can reuse the model that's been trained by TensorFlow in other frameworks and vice versa.

Of course, TensorFlow.js has an API set that's compatible with TensorFlow and pretrained models. The TensorFlow community already provides numerous pretrained models, including those that have been a part of cutting-edge research. TensorFlow.js can make use of these resources by converting the model's format into a JSON file that can be read by TensorFlow.js. We will learn how to import a pretrained model into TensorFlow.js in the next chapter.

In addition, the API for TensorFlow.js was made to look similar to TensorFlow's in terms of its appearance and parameter types. It even has the same look and feel, which should make getting used to TensorFlow.js easy.

Data privacy

People are becoming more and more sensitive when it comes to their own data privacy. Collecting data through the cloud is more difficult than it's ever been. This may prevent us from being able to train the machine learning model with data that we've collected from the server side. Client-side machine learning based on TensorFlow.js is a solution to this problem. TensorFlow.js makes it possible for us to train the model without us having to send the training data outside of the client's computer. This means that our users can receive the benefits of such machine learning while keeping their data private. The following diagram shows a scenario where TensorFlow.js is useful:

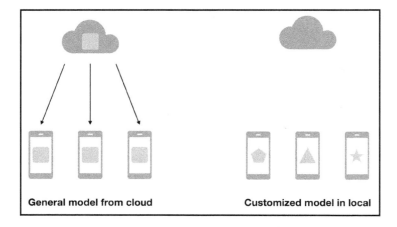

The general model can be distributed from the central cloud server. This model can be applied to most cases, but we need to customize it by fine-tuning it with the user-generated data. By using TensorFlow.js, each client can fine-tune the model with the data that's locally available to them. The model and that data that the model was trained on isn't shared with anyone. In a sense, it is a model that's been personalized for you and that's only available on your local machine. Local-side machine learning can deliver personalized models without having to be concerned about breaching data privacy.

Federated learning can also achieve the same goal. It is capable of updating the model's parameters by gathering the trained models. This technology combines multiple machine learning models without having any knowledge of the input training data, which means that it contributes to protecting private data that's usually tracked on the client side. Although we aren't going to deep dive into federated learning, it shows us that data privacy and security is becoming an interesting topic, even in the field of machine learning.

Installing TensorFlow.js

There are two ways we can set up the TensorFlow.js environment:

- Use the minified JavaScript code that's distributed in the CDN
- Use the bundled package that's distributed by package managers such as npm

Typically, TensorFlow.js should be used on a web platform. Since the prebuilt file is distributed by the global **content distribution network (CDN)** service, we need to add a script tag to the web application:

```
<script
src="https://cdn.jsdelivr.net/npm/@tensorflow/tfjs/dist/tf.min.js"></script
>
```

TensorFlow.js' classes can be found under the tf namespace. The CDN service works fast and is stable enough to provide such static resources to users. This is the easiest way to use TensorFlow.js.

If you want to serve your application in an environment where a public network isn't available, then you need to import TensorFlow.js into your application directly. The framework for doing so is also distributed through npm. You can install TensorFlow.js by running the yarn or npm command. The following code shows how to install TensorFlow.js using the yarn command:

```
yarn add @tensorflow/tfjs
```

The following code shows how to install TensorFlow.js using the npm command:

```
npm install @tensorflow/tfjs
```

Now that you've installed TensorFlow.js, you can bundle it by the tools that make the web application portable, such as Browserify and Parcel. For example, your first application may look as follows:

```
import * as tf from '@tensorflow/tfjs';

const model = tf.sequential();
model.add(tf.layers.dense({units: 1, inputShape: [2]}));

model.compile({loss: 'meanSquaredError', optimizer: 'adam'});

const xs = tf.tensor2d([[0, 0], [0, 1], [1, 0], [1, 1]], [4, 2]);
const ys = tf.tensor2d([0, 1, 1, 0], [4, 1]);

model.fit(xs, ys).then(() => {
```

```
    model.predict(tf.tensor2d([[0, 1]], [1, 2])).print();
});
```

The preceding code creates a multilayer perceptron that predicts the target value using two-dimensional input. As you may have noticed, it has been trained to emulate the **exclusive or** (**XOR**) logical gate to ensure that TensorFlow.js works properly.

tfjs-converter

As we mentioned previously, TensorFlow.js is capable of reusing any existing models that have been trained by TensorFlow. To do so, we need to make `tfjs-converter` runnable in our environment. `tfjs-converter` is a command-line tool that we can use to convert the TensorFlow model. `tfjs-converter` currently supports the following file formats:

File format	Option
Keras HDF5	`keras`
Keras SavedModel	`keras_saved_model`
TensorFlow Hub	`tf_hub`
TensorFlow SavedModel	`tf_saved_model`

Since `tfjs-converter` is a command-line tool that runs in Python, you need to prepare the Python runtime first. `tfjs-converter` internally uses TensorFlow and Keras. To avoid conflicts with the local installation, it is highly recommended that you use `pyenv` or `virtualenv` to isolate it from the local environment:

```
pyenv install 3.6.8
pyenv local 3.6.8

pip install tensorflowjs
```

We need to specify the input and output paths for `tfjs-converter`. While you need to specify `input_format`, you don't need to use `output_format` because `tfjs-converter` automatically infers the output format from the value of `input_format`. In most cases, you can omit `output_format`:

```
tensorflowjs_converter --help
usage: TensorFlow.js model converters. [-h]
                                       [--input_format
{tensorflowjs,keras,tf_hub,keras_saved_model,tf_saved_model,tfjs_layers_mod
el}]
                                       [--output_format
{tfjs_graph_model,tfjs_layers_model,tensorflowjs,keras}]
                                       [--signature_name SIGNATURE_NAME]
```

```
SAVED_MODEL_TAGS]                      [--saved_model_tags

                                       [--quantization_bytes {1,2}]
                                       [--split_weights_by_layer] [--
version]
                                       [--skip_op_check SKIP_OP_CHECK]
                                       [--strip_debug_ops STRIP_DEBUG_OPS]
                                       [--weight_shard_size_bytes
WEIGHT_SHARD_SIZE_BYTES]

                                       [input_path] [output_path]
```

For example, you can convert TensorFlow's SavedModel into a web format that can be read by TensorFlow.js like so:

```
tensorflowjs_converter \
    --input_format=tf_saved_model \
    /path/to/saved_model \
    /path/to/web_model
```

Two types of file format are generated by `tfjs-converter`:

- `model.json`: This defines the structure of the operation graph and weight mapping.
- `group1-shard*of*`: This weighs files that are in binary format.

`model.json` is a human-readable JSON file that describes the structure of the graph of the model. To make weight mapping faster, weight files are sharded so that they can be loaded asynchronously. Since web browsers are significantly optimized to load several resources efficiently, the web model format achieves a good balance between readability and efficiency.

`tfjs-converter` is mainly used for loading existing models into your TensorFlow.js runtime. This tool is indispensable since it not only loads the model that you've trained onto the server-side but also makes use of the models that have been trained by the community. Generally, it takes a significant amount of time to train a model. Reusing pretrained models is far less time-consuming. We will learn how to use existing models and how to fine-tune them in the next chapter.

However, you may want to construct the model from scratch. To do this, you would have to research and invent a new type of machine learning model. How can we construct such a model from nothing?

In the following sections, we are going to introduce two APIs that we can use to construct the machine learning model: the low-level API and the Layers API.

The low-level API

The low-level API is flexible and allows us to construct the operation graph at the lowest level. It is also known as TensorFlow.js Core (`https://github.com/tensorflow/tfjs-core`).

This API allows us to access kernel implementations for each backend directly. Fundamentally, other high-level libraries and ecosystems depend on the Core API. Being familiar with the Core API will help us implement an efficient machine learning model with TensorFlow.js. Although the code base of the Core API was initially separated, TensorFlow.js is now managed by the mono repository. This means we can access any type of API solely from the root of the namespace of the library. Therefore, if we were to use `tf` as the reference to the root namespace, we can import it as follows:

```
import * as tf from '@tensorflow/tfjs';
```

Tensors

Tensors are fundamental data structures in TensorFlow.js. The framework is designed to execute every computation of these generalized vectors and matrices. A tensor contains the following properties:

- `rank`: The dimensions the tensor contains
- `shape`: The size of each dimension
- `dtype`: The data type of the tensor

A tensor is the metadata of a retained data. A tensor only keeps the pointer to the underlying data array so that we can isolate the manipulation of the tensor's shape and the transformation of the actual data array. This leaves a notable amount of room for optimization. The data types that are available in TensorFlow.js are `float32`, `int32`, `bool`, `complex64`, and `string`.

For example, you can create constant tensors using the following code:

```
import * as tf from '@tensorflow/tfjs';

const t1 = tf.tensor1d([1, 2, 3]);
t1.print();
// Tensor
//     [1, 2, 3]

const t2 = tf.tensor2d([1, 2, 3, 4], [2, 2]);
```

```
t2.print();
// Tensor
//     [[1, 2],
//      [3, 4]]
```

To obtain data from the tensor, we can use APIs for synchronous and asynchronous fetching, respectively. The `data` method returns a promise. Data can often be retained in the memory of the GPU, or anywhere else that isn't close to the CPU memory. It is recommended that we use to Asynchronous API so that we can make the most of the resources of the CPU and I/O. Its value is constructed as a `TypedArray` so that we can easily integrate it with other libraries that are able to recognize it. The Synchronous API is often inefficient but is useful for debugging purposes, as shown in the following code:

```
const t = tf.tensor1d([1, 2, 3]);

// Asynchronous API
t.data(d => {
  console.log(d); // Float32Array(3) [1, 2, 3]
});

// Synchonous API
console.log(t.dataSync()); // Float32Array(3) [1, 2, 3]
```

The data is printed immediately, without us having to use the `async` function in JavaScript. The Asynchronous API returns a Promise that must be wrapped with the `async` function, but this can be avoided with the Synchronous API.

 We should use the Asynchronous API as much as possible since it doesn't unintentionally block application execution.

Operations

Operations are programmable units that can be used to manipulate tensors. TensorFlow.js provides various kinds of operations that are suitable for linear algebra and machine learning, just like TensorFlow does. For compatibility purposes, TensorFlow.js supports many of the operations that are implemented by TensorFlow. Due to this, we can import many of the machine learning models that have been implemented by TensorFlow into TensorFlow.js. Operations can be called from the root namespace or the methods of the tensors directly, as follows:

```
const t1 = tf.tensor([1, 2, 3, 4]);
const t2 = tf.tensor([10, 20, 30, 40]);
```

```
t1.add(t2);
// Or
tf.add(t1, t2);
```

All of the operations return the handle of the tensors. When it creates a new tensor, each result is considered to be immutable. This is good practice when we wish to analyze operation graphs and optimization. But how do we manage the memory that's been allocated for each tensor? In particular, tensors with a WebGL backend require the memory to be on the GPU side. It is necessary to control the memory explicitly because there is no garbage collection algorithm running on the GPU memory.

Memory

While the JavaScript runtime has a mechanism for garbage collection, the GPU that's used by WebGL doesn't. This means that no process can automatically free the memory space that's allocated by tensors. Going out of the scope of the tensor is not sufficient if we wish to release the memory that's been allocated for tensors. To destroy the tensor, including its memory, we need to call the dispose method of the tensor itself:

```
console.log(tf.memory());
// -> {unreliable: false, numBytesInGPU: 0, numTensors: 0, numDataBuffers:
0, numBytes: 0}
const a = tf.tensor([1, 2, 3]);
console.log(tf.memory());
// -> {unreliable: false, numBytesInGPU: 0, numTensors: 1, numDataBuffers:
1, numBytes: 12}
a.dispose();
console.log(tf.memory());
// -> {unreliable: false, numBytesInGPU: 0, numTensors: 0, numDataBuffers:
0, numBytes: 0}
```

tf.memory() is an API that inspects the memory information that's used by the backends of TensorFlow.js. As you can see, the memory that's been allocated for the tensor by the backend has been released, as expected. However, you may be thinking that it's troublesome to dispose of each piece of memory by hand. Additionally, you may be wondering how to release the memory that's been allocated to intermediate tensors. As you already know, every operation creates a new tensor so that we can manipulate them in an immutable manner. We must explicitly release the memory that's been allocated to this kind of intermediate tensor in order to avoid a memory leak. But do we need to assign these intermediate tensors to each variable so that we can call the dispose() method?

To solve this problem, TensorFlow.js provides the `tf.tidy` method. This cleans up the memory that's been allocated to all of the tensors in a scope:

```
const a = tf.tensor([1, 2, 3]);

const y = tf.tify(() => {
  const result = a.log().neg().round();
  return result;
});
```

In the preceding code, the memory that's used to keep the tensors of `log` and `neg` is automatically disposed of, but the tensor for `round` is not disposed of because it is assumed to be referenced by `y`, even after it's returned. Generally, `tf.tify` is highly recommended because we don't have to write as much code and it's much less likely to cause leaks.

In some cases, you may want to manage the memory so that it's more flexible and fits your use case. In this case, we would use the `dispose` method explicitly.

 New APIs are added every day. Take a look at the latest API specification on TensorFlow's official site for more details: `https://js.tensorflow.org/api/latest/`.

Eager execution

As you may have already guessed, TensorFlow.js doesn't have a notion of sessions like TensorFlow does. We can execute operations eagerly so that we can control when we run them. The operation graph is naturally constructed by the chain of the operation API. To run the calculation, we only need to get the tensor of the output:

```
const a = tf.tensor([1, 2, 3]);

// Operation chain does not execute the computation by itself.
const result = a.square().log().neg().floor();

// Getting the result will kick the computation of result and all dependent
operations.
result.data().then(d => {
  console.log(d);
});
```

This is another reason why asynchronous data fetching is recommended. The huge operation chain, as is often the case for the machine learning model, can consume a vast amount of CPU time. Using the Asynchronous API can block the execution of the main thread that's running in the browser, which leads to a poor user experience. To avoid this, it is recommended that we use the Asynchronous API in browser applications. That is something we have to be careful with since such issues are caused by running machine learning applications close to the user-facing environment.

The Layers API

In the previous section, we described how to use the Core API of TensorFlow.js, which allows us to construct any operation graph as we like. But this is not always the best choice. You may find yourself in a situation where a high-level API is more relevant when we want to build an application quickly. The Layers API is a Keras-like high-level API that's used to create models in an intrinsic way. You may already be familiar with the style of the Layers API if you've used Keras to construct machine learning models in the past.

There are two ways we can construct a machine learning model with the Layers API:

- By using the sequential model API
- By using the functional model API

As you may have already noticed, the Layers API has been made to look similar to the Keras API. Those of you who are already familiar with Keras will be able to use the Layers API with more ease than the Core API.

Sequential model

With the sequential model API, you can construct the model by piling up each layer. Here, we create the multilayer perceptron or deep learning model, which can be described as the graph of each neural layer. For example, a model that recognizes an input vector with 784 elements to predict the output of 10 categories can be represented as follows:

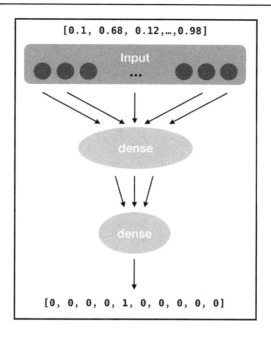

We can use the following code to build a sequential model that connects the two fully connected layers that are shown in the preceding diagram. The sequential model can be expressed as a list of each layer:

```
const model = tf.sequential({
  layers: [
    tf.layers.dense({inputShape: [784], units: 16, activation: 'relu'}),
    tf.layers.dense({units: 10, activation: 'softmax'}),
  ]
});
```

The sequential model shows you how the data flows from the input to the output. Please make sure that you provide the input size with the `inputShape` parameter. The input shape is the size of the input tensor, so if the input shape is `[BatchSize, 784]`, the input shape of each data point would be `[784]`. You can inspect the layers of the model by accessing `model.layers`, `model.inputLayers`, and `model.outputLayers`.

The Layers API has another form of syntax that allows us to add layers later. The following code shows how we can add layers after the sequential model has been constructed:

```
const model = tf.sequential();
model.add(tf.layers.dense({inputShape: [784], units: 32, activation:
'relu'}));
model.add(tf.layers.dense({units: 10, activation: 'softmax'}));
```

Functional model

Another way to create a model with the Layers API is to use the functional model API. This API allows you to add an arbitrary layer to the model, as long as it doesn't have cycles. If you were to rewrite the previous model with the functional model API, we would use the following code:

```
const input = tf.input({shape: [784]});
const dense1 = tf.layers.dense({units: 16, activation:
'relu'}).apply(input);
const dense2 = tf.layers.dense({units: 10, activation:
'softmax'}).apply(dense1);
const model = tf.model({inputs: input, outputs: dense2});
```

In the functional model API, the `apply()` method is used to connect each layer. The value that's returned by the `apply()` method is a `SymbolicTensor` instance, which almost behaves like a tensor, but it doesn't have a pointer to the concrete value. Therefore, we need to create a `SymbolicTensor` for every layer, including the input layer. `tf.input` creates a `SymbolicTensor` so that it can operate consistently with the functional model. Moreover, the functional model API returns a concrete tensor instead of a `SymbolicTensor` if it gets a concrete tensor as input, as shown in the following code:

```
const input = tf.tensor([-2, 1, 0, 5]);
const output = tf.layers.activation({activation: 'relu'}).apply(input);
output.print(); // [0, 1, 0, 5]
```

 Like the sequential model, you can inspect each layer by accessing `model.layers`, `model.inputLayers`, and `model.outputLayers`.

One of the major benefits of using the Layers API is that we can validate the input shape of each layer. The model that's constructed by the Layers API is an instance of `LayersModel`, which runs the validation and notifies us when two layers are incompatible in terms of the shape of the consecutive input and output. Additionally, `LayersModel` automatically infers the shape of each tensor, along with the data flows of the model. Since building the custom model often causes issues, this kind of validation can help us avoid minor mistakes in advance.

Model summary

Inspecting the structure of the model is often helpful if we wish to debug models and ensure they're constructed correctly. The `summary()` method is a tool that we can use to print information about the model's structure, such as the following:

- The name and type of each layer
- The output shape of each layer
- The number of weight parameters in each layer
- The total number of trainable and non-trainable parameters

For example, the model that we created previously, which had one intermediate layer, provides the following summary information:

```
                                                                   layer_utils.ts:62
Layer (type)              Output shape          Param #            layer_utils.ts:152
                                                                   layer_utils.ts:64
=================================================================
dense_Dense1 (Dense)      [null,32]             25120              layer_utils.ts:152
                                                                   layer_utils.ts:74
dense_Dense2 (Dense)      [null,10]             330                layer_utils.ts:152
                                                                   layer_utils.ts:74
=================================================================
Total params: 25450                                                layer_utils.ts:83
Trainable params: 25450                                            layer_utils.ts:84
Non-trainable params: 0                                            layer_utils.ts:85
                                                                   layer_utils.ts:86
```

The structure of the model has a significant impact on its accuracy and performance, so we need to design the model carefully. `summary()` provides an overview of the model, along with the minimum information that's required so that we can improve it. One thing to note is that the null value of the output shape indicates that the dimension is flexible at runtime. TensorFlow.js expects the input tensor to have a batch size in the outermost dimension. Therefore, `[null, 32]` means that it can accept any tensors that have 32 elements.

Custom layers

The Core API provides us with the most flexibility when it comes to machine learning, but the Layers API also supports elasticity. Defining the class of tf.layers.Layer allows us to do custom computing, which can be applied to the Layers API seamlessly:

```
class NegativeLayer extends tf.layers.Layer {
  constructor() {
    super({});
  }

  computeOutputShape(inputShape) { return []; }

  call(input, kwargs) { return input.neg();}

  getClassName() { return 'Negative'; }
}
```

By doing this, you can add a custom layer, as well as other layers:

```
const input = tf.tensor([-2, 1, 0, 5]);
const output = new NegativeLayer().apply(input);
output.print(); // [2, -1, 0, -5]
```

One caveat of using a custom layer is serialization. The model of TensorFlow.js can be saved and loaded using the Layers API like so:

```
const saveResult = await model.save('file://path/to/my-model');
const model = await tf.loadLayersModel('file://path/to/my-model');
```

However, these methods won't work if you create a custom layer since the implementation cannot be serialized. Please be careful, as using custom layers makes the model unportable.

Another thing to note about the Layers API is that it may not be suitable for constructing machine learning models in general. From a technical standpoint, it has been designed for use with deep learning models, which means you may not be able to find an appropriate API to do your desired arithmetic operations. In such cases, the Core API is recommended.

Summary

In this chapter, we have learned about the benefits of constructing a machine learning model on the web and how to use TensorFlow.js to build it. There are two ways we can build a model with TensorFlow.js. The first way is to use the Core API, which helps us build flexible models and optimize their performance as much as possible. The other way is to use the Layers API. This API is similar to Keras, which means we can construct deep learning models more intuitively. We don't need to construct our own model if it is already publicly available.

We also learned that it's possible to import an existing model into TensorFlow.js by using `tfjs-converter`. By completing this chapter, you know how to construct your own models with TensorFlow.js and import existing models into TensorFlow.js.

In the next chapter, we will learn how to import pretrained models into TensorFlow.js.

Questions

1. What is the benefit of building a machine learning model on the web?
2. When we give the TensorHub model to `tfjs-converter`, what type of format will be generated?
    1. Layers model
    2. Graph model
3. How many ways can we release the memory that's been allocated to a tensor in a model in TensorFlow.js?
4. How can we inspect the structure of the model?
5. Describe the major difference between the Core API and the Layers API. When should we use them?
6. Construct a multilayer perceptron with the following layers:
    - The input is a vector with 784 elements.
    - The first intermediate layer is a fully connected layer whose output is a rectified linear unit and has a size of 32.
    - The second intermediate layer is a fully connected layer whose output is a rectified linear unit and has a size of 16.
    - The output is a softmax layer.
7. Is it possible to save a model that contains a custom layer?

Further reading

Refer to the following resources to learn more about the topics that were covered in this chapter:

- tfjs-converter: https://github.com/tensorflow/tfjs-converter
- Tensors and operations: https://www.tensorflow.org/js/guide/tensors_operations
- Models and layers: https://www.tensorflow.org/js/guide/models_and_layers
- TypeScript: https://www.typescriptlang.org/
- Federated learning: https://www.tensorflow.org/federated/federated_learning
- Teachable machine: https://teachablemachine.withgoogle.com/

2
Importing Pretrained Models into TensorFlow.js

In the first chapter, we saw why machine learning on the web platform is so important in general and looked at the design and basic use of TensorFlow.js. In this chapter, we are going to focus on how to import pretrained models into TensorFlow.js. Importing existing machine learning models is so important, especially in the deep learning field, because deep learning models can be reused and combined with other models. Knowledge about importing pretrained models gives us a chance to *stand on the shoulder of a giant* so to speak.

The following topics will be covered in this chapter:

- The portable model format
- Exporting a model from TensorFlow
- Converting models using tfjs-converter
- Loading a model into TensorFlow.js

Technical requirements

In this chapter, you need to build an environment containing the following things:

- Python 3
- JavaScript/TypeScript
- A web browser (for accessing Google Colab)
- TensorFlow 1.13
- `tfjs-converter 0.8.6`

The portable model format

A machine learning model retains the mapping from the parameter name and its value. It is a type of key-value structure in general. Technically, it can be written in any kind of format that can express structured data, but it is important to make the model portable, so that we can reuse it somewhere different to where the model is trained. Here are the characteristics the portable model format should have:

- **Lightweight**: Small enough to be stored in limited memory capacity
- **Serializable**: Sharable through the disk or network I/O
- **Compatible**: Usable by multiple platforms

Nowadays, the range of platforms where machine learning can run is diverse. A machine learning algorithm is expected to run not only on a typical server-side machine but also on edge devices such as mobile or embedded systems. Even with the limited memory capacity of edge devices, the model itself should be compact in its memory footprint. The model is also assumed to be distributed through the commodity network infrastructure. The smaller the model size is, the more efficiency we can gain when transferring the model through the network.

Due to the emergence of various kinds of machine learning frameworks, the model compatibility of these frameworks is seen as significant to developers. That is because we do not want to spend time on redundant work training similar machine learning models. It is natural to use one model everywhere once it is trained in a sufficiently general manner. Therefore, the model format needs to be as compatible and platform-agnostic as possible. As TensorFlow is one of the most used machine learning frameworks, quite a few frameworks support the format TensorFlow generates. Let's see what the TensorFlow model looks like in the following sections.

Protocol buffers

A **protocol buffer** is a language-neutral serializable data format developed mainly by Google. The binary format is used by many products published by Google and, of course, TensorFlow is not an exception. All of the files generated by TensorFlow are based on protocol buffers. A protocol buffer is a serialization format that is readable by various kinds of programming languages. Once you define the schema of the protocol in the protocol buffer DSL, the protocol buffer compiler can generate serializers in various kinds of programming languages. This allows us to write a system to exchange data between services in a heterogeneous system smoothly.

Due to the nature of the protocol buffer, TensorFlow can make use of it in order to construct the model format supported by a variety of platforms seamlessly, as shown in the following diagram:

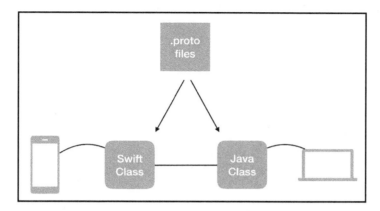

This indicates that the TensorFlow model can also be supported by a lot of platforms without many difficulties.

A platform-agnostic format also leads us to develop diverse tools to analyze TensorFlow models. It must expand the possibility of the application running on the TensorFlow model. **Open neural network exchange (ONNX)** is a good example. ONNX is an open standard to represent the neural network model in a platform-agnostic manner. Technically, you can run the model with various types of frameworks once it is trained. A model trained by TensorFlow can be exported to PyTorch and MXNet, for example. This type of tool is realized by the open model format of each framework, including the protocol buffer.

GraphDef

The core component of TensorFlow is definitely the graph structure representing the operation graph literally. GraphDef is a definition to describe the graph structure in the protocol buffer. As the definition shows, it is just a collection of operation nodes:

```
message GraphDef {
  repeated NodeDef node = 1;
  VersionDef versions = 4;
  FunctionDefLibrary library = 2;
}
```

This is part of the definition of `GraphDef` in TensorFlow. As you can see, it contains a collection of operation node definitions. That is the most important part of `GraphDef` because it defines the structure of the operation graph. Understanding the information contained in `GraphDef` is helpful for debugging and analyzing your model in general. Next, let's see what `NodeDef` looks like.

NodeDef

`NodeDef` is a component in the graph representing an operation. It is the fundamental building block in the graph and is also defined by the protocol buffer. The properties `NodeDef` has are as follows:

- `name`: Every operation node should have a unique identifier to explicitly specify the connection between operation nodes.
- `op`: The pointer to the actual operation implementation. The `op` name is used to look up the actual implementation in the runtime.
- `input`: A list of the names of input nodes.
- `device`: This is used to specify where to run the operation, the CPU or GPU.
- `attr`: Key-value pairs that hold the attributes of the operation. This is a property to provide additional information to define the structure of the operation (such as a data type or properties in the convolutional layer).

Overall, `GraphDef` is a data structure holding all operation nodes in the graph. The connection between nodes and the implementation is managed by each node respectively:

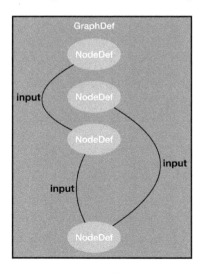

But one thing we need to be careful of is that there is no weight in `GraphDef` itself. As the `weight` parameter in machine learning (especially deep learning) can be huge in total, it is performance oriented, to have them separate from the graph definition. Considering the life cycle of one model, the `weight` parameter may be optimized continuously as the training goes on. On the other hand, the structure of the model itself is rarely changed because it is usually unchanged by each iteration. Separating them keeps us from updating `GraphDef` unnecessarily frequently. It also makes it more efficient to load multi-version models. Let's say you want to compare the accuracy of models trained through a different number of iterations. Switching only the `weight` parameters is sufficient because the definition of the model structure can be completely shared in this case. Since the size of the model definition can often be large, it definitely contributes to minimizing the memory footprint of the model.

We are now going to see how to save the model as a file with the model definition (`GraphDef`) and the `weight` parameters.

Exporting a model from TensorFlow

`GraphDef`, as you can see, only contains the minimum information to construct the model, which is not actually suitable for practical use cases. We may need a more comprehensive, platform-agnostic format to represent the machine learning model. **SavedModel** is the latest way to serialize a machine learning model in TensorFlow. Currently, using SavedModel is the recommended option to export a model trained by TensorFlow.js. This is because SavedModel contains not only the graph definition but also variables and graph metadata, so that higher-level systems or tools can consume the model and reuse it immediately.

Another major way to export the model is by using Keras. Keras is a high-level TensorFlow API that enables us to construct our model more intuitively. The usage of Keras is very similar to the TensorFlow.js Layers API. Many data scientists work with Keras because of its usefulness and simplicity. However, the format saved by a Keras model is completely different from SavedModel. **HDF5** is the data format used by Keras models. As HDF5 is a general binary format mainly maintained by the HDF group, it is also a portable format that is runnable on multiple platforms.

We are now going to dive into the details of these two model formats.

TensorFlow's SavedModel

TensorFlow's SavedModel is a primary model format used in TensorFlow. Even a Keras model, which will be described later, can be exported to SavedModel. If you are building a TensorFlow graph by hand, SavedModel must be the way you choose to export your model because of its flexibility. TensorFlow provides us with two APIs to export SavedModel—the `simple_save` API and `SavedModelBuilder`. Firstly, let's see what the format of SavedModel looks like.

The SavedModel format

SavedModel is a hierarchical data structure that stores multiple directories inside. `MetaGraphDef` is a data flow graph that also contains the mapping to the variables and assets the graph depends on. We can regard the data structure as an operation graph in the SavedModel context. The following diagram shows the high-level structure of SavedModel:

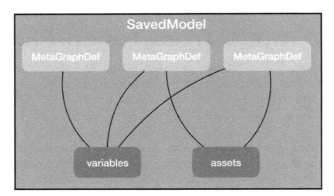

As this diagram shows, the `MetaGraphDef` instances are able to share the variables and assets. Each operator in the graph is associated with a variable contained in SavedModel so that we can save the space allocated for variables. Generally speaking, the `weight` variables for machine learning models may consume a lot of memory space. For example, **ResNet-50**, which is one of the major deep learning models for image classification, takes up 100 MB. Sharing the variables with multiple graph definitions can save a significant amount of space.

Assets are the auxiliary contents to provide additional model resources such as vocabulary for NLP or attributes for images. If a model depends on these assets, having them in a model file totally makes sense in order to make the model portable. The assets can be loaded along with `MetaGraphDef` in SavedModel.

Simple save

You should use this API if you do not have any requirement to do complicated things such as saving multiple models in one file. It is a simple and quick way to export your model in SavedModel format. The parameters to be given to the simple save API are as follows:

- Session
- Input tensors
- Output tensors

The code looks as follows. Your operation graph should be constructed in the session (sess):

```
import tensorflow as tf

with tf.Session() as sess:
    tf.saved_model.simple_save(sess,
            './my_tensorflow_model',
            inputs={"x": x, "y": y},
            outputs={"z": z})
```

You will see the my_tensorflow_model directory in your current directory where the program runs. It should contain a graph definition in the protocol buffer format and variables in the binary format. For example, this is the structure of the SavedModel directory created by the simple_save API. We will introduce the details of each file in the following sections:

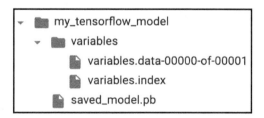

In this case, my_tensorflow_model is a directory storing all information about SavedModel. If you need to pass SavedModel into other tools, you can pass the path to the directory or archive it to share it remotely. For instance, the input path of tfjs-converter can be ./my_tensorflow_model, as will be shown later in this chapter.

The SavedModelBuilder API

If you want to export a complicated model in a more fine-grained manner, SavedModelBuilder is the API you can use, as the API has the functionality to save multiple MetaGraphDef instances, as shown in the first diagram. It is a general way to export a more compact and efficient model. It is also able to contain some assets that are auxiliary files, such as vocabulary for an NLP application. Each MetaGraphDef in SavedModel should be attached to user-defined tags in order to identify the specific model to load when it is used. By using annotation, you can also use SavedModel in different use cases. For example, you can contain models for fine-tuning and inference in one SavedModel file:

```
export_dir = './model_builder'

builder = tf.saved_model.builder.SavedModelBuilder(export_dir)

# Add first MetaGraphDef
with tf.Session(graph=tf.Graph()) as sess:
 x = tf.constant(1)
 y = tf.Variable(2)
 z = x + y
 sess.run(tf.global_variables_initializer())
  builder.add_meta_graph_and_variables(sess,
[tf.saved_model.tag_constants.TRAINING])

# Add a second MetaGraphDef for inference.
with tf.Session(graph=tf.Graph()) as sess:
  x = tf.constant(1)
  y = tf.Variable(2)
  z = x + y
  sess.run(tf.global_variables_initializer())
  builder.add_meta_graph([tf.saved_model.tag_constants.SERVING])
builder.save()
```

First, you need to call the add_meta_graph_and_variables method to save the graph with variables. It saves the graph definition with variables in the given session. In one SavedModelBuilder context, the method must be called only once and prior to all the subsequent graph additions. In order to add additional MetaGraphDef instances, it is necessary to use the add_meta_graph method. The add_meta_graph method is a method to save the graph in the current scope. The save method will write files, variables, and graph definitions in the protocol buffer, as seen in the previous section.

Here is an option you may need to know about in order to debug the model definition efficiently. You can pass the `as_text` option to the `save` method so that you can see the graph definition in a human-readable format:

```
builder.save(as_text=True)
```

The final output is JSON-like plain text:

```
saved_model_schema_version: 1
meta_graphs {
  meta_info_def {
    stripped_op_list {
      op {
        name: "Add"
        input_arg {
          name: "x"
          type_attr: "T"
        }
        // ...
    }
  }
}
meta_graphs {
  meta_info_def {
    // ...
  }
}
```

You can check the name of the operation node and attributes here.

The Keras HDF5 model

Keras is one of the most popular high-level TensorFlow libraries. Most readers may already use Keras in their daily projects. TensorFlow.js also supports model files exported by Keras. Unlike SavedModel, Keras uses HDF5, which is a hierarchical data structure format. It can represent the nested data structure, thus it is very similar to the protocol buffer in that sense.

Here is a simple diagram showing the rough structure of HDF5:

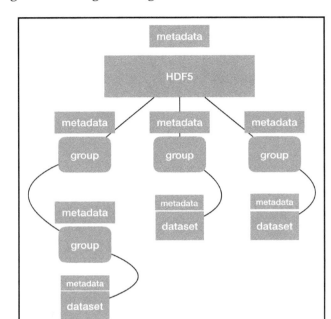

As the Keras API itself is simple, the way to export the model by Keras is also simple. The model created by Keras has a `save` method. Just calling the API will save the model in HDF5 format:

```
from tensorflow.keras import layers

model = tf.keras.Sequential()
model.add(layers.Dense(16, activation='relu'))
model.add(layers.Dense(10, activation='softmax'))

model.save('my_keras.h5')
```

You will find the `my_keras.h5` file in the current directory. As HDF5 is the format that is able to contain hierarchical structure, there is sufficient information to restore the model in the format:

- The structure of the operation graph
- Variables
- Hyperparameters (such as optimizers)
- The state of the optimizer to resume the training

The major difference from SavedModel is that the Keras HDF5 format is a file storing all information so that it is easier to move around. Also, HDF5 is an open format, which indicates that you can get support from many existing frameworks or libraries. Like `SavedModelBuilder`, it has a method to dump the graph structure in a human-readable format:

```
model.to_json()
```

Additionally, it is possible to save only variables or hyperparameter configurations in the file. However, the API is mainly designed to be used by Keras itself. A HDF5 file that contains only some configuration is hard to use in other frameworks due to the lack of information. In order to use the exported model in TensorFlow.js, we need to export all information into an HDF5 file.

Converting models using tfjs-converter

Unfortunately, models such as SavedModel of HDF5 created by TensorFlow cannot be used in the world of TensorFlow.js directly. It is inevitable that you will have to convert the model into a format readable by the web platform.

Converting a TensorFlow SavedModel

Once the SavedModel is created, you can convert the SavedModel into TensorFlow.js format as follows:

```
$ tensorflowjs_converter \
    --output_node_names=output \
    --input_format=tf_saved_model \
  ./my_saved_model ./my_tfjs_model
```

The input path and output path are required as positional arguments. (`my_saved_model` and `my_tfjs_model`). The model will be generated in the `my_tfjs_model` directory. The options specified in the preceding example are the minimum requirements. The `input_format` option is especially important to specify the format explicitly. `tfjs-converter` automatically infers the compatible output format from this value.

The following is a table showing all the options that can be used with `tfjs-converter`:

Option	Description
`--input_format`	The format of the input model. The `tf_saved_model`, `tf_hub`, `keras_saved_model`, `keras`, and `tf_frozen_model` formats are mainly supported.
`--output_format`	The output format. It is mostly inferred automatically.
`--saved_model_tags`	The tag of the target `MetaGraphDef` in the saved model. The default value is `serve`.
`--signature_name`	The common signature to load.
`--stripe_debug_opts`	An option to specify whether we remove debug-type operations such as print and assert.
`--quantization_bytes`	The bytes to be quantized for the weight variables. The default size is 4 bytes.

As quantization bytes show, using tfjs-converter does not only the conversion but also some optimization at the same time by using the optimization tools implemented in TensorFlow. For example, tfjs-converter shows the following message in the middle of the conversion. You will be able to get a more efficient model just by converting your model using tfjs-converter:

```
Optimization results for grappler item: graph_to_optimize
  debug_stripper: Graph size after: 4 nodes (0), 3 edges (0), time =
0.005ms.
  model_pruner: Graph size after: 3 nodes (-1), 2 edges (-1), time =
0.048ms.
  constant folding: Graph size after: 1 nodes (-2), 0 edges (-2), time =
0.484ms.
  arithmetic_optimizer: Graph size after: 1 nodes (0), 0 edges (0), time =
0.078ms.
  dependency_optimizer: Graph size after: 1 nodes (0), 0 edges (0), time =
0.016ms.
  model_pruner: Graph size after: 1 nodes (0), 0 edges (0), time = 0.009ms.
  remapper: Graph size after: 1 nodes (0), 0 edges (0), time = 0.008ms.
  constant folding: Graph size after: 1 nodes (0), 0 edges (0), time =
0.399ms.
  arithmetic_optimizer: Graph size after: 1 nodes (0), 0 edges (0), time =
0.07ms.
  dependency_optimizer: Graph size after: 1 nodes (0), 0 edges (0), time =
0.015ms.
```

Let's look at the example code to export the model and the options to convert SavedModel into TensorFlow.js format. It's very similar to the previous one but we specify the name of the output node and the MetaGraphDef tag for simplicity:

```
export_dir = './my_saved_model'

builder = tf.saved_model.builder.SavedModelBuilder(export_dir)

# Add first MetaGraphDef
with tf.Session(graph=tf.Graph()) as sess:
  x = tf.constant(1)
  y = tf.Variable(2)
  z = tf.add(x, y, name='my_output1')
  sess.run(tf.global_variables_initializer())
  builder.add_meta_graph_and_variables(sess, ['model1'])

# Add first MetaGraphDef
with tf.Session(graph=tf.Graph()) as sess:
  x = tf.constant(2)
  y = tf.Variable(2)
  z = tf.add(x, y, name='my_output2')
  sess.run(tf.global_variables_initializer())
  builder.add_meta_graph(['model2'])
```

You can see the first model has the output named my_output1 and that is associated with the model1 tag. The second one has the output node named my_output2 and it is associated with the model2 tag. Let's say we want to convert the first model into a web format. The command-line option looks like this:

```
$ tensorflowjs_converter \
    --output_node_names=my_output1 \
    --input_format=tf_saved_model \
    --saved_model_tags=model1 \
    ./my_saved_model ./my_tfjs_model
```

The web format model is generated in the my_tfjs_model directory. If you want to convert the second model, you can change the options as follows:

```
$ tensorflowjs_converter \
    --output_node_names=my_output2 \
    --input_format=tf_saved_model \
    --saved_model_tags=model2 \
    ./my_saved_model ./my_tfjs_model
```

As you might have already noticed, the web format only contains one graph definition in one format. We need to create the directories of the web format respectively if we want to use multiple models in our web application. The output of the conversion will look like this:

```
$ ls my_tfjs_model
group1-shard1of1 tensorflowjs_model.pb weights_manifest.json
```

A `weights_manigest.json` file is a file to store the information about the location of weight files. In this case, that is `group1-shard1of1`. As the name suggests, the `weight` parameters are sharded so that the browser can load the weight files in a parallel manner.

The Keras HDF5 model

To convert a Keras HDF5 model into the web format, you need to specify the `keras` input format option. Let's assume we want to convert the following model trained through the Keras API into the web format:

```python
import tensorflow as tf
from tensorflow.keras import layers
import numpy as np

model = tf.keras.Sequential()
model.add(layers.Dense(32, activation='relu'))
# Add another:
model.add(layers.Dense(10, activation='softmax'))

model.compile(optimizer=tf.train.AdamOptimizer(0.001),
              loss='categorical_crossentropy',
              metrics=['accuracy'])

data = np.random.random((1000, 32))
labels = np.random.random((1000, 10))

model.fit(data, labels, epochs=10, batch_size=32)

model.save('my_keras_model.h5')
```

You do not need to specify additional options such as `output_node_names`. Just specifying the input format works in most cases, as follows:

```
$ tensorflowjs_converter \
    --input_format keras \
    my_keras_model.h5 my_tfjs_model
```

You will see the model file in the web format in the `my_tfjs_model` directory:

```
# ls my_tfjs_model/
group1-shard1of1 model.json
```

The structure of the format is a little bit different from the previous one. It does not contain a protocol buffer file and the schema of the manifest JSON file is also different. How can these two types of format be read in TensorFlow.js? Actually, we need to use different APIs in TensorFlow.js to load these two types. We are going to explain the process to load the model into TensorFlow.js in the last section of the chapter.

The TensorFlow Hub module

tfjs-converter is also able to recognize the TensorFlow Hub module. TensorFlow Hub is a library to discover the reusable part of machine learning models. We may regard TensorFlow Hub as the central repository of the machine learning model so that we can share our pretrained model with researchers or developers around the world. Converting the model using tfjs-converter from TensorFlow Hub means we can use the model published on the internet directly. For example, you can make the web format of the pretrained MobileNetV1 as follows. It is necessary to specify `tf_hub` as an input format option:

```
$ tensorflowjs_converter \
    --input_format=tf_hub \
'https://tfhub.dev/google/imagenet/mobilenet_v1_100_224/classification/1' \
    ./my_tfjs_model
```

You can find the input path in the TensorFlow Hub main repository: `https://tfhub.dev/`.

It stores not only pretty mature models such as inception networks, but also cutting-edge models such as deep GANs. Training a huge model is time-consuming work and also cannot be achieved without knowledge about the model itself and some programming skills. TensorFlow Hub is, so to speak, a tool allowing us to *stand on the shoulders of a giant*. If you just want to use TensorFlow.js as a platform to host existing deep learning models, using TensorFlow Hub can be the most efficient solution.

Loading the model into TensorFlow.js

The model generated by tfjs-converter can be finally loaded by TensorFlow.js. TensorFlow.js provides us with some dedicated APIs to load the specific model format, `loadGraphModel` and `loadLayersModel`. If the model file is created from SavedModel, `loadGraphModel` can be used. On the other hand, if the original model is Keras, `loadLayersModel` should be used. These APIs are able to load the model via both HTTP and a local filesystem:

```
import * as tf from '@tensorflow/tfjs';

const MODEL_URL = 'https://path/to/model.json';
const model = await tf.loadGraphModel(MODEL_URL);

// Or

const MODEL_PATH = 'file://path/to/model.json';
const model = await tf.loadGraphModel(MODEL_PATH);
```

Model loading can be done asynchronously to prevent the loading of a large-size model from blocking the main thread. While browsers usually support loading 100-500 MB models, it can worsen the user experience significantly. It may consume a notable amount of memory and CPU time of browsers. In order to avoid the deterioration of the application's performance, loading a model smaller than 30 MB is highly recommended. Although TensorFlow.js is a powerful tool, we need to use it as a machine learning platform on the edge side. Being aware of the limited resources in such an environment may contribute to writing an efficient application with TensorFlow.js.

Both `GraphModel` by `loadGraphModel` and `LayersModel` from `loadLayersModel` implement `InferenceModel` in the TensorFlow.js core API. Thus, we can use these models transparently without caring about the details of the loaded model.

Supported operations

One caveat to be mentioned here is that tfjs-converter and TensorFlow.js do not fully support all TensorFlow operations. This indicates that models using unsupported TensorFlow.js operations may fail to convert into the web format. Model conversion is done just to structure the operation graph and the manifest of the `weight` parameters, not operation implementations. If an operation is not implemented in TensorFlow.js, we cannot use the model in the web world.

Implementations are processed on a request basis. If the community and open source maintainers find many developers are waiting for an operation, they prioritize the implementation. Currently, image-based models such as MobileNet, SqueezeNet, and others are the most supported models. Basically, tfjs-converter does some validation against the target model. If the model uses an unsupported operation, it can throw an error. All operations supported by tfjs-converter are described at `https://github.com/tensorflow/tfjs-converter/blob/master/docs/supported_ops.md`.

If you find an operation you need is unsupported, please file an issue on the GitHub page so that the community can recognize the necessity of the operation.

Summary

In this chapter, we have introduced how to export your trained model in TensorFlow and convert it into a usable format in TensorFlow.js. TensorFlow exports models mainly in two types of formats. One is SavedModel, which is a low-level format but it enables us to flexibly control variable mapping and share it with multiple graph definitions. If you want to construct a serialized model in a sufficiently optimized manner, SavedModel is the one you need to consider. Another format is Keras HDF5. As Keras is a pretty popular framework running on top of TensorFlow, exporting a model in Keras format could be the optimal solution for developers. Thanks to the limited number of configurations we need to set explicitly, that must be the easiest one to export the pretrained model into the file.

An exported file cannot be used directly in TensorFlow.js. There is a tool named tfjs-converter to turn the exported model into a TensorFlow.js compatible format. By using tfjs-converter, you can create a TensorFlow.js format especially optimized for the web platform. As TensorFlow.js provides two ways to import the converted model, it is important to be aware of the kind of format that is used by tfjs-converter.

In the next chapter, we will learn all about the TensorFlow.js ecosystem.

Questions

1. What is the serialization format used by the model definition file of SavedModel?
2. What kind of file format does the Keras API export?

3. Let's assume we want to convert the following model. Please describe the options for converting it using tfjs-converter:
    1. SavedModel
    2. The model tag is `my_mobilenet1`
    3. The output node name is `y`

4. Write code to import a pretrained MobileNet into TensorFlow.js. The model is uploaded to TensorFlow Hub: `https://tfhub.dev/google/imagenet/mobilenet_v2_100_224/classification/3`.

5. What is the recommended model size to import a model into web browsers in general? Do you think you can optimize the memory footprint of the SavedModel or Keras model?

6. In order to achieve the best performance when loading the model via HTTP, how big should each shard of the `weight` variable file be in the web format?

Further reading

For further references, refer to the following links:

- TensorFlow model files: `https://www.tensorflow.org/guide/extend/model_files`.
- ONNX: `https://github.com/onnx/tutorials`.
- SavedModelBuilder: `https://www.tensorflow.org/guide/saved_model#manually_build_a_savedmodel`.
- GraphDef: `https://github.com/tensorflow/tensorflow/blob/master/tensorflow/core/framework/graph.proto`.
- HDF5: `https://www.hdfgroup.org/solutions/hdf5/`.
- *Advances in deep learning approaches for image tagging. APSIPA Transactions on Signal and Information Processing, Fu, Jianlong and Rui, Yong. (2017)*: `https://www.researchgate.net/publication/320199404_Advances_in_deep_learning_approaches_for_image_tagging`.
- TensorFlow Hub: `https://tfhub.dev/`.

TensorFlow.js Ecosystem 3

Just like TensorFlow, TensorFlow.js has a bunch of ecosystem libraries. These libraries help us to build applications quickly and efficiently because some of them are designed to allow us to develop machine learning applications intuitively. In this chapter, we are going to introduce tools and libraries built on top of TensorFlow.js that we can use to accelerate the development of our application. Because these libraries are available as open source software, you can customize and contribute to them if necessary to meet your requirements.

The following topics will be covered in this chapter:

- Why high-level libraries?
- Using existing machine learning models
  - MobileNet in tfjs-models
  - Supported models by tfjs-models
  - Image classification application
  - Example applications in the community
- Loading the data from various kinds of storage
  - Data sources
  - Webcam
- Pose detection with ML5.js
  - Supported models
  - PoseNet in ML5.js
- Drawing cats with Magenta.js
- XOR classification by machinelearn.js

Technical requirements

You require the following to complete the tasks in this chapter:

- Web browser (Chrome is recommended)
- TensorFlow.js (tfjs-models)
- TypeScript
- Node.js
- ML5.js
- machinelearn.js

Check out the following video to see the Code in Action:
`http://bit.ly/3465VJJ`

Why high-level libraries?

Standing on the shoulders of giants is a famous proverb. In software engineering, it reminds us of the importance of reusing resources that already exist in the public domain.

There is no doubt that TensorFlow.js is a powerful and practical machine learning library running in the JavaScript environment. Technically, we can build any kind of machine learning model by combining the operations implemented in TensorFlow.js. However, working with raw operations is not always easy, and not even the best practice. If you only desire to use pretty mature existing algorithms, implementing a model by yourself is actually not what you want to do. The libraries we are going to introduce already have implementations of the basic machine learning and deep learning algorithms so that you can try them immediately.

Another reason is for learning purposes. There are too many papers that show interesting results in machine learning and deep learning to keep up with the state of the art. Of course, we should be able to implement an algorithm by ourselves once we've seen the description on paper, but writing efficient code to realize the concept described on paper requires decent knowledge of the field. If you just want to try the result of the research, it is too difficult. The good news is that ecosystems and popular high-level libraries quickly incorporate the new achievements of research. Thanks to the many skillful developers in the community, that kind of model development can be done promptly. You can not only make use of the implemented model, but you can also learn how to write the code to implement the model. It is a common practice to learn how to write good code in general. As open source software is a good resource to study writing code, high-level machine learning libraries provide a chance to see how algorithms are implemented.

These libraries depend on TensorFlow.js to reuse the primitives to construct a higher-level model. Some of them just provide pre-trained models, and others implement more intuitive APIs that can be integrated with the browser **document object model** (**DOM**) quite easily. Thus, you can build your application by combining several libraries, as we do with web applications, by combining several publicly available web APIs:

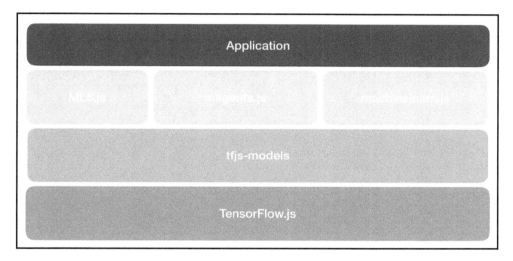

In the following sections, we are going to introduce popular high-level libraries built on top of TensorFlow.js. As we are going to use these libraries in the later chapters to implement some algorithms, please become familiar with the usage and overview of the libraries.

Using existing models

The TensorFlow.js project has its own repository to collect machine learning models that are compatible with the latest in TensorFlow.js. The repository is named tfjs-models: `https://github.com/tensorflow/tfjs-models`.

These models are pre-trained and uploaded in `npm`, `unpkg`, or `jsDelivr` so that we can quickly use the model in our application. As you may already know, `npm` is a package manager for the Node.js environment. It is easy to install the model in your Node.js application by using the `npm` or `yarn` CLI. For web applications, `unpkg` is a good option. It is an open source project providing a global CDN that is designed to serve every `npm` package. tfjs-models and TensorFlow.js core are served via `unpkg`. `jsDelivr` is a similar application that serves static content on our behalf.

MobileNet in tfjs-models

For example, here is some code that uses the MobileNet model. It's a small, low-latency model parameterized for a resource-constrained environment:

```
<script src="https://cdn.jsdelivr.net/npm/@tensorflow/tfjs@1.0.1">
</script>

<!-- Load the MobileNet model from jsDelivr -->
<script
src="https://cdn.jsdelivr.net/npm/@tensorflow-models/mobilenet@1.0.0">
</script>

<script>
  const img = document.getElementById('img');

  // Load the model asynchronously.
  mobilenet.load().then(model => {
    // Classify the image.
    model.classify(img).then(predictions => {
      console.log('Predictions: ');
      console.log(predictions);
    });
  });
</script>
```

As it shows, you can use TensorFlow.js and the MobileNet model without training a model or even installing the core packages. This is a good way to host an application instantly while keeping the cost of hosting low. Another option is installing the tfjs-models package into your application. The following command will install the package for MobileNet into the location your application can refer to:

npm install @tensorflow-models/mobilenet

The code for that is pretty similar to what we wrote with `jsDelivr`:

```
import * as mobilenet from '@tensorflow-models/mobilenet';

const img = document.getElementById('img');

const model = await mobilenet.load();

const predictions = await model.classify(img);

console.log('Predictions: ');
console.log(predictions);
```

Supported models

In addition to MobileNet, tfjs-models provides various kinds of models. This is the list of models that are currently supported:

Application type	Model	Description
Image	MobileNet	Pre-trained model based on the ImageNet dataset
Image	PostNet	A model that estimates human poses in real time
Image	Coco SSD	A model designed to localize and identify multiple objects
Image	BodyPix	A model for body segmentation
Audio	SpeechCommand	A model that recognizes simple English words using the WebAudio API
Text	Universal Sentence Encoder	A lightweight model that embeds text into a 512-length vector space
Text	Toxicity Classifier	A model that detects toxic content, such as threatening language
Classification	KNN Classifier	Classifier using the K-nearest-neighbors algorithm

Generally, these models are constructed to hide internal data structures such as tensors, which enables non-machine learning experts to use these models in their application. Just passing the data to be predicted to the model works in most cases.

Image classification application

Let's see how it works by creating an image classification application with the MobileNet model. As we have already seen, MobileNet is a lightweight model designed for image classification tasks on edge devices. The model was invented by Google in 2017. As it tries to solve the trade-off problem between efficiency and accuracy, it achieves optimal model fitting in resource-constrained environments such as mobile devices without losing much accuracy. TensorFlow.js is categorized as the framework running on the edge device. MobileNet matches the primary use cases of TensorFlow.js.

First, we need to install the model via npm. You can do this using npm install @tensorflow-models/mobilenet or yarn add @tensorflow-models/mobilenet. It will automatically clear the dependency in the package.json file.

The core script for loading the model and prediction is written as follows:

```
import * as mobilenet from '@tensorflow-models/mobilenet';

async function loadAndPredict() {
  const img = document.getElementById('cat');
```

```
  // As usual, the model is loaded asynchronously.
  const model = await mobilenet.load();

  // Classify the image. We can pass DOM element directly.
  const predictions = await model.classify(img);

  console.log('Predictions: ');
  console.log(predictions);

  // Display the prediction result.
  const preds = document.getElementById('predictions');
  preds.innerHTML = predictions.map((p) => {
    return p['className'];
  }).join('<br>');
}

loadAndPredict();
```

This application script loads the MobileNet model asynchronously to avoid blocking the main thread of the application running in the browser. In TypeScript and JavaScript, an asynchronous function call with `await` should be put inside the `async` function. `Model.load` returns the `Promise` data structure. In this application, it is called with the `await` keyword so that the execution is blocked at the specified function call. We expect the prediction to happen after the model is completely prepared. The `await` keyword is used to fulfill the returned Promise. As well as model loading, the inference may also take some time. Therefore, it is also designed to return the result as Promise. In order to set the prediction result properly, please ensure to use the `await` keyword as well.

Next, let's write some code to show the prediction result in a web page in the browser:

```
<!DOCTYPE html>
<html>
  <head>
    <meta charset="utf-8">
    <meta http-equiv="X-UA-Compatible" content="IE=edge,chrome=1">
    <meta name="viewport" content="width=device-width, minimum-scale=1.0,
initial-scale=1, user-scalable=yes">
    <title>Image Classifier with Mobilenet</title>
    <script src="mobilenet.ts" defer></script>
  </head>
  <body>
    <h1>Image Classifier with Mobilenet</h1>
    <p id='predictions'></p>
    <img src="cat.jpg" id="cat">
  </body>
</html>
```

This code will result in the following page, which shows the result of the prediction. You can put any image in the `img` tag for prediction:

The messages described in the preceding image is the result of predictions:

- **tabby, tabby cat**
- **quilt, comforter, comfort, puff**
- **tiger cat**

As it says, the image includes a cat and a comforter too. The model more or less returns a correct prediction result.

This application demonstrates that you can start the inference immediately after you download the model, as the MobileNet model is trained with the ImageNet dataset publicly. The training dataset and selected labels in ImageNet are limited. It does not cover every category in the world. Therefore, you need to retrain with your own data. This process is called **fine-tuning**. We are going to explain how to fine-tune the pre-trained model with TensorFlow.js in the following chapters.

Example applications in the community

Due to the nature of open source projects, new models are submitted more and more from the community. The criterion for accepting a new model in the repository is how much interest the model is generating in the community. If you are interested in contributing to the community by sharing a model, it would be great to submit it to GitHub. If you find it difficult to use these models, tfjs-examples would be helpful (`https://github.com/tensorflow/tfjs-examples`).

This repository is a community-driven collection of interesting applications using models trained by TensorFlow.js. It can give you an idea of how to use pre-trained TensorFlow.js models in your applications.

tfjs-models are mainly developed by the TensorFlow.js community. Actually, the repository is hosted in the TensorFlow organization on GitHub. But there are many libraries running with TensorFlow.js even outside the TensorFlow community. Let's see what they look like in the following sections.

Loading the data from various kinds of storage

The training dataset is a fundamental building block of the machine learning pipeline. Importing the variety of datasets without difficulty surely improves our productivity. tfjs-data is an analog library of tf.data in TensorFlow. It makes data loading simply by providing a uniform way of accessing the training data. As the library is contained by the core library of TensorFlow.js, tfjs-data will be available when you install @tensorflow/tfjs:

```
yarn add @tensorflow/tfjs
```

Data sources

TensorFlow.js provides you with a unified access layer for various kinds of data sources represented by tf.data.Dataset. The data structure is an ordered collection of each sample that allows us to run data transformations lazily:

- tf.data.array: Dataset generated from a JavaScript array
- tf.data.csv: Dataset generated from a CSV file
- tf.data.generator: Dataset generated from a JavaScript generator function
- tf.data.webcam: Dataset created from webcam input

We can ingest these data formats into TensorFlow.js models efficiently by using tfjs-data.

Webcam

One of the biggest benefits of using TensorFlow.js is that we can use a web browser as a data source. Most web browsers support API to manipulate webcams. tfjs-data implements an instinctive wrapper to access the webcam, tf.data.webcam:

```
import * as tf from '@tensorflow/tfjs';

async function webcamLaunch() {
  const display = document.getElementById('display');
  const videoElement = document.createElement('video');

  // Add element to display the webcam image.
  display.appendChild(videoElement);
  videoElement.width = 500;
  videoElement.height = 500;

  const webcamIterator = await tf.data.webcam(videoElement);

  // img is a tensor showing the input webcam image.
  const img = await webcamIterator.capture();
  img.print();
}

webcamLaunch();
```

This API builds the object that accesses webcam data. `webcamIterator.capture()` returns the tensor representing the camera image at the time it was captured. In the example, the image is a three-dimensional tensor, [500, 500, 3], which is the width, height, and length of the channel. Since it is just an ordinal multiple-dimensional tensor, we can pass it to any machine learning model that is compatible with the tensor data structure of TensorFlow.js.

In this example, the webcam input is directly connected to the DOM appended as a child of the `video` element. The output is shown on the page in the browser in real time:

```
<!DOCTYPE html>
<html>
  <head>
    <meta charset="utf-8">
    <meta http-equiv="X-UA-Compatible" content="IE=edge,chrome=1">
    <meta name="viewport" content="width=device-width, minimum-scale=1.0,
initial-scale=1, user-scalable=yes">
    <title>tfjs-data</title>
    <script src="data-load.ts" defer></script>
  </head>
  <body>
    <div id='display'></div>
  </body>
</html>
```

As you are going to see in the next section, this kind of real-time data source makes it possible to create an application that continues predicting with webcam input. Let's see how webcam input can be used to predict the pose of the human body.

Pose detection with ML5.js

ML5.js is a widely used high-level machine learning framework running on top of TensorFlow.js. It is designed to make machine learning accessible to a broad audience, such as students and artists. Those who are not familiar with machine learning tend to be only interested in the output of the algorithm, not the internal details of the algorithm. They are likely to want to write an efficient application without having to care too much about the optimization of the algorithm. ML5.js achieves good performance by using TensorFlow.js internally while providing an intuitive interface to developers.

As well as TensorFlow.js, ML5.js is distributed on the CDN, unpkg. Technically, you do not need to install anything in your application, you just need the following code:

```html
<!DOCTYPE html>
<html lang="en">
  <head>
  <title>Your ML5 application</title>
    <!-- You can load ML5 from unpkg -->
    <script src="https://unpkg.com/ml5/dist/ml5.min.js"></script>
  </head>
  <body>
    <script>
      console.log('ml5 version:', ml5.version);
    </script>
  </body>
</html>
```

Supported models

As several developers of TensorFlow.js are involved with ML5.js project too, we can reasonably expect the project to catch up with the latest TensorFlow.js enhancement and features. The latest ML5.js includes the following algorithms:

Type	Model	Description
Image	BodyPix	Segmentation for the body in an image
Image	CVAE	A generative model for the image
Image	DCGAN	A generative model for the image
Image	MobileNet	A model for image classification
Image	PoseNet	A model for estimating the human pose in real time
Image	StyleTransfer	Mixing different styles in two images
Image	YOLO	Fast state-of-the-art model for object detection
Image	Pix2Pix	A model for image conversion
Image	KNN	A classification model using the K-nearest-neighbors algorithm
Text	Sentiment	The model for inferring the sentiment of text
Text	Word2Vec	Embedding text into the vector space
Audio	SpeechCommand	A model recognizing simple English words using the WebAudio API
Audio	PitchDetection	A model for discovering the specific pitch of a sound

These algorithms are implemented in the `ml5-examples` repository, which shows the code you need to use to apply the model in an application (`https://github.com/ml5js/ml5-examples`).

Let's see how PoseNet from ML5.js works by looking at some example code.

PoseNet in ML5.js

PoseNet is a machine learning model for estimating the poses of people in an image or video. Although the core model is included in tfjs-examples, ML5.js provides a more intuitive way to use the model in combination with the `p5.js` library. p5.js makes it far easier to write an interactive application running in the browser. As p5.js can powerfully manipulate video, sound, and images, most ML5.js applications are integrated with p5.js. PoseNet is not an exception. It gets the input video from the p5.js API. This code loads the PoseNet model and estimates the pose of the input video:

```
// Setup the video
video = createCapture(VIDEO);
video.size(width, height);

// Load the PoseNet model from ML5.js.
// It gets the input from the webcom video previously created.
poseNet = ml5.poseNet(video, modelReady);

// PoseNet model is triggered when the new pose is detected.
// The estimation result is returned to the callback function.
poseNet.on('pose', function(results) {
  poses = results;
});
```

The `poses` global variable is used to draw key points in the pose. The following function is called periodically to render the key points in the video. It also uses the various APIs in `p5.js`, such as `fill`, `noStroke`, and `ellipse`:

```
function drawKeypoints() {
  // PoseNet can detect multiple poses at once.
  for (let i = 0; i < poses.length; i++) {
    let pose = poses[i].pose;
    for (let j = 0; j < pose.keypoints.length; j++) {
      let keypoint = pose.keypoints[j];
      // Taking only highly possible keypoints
      if (keypoint.score > 0.2) {
        fill(255, 0, 0);
        noStroke();
        // Draw the points in the image
```

```
        ellipse(keypoint.position.x, keypoint.position.y, 10, 10);
      }
    }
  }
}

function drawStrokes() {
  for (let i = 0; i < poses.length; i++) {
    // Skelton is the stroke between keypoints.
    let skeleton = poses[i].skeleton;
    for (let j = 0; j < skeleton.length; j++) {
      let start = skeleton[j][0];
      let end = skeleton[j][1];
      stroke(255, 0, 0);
      line(start.position.x, start.position.y, end.position.x,
end.position.y);
    }
  }
}
```

The drawKeypoints function renders the important points in the pose, and drawStrokes is for rendering the lines between key points.

It renders the following image in real time:

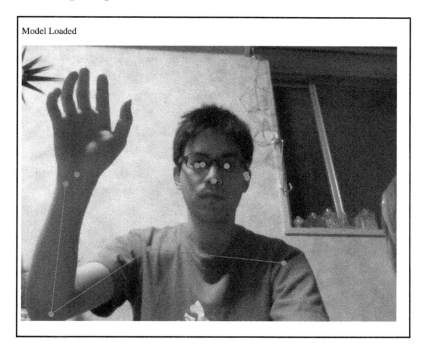

The red circles are the key points of this pose. You will experience how fast the ML5.js estimation and p5.js rendering is, and you will see that these libraries are powerful enough to build performant machine learning applications on the web.

Every demo application using ML5.js in `ml5-examples` is available on the internet, but it is also easy to run it using your own laptop. These applications are just a single file. Hosting the file by running an HTTP server is sufficient to serve an application:

```
git clone https://github.com/ml5js/ml5-examples.git
cd ml5-examples
python -m http.server # For Python 3
```

ML5.js is a general machine learning framework supporting a variety of application types, such as image, audio, and text. ML5.js is a Swiss army knife for machine learning applications on the web. As you have already seen, there are many cases in which we can use ML5.js. But there is another framework designed for special use cases. Magenta.js is one such library. Let's use Magenta and Magenta.js in the next section.

Drawing cats with Magenta.js

Magenta is an open source project that you can use to apply machine learning technology in the fields of art and music. It is mainly used by researchers or artists who are enthusiastic about making use of machine learning technology in the artistic field. Magenta was originally developed on the TensorFlow Python API, but the web platform is regarded as the best place to run the audio and image application. Then, Magenta was also integrated into the web with TensorFlow.js. Like ML5.js, Magenta.js is just a collection of models that can be utilized in the machine learning applications, especially for music and image processing. Pre-trained models are available so that we can save time while training the model from scratch.

There are three main types of modules in Magenta.js, `@magenta/music`, `@magenta/sketch`, and `@magenta/image`. As the name suggests, the first one is for audio applications, while the others are for image processing, especially for sketch drawing and style transfer. Let's see how Magenta.js helps us construct an image application by looking at a sketch drawing application.

Sketch drawing

You can try the demo application of the sketch drawing here: `https://magenta.tensorflow.org/assets/sketch_rnn_demo/index.html`.

The application tries to draw a picture of a specific object by adding strokes and curves to the object in the middle. Even if we only draw a simple square, the application keeps on working to complete the illustration of a crab, as follows:

sketch-rnn demo

permalink to drawing

The application uses a model called SketchRNN. **Recurrent neural networks (RNNs)** are neural networks that are especially useful for sequential data such as text or strokes. By keeping past information, it predicts the possible future. In this case, the SketchRNN model constructs a probability distribution function based on past stroke movement.

This is a diagram showing how SketchRNN works:

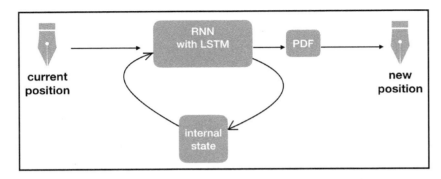

The RNN receives the current position with a two-length vector representing the x and y position in two-dimensional space. The RNN generates the internal state, which is passed to the RNN in the next phase and then to the **probability distribution function (PDF)**. The RNN with **long short-term memory (LSTM)** receives the internal state generated in the previous step so that it can keep the information over time. LSTM is a type of neural network that's designed to keep a memory to represent the dependencies of the previous data points. Generally, a data point in sequential data tends to depend on the data point in the previous step. The RNN with LSTM is predicting the next state based on past historical data points. However, SketchRNN constructs the PDF instead of directly predicting the next position. PDF is a function estimated by the RNN to emulate the space of the possible stroke. The next data point drawn by the application is sampled from the PDF. Therefore, the RNN constructs the PDF based on the current position and the internal state generated in the previous step. The new point is sampled from the PDF.

Once you have installed the SketchRNN package via yarn or npm, the following code loads the pre-trained model through the network:

```
import * as ms from '@magenta/sketch';

// Load the model for drawing the bird sketch.
const model = new ms.SketchRNN(
'https://storage.googleapis.com/quickdraw-models/sketchRNN/large_models/bir
d.gen.json');
```

This model is for drawing a sketch of a bird. As the model is loaded asynchronously, we need to make sure to write the code to use the model after the loading is completed. The `initialize()` method returns a Promise object, so it is sufficient to write the callback function to wait for the model to load:

```
model.initialize().then(function() {
  // Scale factor adjusts the scale between neural network output and pixel
space.
  model.setPixelFactor(3.0);

  // The state represents [dx, dy, penDown, penUp, penEnd] in a stroke.
  let [dx, dy, ...pen] = model.zeroInput();
  let modelState = model.zeroState();

  for (let i = 0; i < 10; i++) {
    // RNN needs to receive current stroke position and the previous state.
    modelState = model.update([dx, dy, ...pen], modelState);

    // Build the PDF
    let pdf = model.getPDF(modelState, 0.45);

    // Sample the final output from PDF
    [dx, dy, ...pen] = model.sample(pdf);
    console.log(model.sample(pdf));
  }
});
```

As you can see, it is necessary to pass the current stroke position (`dx`, `dy`, and `pen`) and the previous internal state (`modelState`) in every model update. Drawing the generated stroke will show the sketch of a bird. The preceding code only generates 10 samples. You can use `p5.js` to visualize the points generated by the PDF. To do so, we need to prepare two functions, `setup` and `draw`. These methods are used by `p5.js` to initialize the drawing environment and update the strokes in every frame update:

```
import * as ms from '@magenta/sketch';
import p5 from 'p5';

function sketch(p) {
  let modelLoaded = false;
  // Offset of the pen movement
  let dx, dy;
  // Initial position
  let x = p.windowWidth / 2.0;
  let y = p.windowHeight / 3.0;


  let pen = [0,0,0]; // Representing pen state [pen_down, pen_up, pen_end].
```

```
    let previousPen = [1, 0, 0]; // Previous pen state. Initial state is pen
down.
    const PEN = {DOWN: 0, UP: 1, END: 2};
    let modelState;

    const model
      = new
ms.SketchRNN("https://storage.googleapis.com/quickdraw-models/sketchRNN/mod
els/cat.gen.json");

    p.setup = () => {
      const containerSize =
document.getElementById('sketch').getBoundingClientRect();
```

Initialize the canvas and construct the canvas element on the page:

```
const screenWidth = Math.floor(containerSize.width);
    const screenHeight = p.windowHeight / 2;
    p.createCanvas(screenWidth, screenHeight);
    p.frameRate(60);

    model.initialize().then(() => {
      modelLoaded = true;
      model.setPixelFactor(3.0);
```

Set the initial pen movement and state:

```
[dx, dy, ...pen] = model.zeroInput();
      modelState = model.zeroState();
    });
  }

  p.draw = () => {
    if (!modelLoaded) {
      return;
    }
```

Update the internal state in SketchRNN and build the probability distribution function for the output sample. Then, sample the PDF using the following code:

```
modelState = model.update([dx, dy, ...pen], modelState);
    const pdf = model.getPDF(modelState, 0.45);
    [dx, dy, ...pen] = model.sample(pdf);
```

If the pen needs to be put down on the paper, draw the line:

```
if (previousPen[PEN.DOWN] == 1) {
        p.line(x, y, x+dx, y+dy);
    }

    x += dx;
    y += dy;

    previousPen = pen;
  }
}

// p5.js automatically call the drawing function.
new p5(sketch, 'SketchRNN');
```

It is necessary to prepare an HTML page to use the model's code. The canvas area is added in the DOM whose id is sketch:

```
<!DOCTYPE html>
<head>
  <script src="scripts/ch3.ts" defer></script>
</head>
<body>
  <div id='sketch'></div>
</body>
```

As the model used by this application is for drawing a cat, the image drawn by the application looks like this:

It is amazing that we can build such a creative application by writing just a few lines of code. Thanks to the pre-trained model and flexible framework, it is easy to create such an application quickly. We can make use of the library not only for images but also for audio.

Lastly, we are going to look at one more library that can be widely used.

XOR classification with machinelearn.js

machinelearn.js is yet another machine learning framework running on the web platform. The primary characteristic of this framework is simplicity. machinelearn.js is originally designed to solve complicated problems by running a machine learning algorithm in a simple manner. Simplicity attracts many developers who are not familiar with machine learning. The latest version of machinelearn.js includes the following algorithms:

- Clustering:
    - K-Means
- Decomposition:
    - PCA
- Classification:
    - Bagging
    - Random forest
    - Logistic regression
    - SGD
    - Naive Bayes
    - Support vector machine
    - K-nearest-neighbors
    - Decision trees
- Regression:
    - Lasso
    - Linear regression
    - Ridge
    - SGD
- Model selection:
    - K-fold
    - Train and test split

As you can see, machinelearn.js is very similar to the traditional machine learning framework. The algorithms implemented by the library are pretty mature compared to ML5.js and Magenta.js. We can regard it as a framework for more general purposes. The API interface is designed to resemble the scikit-learn API. For example, a model is trained via the `fit` method of the algorithm in the same manner as scikit-learn.

Random forest classifier

In this section, we will look at how to classify using a random forest classifier. For instance, this code emulates the output of XOR logic by using `RandomForestClassifier`:

```
import { RandomForestClassifier } from 'machinelearn/ensemble';

async function trainAndPredict() {
  // The 2-dimensional input
  const X = [
    [0, 0],
    [0, 1],
    [1, 0],
    [1, 1]
  ];

  // Target value for the output of XOR
  const y = [
    0,
    1,
    1,
    0
  ];

  const model = new RandomForestClassifier();
  model.fit(X, y);

  const result = model.predict(X);
  console.log(result);
}

trainAndPredict();
```

Simply passing the input data and target value to the model in the `fit` method gives you a trained model. Not all models in machinelearn.js use TensorFlow.js as the backend, but the project tries to enhance the library to use TensorFlow.js as the core implementation so that it can receive the benefit when TensorFlow.js improves its own performance.

The following code exports the model in JSON format, converts it from a JSON string to a JSON object, and then loads it from the JSON object:

```
// Export the model in plain JSON format.
const modelStr = JSON.stringify(model.toJSON());

// Convert the JSON string to JSON object.
const loadedModel = JSON.parse(modelStr);

// Load the model from the given JSON object.
model.fromJSON(loadedModel);
```

machinelearn.js defines a model serialization format that is human-readable. It gives us the power to exchange the trained model through network flexibly because we can utilize the existing web API platform supporting JSON format.

Summary

In this chapter, we have introduced several machine learning frameworks running on the web. Since tfjs-models and Magenta.js are mainly developed by the same community as TensorFlow.js, they can be naturally integrated with TensorFlow. These libraries contain many state-of-the-art machine learning models and even include pre-trained model parameters. While tfjs-models contain various kinds of models for general purposes, Magenta.js is for more artistic applications. You will be able to find the appropriate machine learning model for your application type.

On the other hand, ML5.js and machinelearn.js are higher-level libraries. They provide tools and workflows that are indispensable for building common pipelines to train machine learning models such as preprocessing and dimensionality reduction. In addition to that, their usage and interface are similar to popular libraries such as scikit-learn and NumPy. It should be attractive to those who are creating a machine learning system in their daily work and are already familiar with these libraries. If you are seeking a library that implements mature machine learning models, ML5.js and machinelearn.js are solid options.

In the following chapters, we are going to implement machine learning algorithms by using these libraries if it is straightforward and practical. Bear in mind that even if we use a higher-level library, it does not mean we do not need to understand the characteristics of and when to use the algorithm. Recognizing the underlying details of an algorithm is always crucial to achieving the best performance. Writing code for using a machine learning model with knowledge of how it works will provide you the deepest insight that you can get.

In the next chapter, we will explore classification with logistic regression.

Exercises

1. Find the PoseNet demo application in tfjs-models and run it in your local machine: `https://github.com/tensorflow/tfjs-models/tree/master/posenet`.

2. Write an application that draws a circle where you click in the canvas area.

3. Build an application that classifies the given image by using:
    1. MobileNet in tfjs-models
    2. Image Classifier in ML5.js (`ml5.imageClassifier`)

4. Use the SketchRNN application to:
    1. Use the model for drawing a bird.
    2. By adjusting the temperature parameter of PDF, look into how the generated image is changed.

5. Train `RandomForestClassifier` from machinelearn.js to predict the output value of OR, AND, and NAND logic.

6. Build a pipeline, including preprocessing, as follows by using machinlearn.js:
    1. The input Iris dataset is available in machinelearn.js.
    2. The model is `RandomForestClassifier`.
    3. The model is evaluated by using `train_test_split`.
    4. The metric to evaluate the model is `accuracyScore`.

Further reading

- tfjs-models: `https://github.com/tensorflow/tfjs-models`
- MobileNet: `https://arxiv.org/abs/1704.04861`
- tfjs-data: `https://github.com/tensorflow/tfjs-data`
- tfjs-examples: `https://github.com/tensorflow/tfjs-examples`
- unpkg: `https://unpkg.com/`
- jsDelivr: `https://www.jsdelivr.com/`
- ml5.js: `https://ml5js.org/`
- p5.js: `https://p5js.org/`
- Magenta: `https://magenta.tensorflow.org/`
- LSTM: `ftp://ftp.idsia.ch/pub/juergen/lstm.pdf`
- A Neural Representation of Sketch Drawings: `https://arxiv.org/abs/1704.03477`
- machinelearn.js: `https://www.machinelearnjs.com/`

2

Section 2: Real-World Applications of TensorFlow.js

This section of the book will demonstrate how to write applications with TensorFlow.js. It includes some interesting cases, including image classification. We will learn how TensorFlow.js APIs are used. Readers will also learn how to implement k-means in TensorFlow.js and how to apply the Bellman equation to solve the Markov decision process problem.

This section contains the following chapters:

- Chapter 4, *Polynomial Regression*
- Chapter 5, *Classification with Logistic Regression*
- Chapter 6, *Unsupervised Learning*
- Chapter 7, *Sequential Data Analysis*
- Chapter 8, *Dimensionality Reduction*
- Chapter 9, *Solving the Markov Decision Process*

4
Polynomial Regression

This book aims to act as a comprehensive guide to help you implement machine learning applications using TensorFlow.js. Thus far, we have looked at the basics of the web platform and an overview of TensorFlow.js. Although further knowledge and building blocks to implement a machine learning application will be introduced later, what you've learned so far will be the basis for that.

From this chapter onward, we are going to implement real machine learning applications using TensorFlow.js. In this chapter, we are going to discuss how to implement a simple polynomial regression model with TensorFlow.js. You will learn about the basic building blocks of machine learning applications, such as the optimizer and the loss function to be optimized, and how they are used in the TensorFlow.js platform. To do this, we will implement a polynomial regression model that will fit the two-dimensional sine curve.

In this chapter, we will cover the following topics:

- What is polynomial regression?
- Two-dimensional curve fitting

Technical requirements

You will need the following tools for this chapter:

- TensorFlow.js
- A web browser (Chrome is recommended)
- JavaScript/TypeScript

Check out the following video to see the Code in Action:
http://bit.ly/2OzDbTk

What is polynomial regression?

First of all, let's explain what polynomial regression is. Polynomial regression is a machine learning algorithm that's used to predict the target value of a given dataset. It is a form of **supervised learning**. In supervised learning, the algorithm is given the training dataset with feature vector and target values. The algorithm constructs a model that is capable of predicting the new target value, which corresponds to new incoming features. Before we learn about polynomial regression, let's take a look at what supervised learning is.

Supervised learning

A machine learning problem whose training dataset is composed of a feature vector and a target vector (also known as a label) is called **supervised learning**. Supervised learning is a type of machine learning that requires us to specify the target value explicitly. The training dataset must contain the target vector, as well as feature vectors. As shown in the following diagram, the algorithm generates the model in the training phase with the given training dataset, including the feature vector and target values. In the prediction phase, the model is asked to estimate the target value that corresponds to the given feature vector:

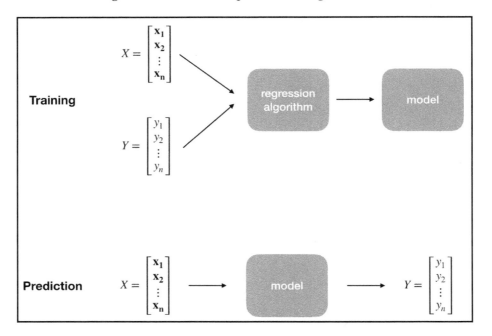

Roughly, there are three types of machine learning application processes: supervised learning, unsupervised learning, and reinforcement learning. Typical problems that occur with supervised learning include classification and regression problems. Just like handwritten digit recognition, in classification, it's difficult to map the input vector to the discrete category. If the output is a continuous value, it's called a regression problem.

Therefore, with regression problems, it's our task to predict the target continuous value from the given multidimensional vector that's not contained in the training dataset. Naturally, the model should get some amount of generality to predict the unknown target precisely. That is the primary goal of supervised learning.

The simplest linear model

A regression model is a machine learning model that estimates the target value using information from a set of given variables. The purpose of the model is to describe the relationship between explanatory variables and the target value as a statistical model.

As an example, let's assume we want to construct a linear model with only one explanatory variable. In the following example, x is a variable and y is the target value to be predicted. The samples we obtained for training are represented as gray dots in the following graph:

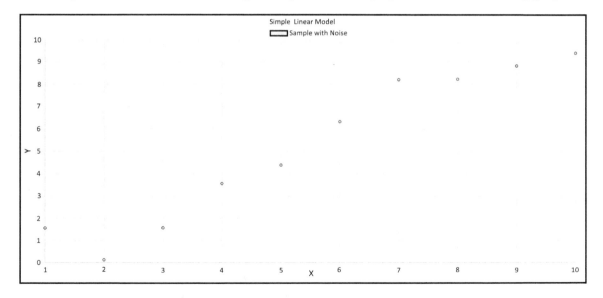

Our goal is to construct a line that fits the sample dataset as much as possible. The simplest linear model is expressed as follows:

$$y = ax + b$$

The parameter that needs to be trained has a linear relationship with the features and is known as a **linear model**. This model is described as a straight line in the two-dimensional chart. We need to estimate a and b to fit the line with the given x and y as much as possible. The following graph shows what the correct estimation result looks like. The straight line labeled `Target` in the legend in the chart is close to most of the points in the sample dataset, so it's regarded as the model showing the underlying structure of the samples. Once the model has been constructed and is sufficiently general, we can predict the target value, y, for the unknown x using the model. For example, our estimation gives us a = 1.0, and b = 0.0. Therefore, we can predict the target value for x = 11 by calculating *1.0 * 11 + 0.0 = 11*. This is exactly what we want to do with the machine learning model:

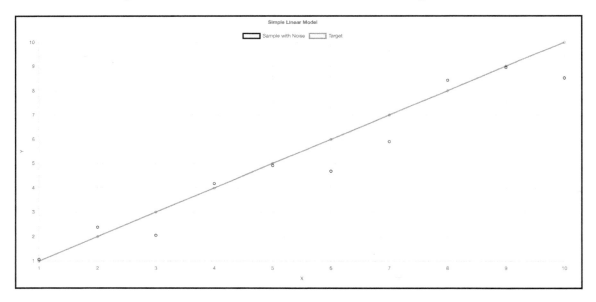

As you may have already noticed, the model we are talking about is not very expressive when it comes to representing the complicated structure of the dataset. The capability of a 1-degree polynomial is limited due to its small number of free parameters. It only has a and b. Do you think it is possible to predict the target value with the following samples in the curve? For example, is it capable of predicting the correct value from the sample in the following sine curve?

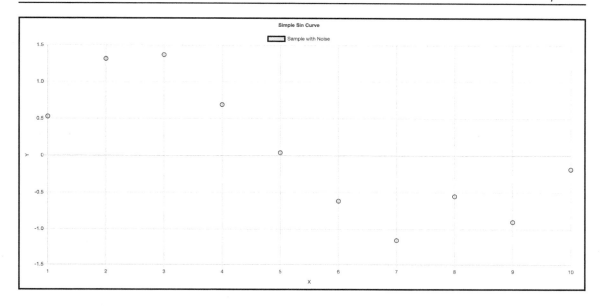

Technically, the simplest linear model will give us a significantly poor result for this sample dataset. In the next section, we are going to look into a more general model, called the polynomial model, to estimate a more complicated data structure.

General polynomial model

A polynomial model is a general form of linear regression model. The linear regression model can be described as a linear equation that has the first-degree term of the explanatory variable. The polynomial regression model needs to have higher degree terms to have more expressive power. Polynomial regression can be described mathematically as follows:

$$f(x) = y = w_0 + w_1 x + w_2 x^2 + \cdots + w_n x^n = \sum_{j}^{M} w_j x^j$$

Theoretically, the infinite number of the sum of polynomial terms can express any function. This indicates that the model can fit any kind of sample by adding more terms. Let's see how the model can represent a more complicated curve, as shown in the previous section.

However, there is still one problem we need to discuss. How can we calculate the appropriate value, that is, ws, in the equation to fit the given samples? Generally, it is essential to define two components to complete the process of finding the optimal parameter (ws) in a machine learning algorithm. These are the loss function and the optimizer.

The loss function

The loss function is a function that defines the error between the prediction result and the sample dataset. The function value is calculated based on model parameters (w_j), sample datasets (X), and target values (Y). Therefore, the loss function to be minimized can be expressed as follows:

$$E(\mathbf{w}, X, Y)$$

Since the feature dataset and target values (X and Y) are given in advance, the parameters we can control in the optimization process are only model parameters, w. Our goal is to find the parameter that gives us the optimal (minimal) value of E. In short, the task of machine learning is finding the model parameter that provides the minimal value of the loss function.

The loss function for the aforementioned curve-fitting problem can be defined as the sum of the mean squared error:

$$E(\mathbf{w}) = \frac{1}{2N} \sum_{n}^{N} (f(x) - y)^2$$

The prediction value that's given by the model is calculated using the parameters ($\mathbf{w}$) and given features (x). In this case, you may find that we can calculate the optimal value by calculating the derivative function of E. But generally, it is pretty hard to find the optimal value and parameters by giving that value analytically. The loss function can be any kind of function that helps find or approximate the optimal values since they can't always be computed analytically.

Therefore, an iterative method for optimizing the objective function is a typical solution if we want to seek the optimal parameter in the machine learning model. Although the iterative method doesn't always reach the global optima, it is possible to apply it to almost any type of objective function, as long as it is differentiable, because the algorithms for iterative optimization use the gradient that's calculated from the derivative function.

Now, our goal is clear: finding the optimal value of the differentiable loss function, E. But what kind of algorithm gives us the optimal value efficiently?

Optimizer for machine learning

An algorithm that decides how the iterations are processed is called an **optimizer**. The optimizer uses an initial guess of the value and keeps improving the approximate optimal value continuously. In each iteration, the optimizer provides a better value than the previous value so that we can find the optimal value along with the iterations. The optimization algorithms that are mainly used in machine learning are derived from **gradient descent**. Gradient descent is a first-order iterative optimization algorithm that uses the first-order gradient of the objective function to find the direction we should move in in the next iteration. Let's say the objective function is $E(\mathbf{w})$ and that the parameter to be adjusted is $\mathbf{w}$. The gradient descent algorithm is described as follows:

$$\mathbf{w}_{i+1} = \mathbf{w}_i - \alpha \nabla E(\mathbf{w}_i)$$

i represents the iteration, α is a hyperparameter that specifies how much the parameter is updated in one iteration, and ∇E is the gradient of the current point. This indicates that $\mathbf{w}_i$ is updated by subtracting the gradient in each iteration. The next parameter, $\mathbf{w}_{i+1}$, will give us the smaller value of the objective function, E, if the hyperparameter, α, is small enough. Why? According to Taylor's theorem, the difference between the current value and the next value can be described as follows:

$$E(\mathbf{w}_{i+1}) - E(\mathbf{w}_i) = E(\mathbf{w}_i - \alpha \nabla E(\mathbf{w}_i)) - E(\mathbf{w}_i)$$
$$= \alpha \left(\nabla E(\mathbf{w}_i)^T (-\nabla E(\mathbf{w}_i)) + \frac{o(\alpha)}{\alpha} \right)$$
$$= \alpha \left(-|\nabla E(\mathbf{w}_i)|^2 + \frac{o(\alpha)}{\alpha} \right)$$

We will see that the value of E is decreased if α is small enough. This is because $o(\alpha)/\alpha \to 0$ if $\alpha \to 0$. Therefore, setting the alpha to an appropriate value is another challenge in the optimization problem. This is the process of hyperparameter tuning. Although we aren't going to deep dive into the details of how to calculate the alpha in this book, bear in mind the necessity to adjust the alpha parameter if the optimization process doesn't show good progress. Some good and simple practices are as follows:

- If the loss vibrates, use the smaller alpha.
- If the loss doesn't converge for long iterations, use the larger alpha.

Overall, the pseudocode of the algorithm is as follows. Once we set the initial parameter with a random value, the algorithm keeps updating the parameter by each iteration and is expected to reach the optimal value:

```
Initialize w, alpha
i = 0
while true
   if w is providing the sufficient optimal value return it.
   d = gradient(E, w, i)
   w = w - alpha * d
   i += 1
end
```

When the objective function is described as multiple level sets, the act of the algorithm moving the parameter can be expressed as follows:

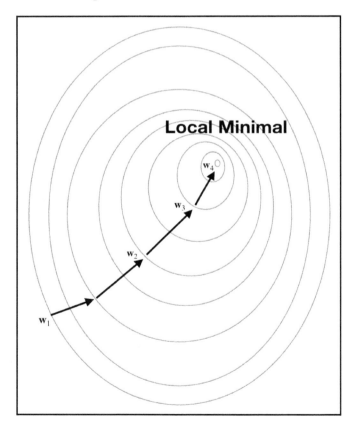

If we decrease the objective function in every iteration, the move is a monotonically decreasing process:

$$E(\mathbf{w}_1) > E(\mathbf{w}_2) > E(\mathbf{w}_3) > \cdots > E(\mathbf{w}_i) > \ldots$$

Hopefully, the sequence of $\mathbf{w}_i$ will converge to the desired local minimum. Although the objective function needs to have certain assumptions to complete this process successfully (differentiable, convex, and more), the loss functions that are commonly used in machine learning applications have such characteristics by nature.

In this case, the goal of optimization is to find the minimal value of the loss function, E. However, you may want to find the maximum value of the objective function in some cases. If you want to increase the value of the objective function, just rewriting the objective function so that it returns the negative value of the original function works:

$$E'(\mathbf{w}) = -E(\mathbf{w})$$

By using optimizers, we can find the optimal value without caring too much about the shape of the objective function. Generally, what we need to do is define the loss function and choose an optimizer from the list of optimizers that's provided by the library you are using. At a practical level, the choice of optimizer sometimes has a significant impact on the final accuracy and speed of convergence.

Optimizers in TensorFlow.js

Actually, there are many improved versions of the gradient descent algorithm. The following is the list of optimizers provided by TensorFlow.js:

- Stochastic gradient descent
- Momentum
- AdaGrad
- AdaDelta
- Adam
- Adamax
- RMSprop

Basically, they are derived from the original gradient descent algorithm, but the differences exist in the way we calculate the updated value in the training iteration. For example, Momentum is an algorithm that helps us avoid vibration, which tends to happen close to the local minimum and is expected to make convergence faster. The updated value of the momentum algorithm is calculated as follows:

$$\Delta \mathbf{w}_i = -(1 - \mu)\alpha \nabla E(\mathbf{w}_i) + \mu \Delta \mathbf{w}_{i-1}$$
$$\mathbf{w}_{i+1} = \mathbf{w}_i + \Delta \mathbf{w}_i$$

The most notable change exists in the first equation. In addition to the gradient of the current iteration, it calculates the weighted average of the gradient and the previously updated value. It keeps the updated value in the previous iteration so that the weight parameter is kept updated, even in the space where the gradient is small.

As we can see, each optimizer has different performance characteristics, and the hyperparameters of the optimizer should also be tuned in accordance with the model you are using. In the deep learning model, the Adam algorithm is commonly used because it converges quickly and achieves high accuracy in general. With so many options, you can find the best optimizer fitting for your use case.

Now, we will learn how to derive the polynomial equation by emulating the given sine curve.

Two-dimensional curve fitting

In this section, we are going to implement an application so that we can fit the given two-dimensional curve using the polynomial model. Previously, we saw that the polynomial model can emulate any function if we can calculate the sum of its terms infinitely. Let's see what prediction looks like with the two-degree polynomial model.

Preparing the dataset

First, we are going to prepare the dataset. The dataset is two numerical sequences representing x and y values in a two-dimensional space. The target value to be predicted by the model is a sine curve in each point. To make the situation as close to the real world as possible, we have added Gaussian random noise to the target value.

`tf.randomNormal` is a function that samples values from the normal distribution so that we can create noisy data just by adding it to the original sine values:

```
import * as tf from '@tensorflow/tfjs';

const doublePi = tf.scalar(2.0 * Math.PI);

// Sequence of x
const xs = tf.mul(doublePi, tf.range(-0.5, 0.5, 0.01));

// y is a sine curve with gaussian noise
const noise = tf.randomNormal([xs.size]).mul(0.05);
const ys = tf.sin(xs).add(noise);
```

This results in the following output:

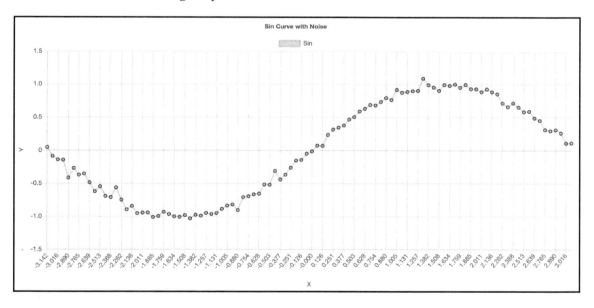

This is the sine curve in the range $(-\pi, \pi)$. You can see that each point is vibrating with the noise. Our task is finding the function $f(x)$ that satisfies the following condition:

$$y = f(x) = \sin(x)$$

A polynomial model is one that fits the given two-dimensional curve.

Applying the 2-degree polynomial model

Once our model is able to emulate the sine function, we are able to predict the sine value with any given input. The 2-degree polynomial regression model is constructed as follows:

```
const w0 = tf.scalar(Math.random() - 0.5).variable();
const w1 = tf.scalar(Math.random() - 0.5).variable();
const w2 = tf.scalar(Math.random() - 0.5).variable();

// f(x) = w2*x^2 + w1*x + w0
const f_x = x => {
  return w2.mul(x).mul(x)
  .add(w1.mul(x))
  .add(w0);
}
```

Now, we have defined the 2-degree function that will be adjusted by the optimization process. To specify the trainable variable explicitly, it is necessary to use the `variable` method in tensor in TensorFlow.js. We have initialized the variables with the random variable that we sampled from the uniform distribution. The optimizer automatically finds the trainable variable and adjust the parameters in the iterative process. In this case, *a*, *b*, and *c* are the trainable parameters:

$$f(x) = w_2 x^2 + w_1 x + w_0$$

Loss function by mean squared error

Next, we need to define the loss function as the objective function to be optimized. The loss function that's commonly used for regression problems is **mean squared error** (**MSE**). This can be calculated as follows:

$$E(\mathbf{w}) = \frac{1}{n} \sum_i^n (y_i - f(x_i))^2$$

It is just an average of the difference between the target value and the predicted value from the model. The gradient of the loss function is calculated like this so that we can apply the updating logic:

$$\mathbf{w} = \begin{pmatrix} w_2 \\ w_1 \\ w_0 \end{pmatrix}$$

$$\nabla E(\mathbf{w}) = -\sum_{i}^{n} 2(y_i - f(x_i)) \begin{pmatrix} x^2 \\ x \\ 1 \end{pmatrix}$$

We can define the MSE loss function in TensorFlow.js as follows:

```
const loss = (pred, label) => pred.sub(label).square().mean();
```

Here, we've defined the polynomial model and loss function. Then, we can construct the optimizer for the model so that we can keep updating the parameter iteratively. This time, let's try to use the Adam optimizer to converge the optimal value quickly:

```
const learningRate = 0.3;
const optimizer = tf.train.adam(learningRate);
```

The Adam optimizer needs to have four hyperparameters configured:

- `alpha`: Learning rate
- `beta1`: Exponential decay rate for the first moment estimation
- `beta2`: Exponential decay rate for the second moment estimation
- `epsilon`: A small constant that's used for numerical stability

If the final value that's given by the loss function doesn't show a satisfying result, it may be time to tune these parameters. The learning rate alpha is the one we should try to tune first because the learning rate is the common hyperparameter configuration most optimizers have. Let's take a look at how the iteration progresses as we change the learning rate.

Looking into the optimization process

Optimization is processed by the `minimize` method of the optimizer. The method is called per iteration of the optimization process. Thus, it is necessary to call it multiple times until the returned value from the loss function converges:

```
for (let i = 0; i < 100; i++) {
    const l = optimizer.minimize(() => loss(f_x(xs), ys), true);
    losses.push(l.dataSync());
}
```

Since the `minimize` method returns the tensor containing the loss value of the iteration, we can visualize the history of the loss function in the training process. The following chart visualizes the loss values in 100 iterations:

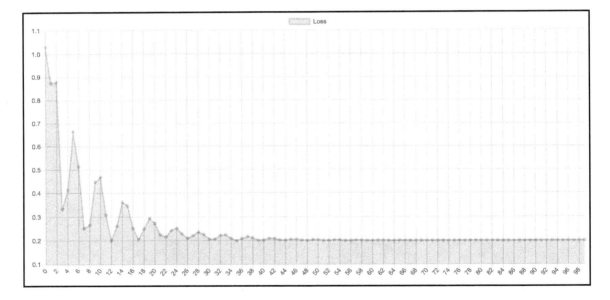

The preceding chart shows that the loss value converges around 0.2. Even if we increase the number of iterations further, the final loss value isn't likely to change. How about changing the learning rate with the same optimizer? Here is the loss value transition with a learning rate of 0.03:

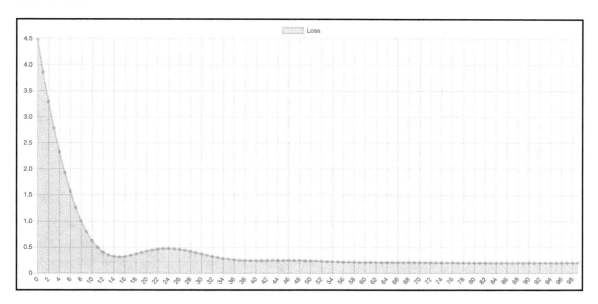

As you can see, the curve is smoother than the previous one. Generally, the large learning rate can cause vibration around the local minimal value because it may keep jumping to the opposite side across the minimal point. Making the learning rate smaller contributes to helping the iteration process consistently decrease so that the graph is likely to be smoother.

Fitting the curve

The final curve that's expressed by the final 2-degree polynomial model is as follows:

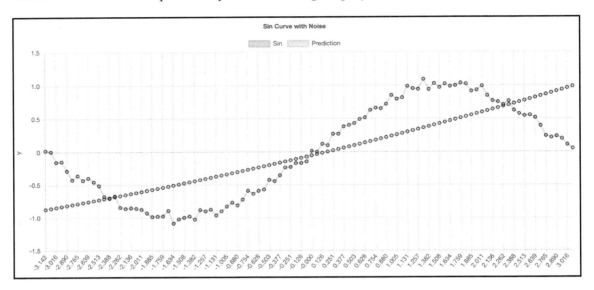

Unfortunately, it is difficult to say that our model fits the sine curve well. The training process seemed to work well because the loss function was constantly decreasing. There's nothing wrong in the training process itself. The problem is our choice of model. The sine curve is too complex to express with a 2-degree simple polynomial model. The model doesn't have sufficient expressiveness to represent the given sine curve. We call this problem **underfitting with the high biased model**. Underfitting is the situation when the algorithm oversimplifies the output model so that it doesn't fit, even with the training dataset. This always leads to a high error rate for both the training and the test datasets. It can happen when we use a very simple model to capture the underlying complex structure of the given dataset or when we have an insufficient amount of data.

To overcome this situation, we need to choose the expressive model rather than the 2-degree one. Let's try the 3-degree polynomial model here:

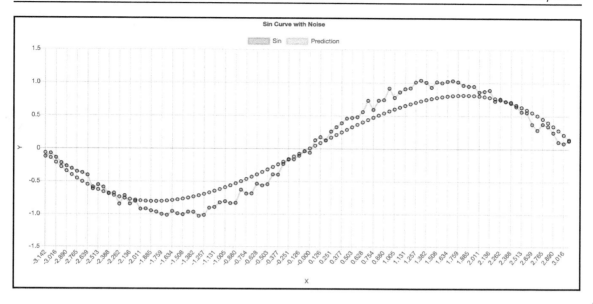

The curve that's been rendered by the model almost fits the sine curve perfectly. Apparently, the two-dimensional polynomial model has two peak points that match the peak of the sine curve. In fact, the total loss (MSE) that was calculated by the predicted result is far less than it was for the two-dimensional model:

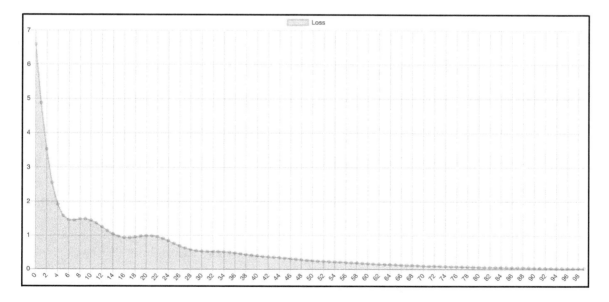

So, if we can increase the degree of the polynomial model, will the loss be far smaller? In this case, this isn't true. Just increasing the complexity of the model will make the situation worse. This is shown in the following chart, which has a 6-degree polynomial model:

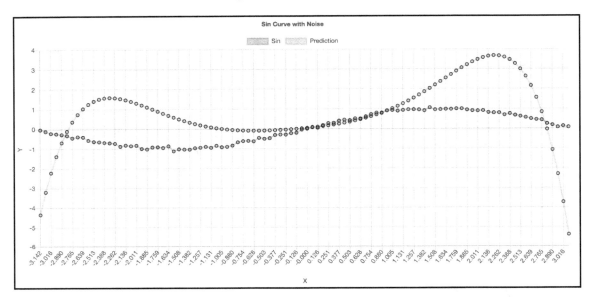

This is a problem known as **overfitting**. To overcome this type of problem, we need to understand the trade-off between bias and variance. We are going to explain this in the chapters that follow.

Summary

In this chapter, we introduced how the regression problem can be solved by TensorFlow.js. The regression problem is common in any machine learning application. Now, you know how to write an application that solves this type of problem.

You have learned what the regression problem is and how the polynomial regression model can be applied to solve the problem. Polynomial regression is a simple mathematical model that predicts the continuous target value. However, it can show a pretty good result if we use a well-tuned optimizer such as Adam. Therefore, you should also learn how iterative optimization works. We will look at this continuously throughout this book.

Regression problems can appear in any kind of format, but for simplicity, we tried to solve the sine curve fitting problem as an example of a regression problem. You saw how your model fit the target curve properly or not by visualizing the result. Of course, you can fit the cosine curve and any curve within any dimensional space.

In addition to the regression problem, classification is another typical use case where machine learning is applied.

In the next chapter, we will cover how to apply TensorFlow.js to solve the classification problem practically.

Questions

1. Which shows the better result in the sine curve-fitting problem? SGD or the Adam optimizer?
2. Try to find the best hyperparameter combination among the following parameter list:
   - Learning rate: 0.01, 0.1, 1.0
3. Run the training process with the 5-degree polynomial model to train the sine curve. Then, answer the following questions:
   - How does the cost that's returned by the model change?
   - What happens if you increase the number in a dataset?
4. How does the result of the prediction change when you use the sine curve without any noise?

Further reading

- Stochastic gradient descent: https://en.wikipedia.org/wiki/Stochastic_gradient_descent
- TensorFlow.js optimizers: https://js.tensorflow.org/api/latest/#Training-Optimizers
- *On the importance of initialization and momentum in deep learning*, by Ilya Sutskever, James Martens, George Dahl, and Geoffrey Hinton: http://www.cs.toronto.edu/~fritz/absps/momentum.pdf
- Bias-variance trade-off: https://en.wikipedia.org/wiki/Bias%E2%80%93variance_tradeoff

5
Classification with Logistic Regression

Logistic regression is one of the most commonly used linear classification models. Although it was developed a long time ago, it is still widely used in the practical field of industries. It is not only powerful but also simple enough that it can be a good resource when it comes to understanding the classification problem of machine learning.

This classification problem is categorized as a supervised learning-type problem and it is the most common setting in the machine learning field. It aims to attach the label to a new incoming instance by using information from past observations. These labels can be interpreted as non-ordered discrete values, unlike continuous values, which we learned about in the previous chapter. In this chapter, we are going to learn about a powerful traditional algorithm called **logistic regression** by trying to solve the binary classification problem. We can naturally apply what we will learn about in this chapter to the multiclass classification problem.

In this chapter, we will cover the following topics:

- Background of binary classification
- What is logistic regression?
- Classifying two-dimensional clusters

Technical requirements

You will need the following to complete the task in this chapter:

- TensorFlow.js
- JavaScript/TypeScript
- Node.js
- A web browser (Chrome)

Check out the following video to see the Code in Action:
`http://bit.ly/2016zCF`

Background of binary classification

Classification is a type of supervised learning. We need a machine learning model in order to predict the correct label for a new instance. For example, the handwritten image recognition problem is categorized as a classification problem. The most popular dataset for handwritten digits is MNIST. MNIST was developed by Yann LeCun, who won the Turing award in 2018 for leading the current boom of artificial intelligence research. This is the prediction result when using TensorFlow.js:

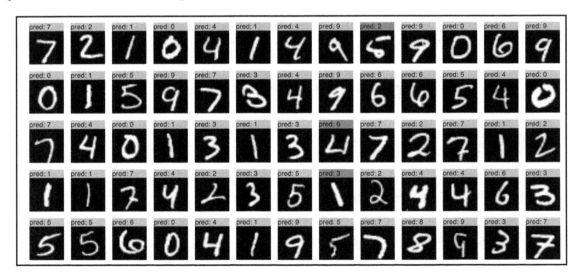

While handwritten digit classification is a multi-label classification problem, the problem we are going to solve in this chapter is binary classification. The target labels to be predicted in the binary classification situation have only two labels: positive and negative. In the following example, there are two classes: a set of rhombuses and circles. If these two classes can be isolated by drawing a line, then they are classed **linearly separable**. The following is an example of something that's linearly separable:

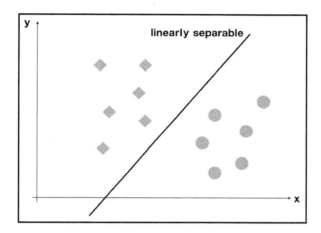

Not only is a linearly separable space easy to illustrate in a two-dimensional space, but it also has several properties that are beneficial when it comes to applying the logistic regression model. Now, let's take a look at what logistic regression is.

What is logistic regression?

Logistic regression is a simple yet powerful model that solves the linear classification or binary classification problem. Due to its simplicity, the algorithm is widely used in the practical industrial field. Although the model is easy to implement, it has enormous power, which can be demonstrated through a linearly separable dataset.

A logistic regression model is generally described as the linear relationship between the input vector and its parameters. Let's take a look at how the model is formulated:

$$p(C_1|\mathbf{x}) = \sigma(\mathbf{w}^T\mathbf{x})$$
$$p(C_2|\mathbf{w}) = 1 - p(C_1|\mathbf{w})$$

$p(C_1|\mathbf{x})$ and $p(C_2|\mathbf{x})$ are conditional probabilities that represent how the input vector belongs to the target class. For instance, if $p(C_1|\mathbf{x})$ is 0.9, then x is highly likely to belong to the C_1 class. In this case, there are only two target classes, and so the sum of them must always be 1. σ is **a logistic sigmoid function** that returns a value between 0 and 1. This function was originally developed by statisticians so that they could describe population growth. It has an S-shaped curve that can map a real input value to a range between 0 and 1:

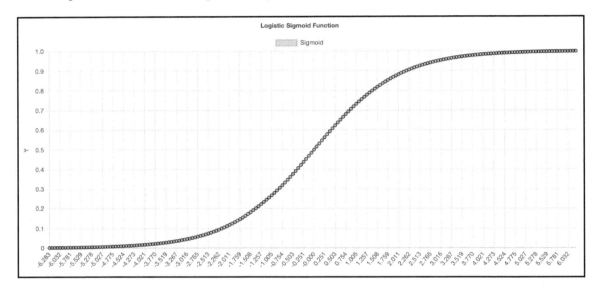

The main benefit of using this function is to be able to represent the probability of a specific condition. Since the output value range from between 0 and 1, it can be used as a probability marker.

But why can we assume that the model can be described as the linear relationship between the input vector (**x**) and the weight parameter? We will discuss this in the next section.

The behavior of the probabilistic generative model

Let's assume that there are two target classes: C_1 and C_2. By using Bayes' theorem, the posterior probability of C_1 can be described as follows:

$$p(C_1|\mathbf{x}) = \frac{p(\mathbf{x}|C_1)p(C_1)}{p(\mathbf{x}|C_1)p(C_1) + p(\mathbf{x}|C_2)p(C_2)}$$
$$= \frac{1}{a + \exp(-a)}$$
$$= \sigma(a)$$

In this case, we are using a logistic sigmoid function, σ, and defining **a** as follows:

$$a = \ln \frac{p(\mathbf{x}|C_1)p(C_1)}{p(\mathbf{x}|C_2)p(C_2)} = \ln \frac{\sigma}{1 - \sigma}$$

This inverted logistic sigmoid function is called the **logit function**, which is the ratio between the probabilities of two classes. Thus, it can be interpreted as the odds in the log scale. Now, we understand that the conditional probability of each class can be described as the logistic sigmoid function. But what kind of assumption is necessary if we wish to represent the model as the linear relationship between the input vector and weight parameters?

To get to this point, we need all the Gaussian distributions of each class to have exactly the same covariance matrix, which indicates that the shape of all the distributions is the same. Let's think about a situation where all the Gaussian distributions share the same covariance matrix:

$$p(\mathbf{x}|C_k) = \frac{1}{(2\pi)^{D/2}} \frac{1}{|\Sigma|^{1/2}} \exp\left\{ -\frac{1}{2}(\mathbf{x} - \mu_k)^T \Sigma^{-1} (\mathbf{x} - \mu_k) \right\}$$

D is the size of the dimension, while μ_k and Σ are the mean and covariance matrices of the distribution of the class, k, respectively. By combining these with the previous formulas, the posterior probability of class 1 can have a linear relationship with the following condition:

$$p(C_1|\mathbf{x}) = \sigma(\mathbf{w}^T \mathbf{x} + w_0)$$

$$\mathbf{w} = \Sigma^{-1}(\mu_1 - \mu_2)$$
$$w_0 = -\frac{1}{2}\mu_1^T \Sigma^{-1} \mu_1 + \frac{1}{2}\mu_2^T \Sigma^{-1} \mu_2 + \ln \frac{p(C_1)}{p(C_2)}$$

Although this formula remains the follow-up question in this chapter, you can see that the conditional probability is the linear function of the input vector, **x**. If we append the constant value 1 to the input vector, we'll get a function that's similar to the one we saw at the beginning of this section:

$$\mathbf{x} = \begin{pmatrix} 1 \\ x_0 \\ \vdots \\ x_{D-1} \end{pmatrix}$$

$$\mathbf{w} = \begin{pmatrix} w_0 \\ w_1 \\ \vdots \\ w_D \end{pmatrix}$$

$$p(C_1|\mathbf{x}) = \sigma(\mathbf{w}^T\mathbf{x})$$

Therefore, the assumption that all the samples are generated from the Gaussian distributions that share the same covariance matrix gives us the linear function of the input vector in the logistic regression model. This assumption may seem natural to us because many types of events in the real world show the properties of Gaussian distributions.

As you will see throughout the rest of this chapter, this property is useful if we wish to optimize the parameters for several reasons. This assumption is also a pretty common observation in the real world. Typically, the data can be regarded as such since it's been sampled from a normal distribution. Sharing the same covariance matrix may seem to be too strict, but it is well-known that logistic regression still works in most cases.

Optimization process

As we saw in the previous chapter, it is necessary to define the optimizer in order to solve problems using a logistic regression model. Here, we need to consider the following:

- The optimization algorithm
- The loss function

The optimization algorithm is simple because any optimization algorithm can be used, just like the one we used for the regression problem. We can use the Adam optimizer, just like we did for polynomial regression. The only thing we need to deal with is the loss function. Of course, we can use the mean squared error as well, but we have a better loss function definition for binary classification.

Let's assume that the dataset is $\{\mathbf{x_n}, t_n\}$, where $t_n \in \{0, 1\}$ specifies the class label that the data belongs to. The likelihood is measured by the following function. It shows the probability of the model returning the correct result:

$$p(\mathbf{t}|\mathbf{w}) = \prod_{n=1}^{N} p(C_1|\mathbf{x}_n)^{t_n} \{1 - p(C_1|\mathbf{x}_n)\}^{1-t_n}$$

The function can be the target function to be maximized, but it is possible to make it a more appropriate format for iterative optimization. The loss function that's commonly used for binary classification is called the **cross-entropy loss function**, and it can be derived from the likelihood function:

$$E(\mathbf{w}) = -\ln p(\mathbf{t}|\mathbf{w}) = -\sum_{n=1}^{N} \{t_n \ln p(C_1|\mathbf{x}) + (1 - t_n) \ln(1 - p(C_1|\mathbf{x})\}$$

This format has a special characteristic that can be used for processing iterative optimization. As you may recall, the updated value is calculated using the gradient of the target function. Since we know the logistic regression model can be represented as $p(C_1|\mathbf{x}) = \sigma(\mathbf{w}^T \mathbf{x})$, the gradient of the cross-entropy loss function can be written like this:

$$\nabla E(\mathbf{w}) = \sum_{n=1}^{N} \{p(C_1|\mathbf{w}) - t_n\}\mathbf{x}_n$$

The gradient's contribution is reduced to multiplication, along with the difference in terms of the prediction result ($p(C_1|\mathbf{x})$), the target label (t_n), and the input vector ($\mathbf{x}_n$). Since the cross-entropy loss function is widely used for binary classification problems, we are also going to use it in the upcoming sections.

Now, let's learn how we can implement a logistic regression model with TensorFlow.js.

Classifying two-dimensional clusters

In this section, we are going to implement the logistic regression model using the core API of TensorFlow.js. This means that we will build the model by combining several kernel ops that are provided by the TensorFlow.js core API. You'll come to fully understand how the model works by implementing the algorithm from scratch.

Preparing the dataset

In this experiment, the dataset is a two-dimensional binary of clusters. The points in each cluster have been sampled from the Gaussian distribution. Although the same standard deviation is shared by all the base distributions that generate each cluster, the center of the distribution is shifted to make them separated clusters. For logistic regression to work well, the samples of each cluster need to be generated from the same shape distribution, as we explained previously. The following screenshot shows the samples from each cluster:

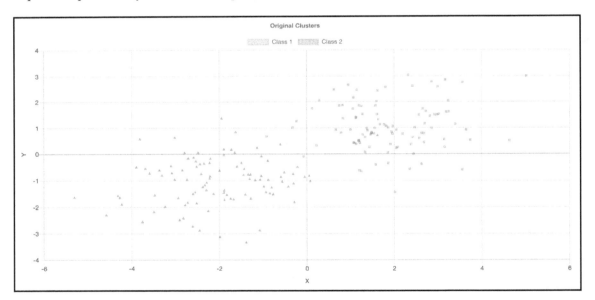

The rectangle points belong to class 1, while the triangle points belong to class 2. Both classes have been sampled from the Gaussian distribution, whose covariance matrix is shared. We can use the `randomNormal` method to generate the data:

```
const N = 100;

// Gaussian distribution whose mean is (2.0, 1.0)
const c1 = tf.randomNormal([N, 2]).add([2.0, 1.0]);

// Gaussian distribution whose mean is (-2.0, -1.0)
const c2 = tf.randomNormal([N, 2]).add([-2.0, -1.0]);

// Labels for the class 1 is 1.
const l1 = tf.ones([N, 1]);

// Labels for the class 2 is -1.
const l2 = tf.zeros([N, 1]);
```

In this case, we generate 100 points for each class. By adding the constant to the sampled data, we can shift the mean of the distribution. Since the output of the sigmoid function is 0 or 1 for each class, the label of class 1 is 1 and the label for class 2 is 0.

The constant value for the `bias` term can be added with the `concat` operation:

```
const xs = c1.concat(c2);
const input = xs.concat(tf.ones([2*N, 1]), 1);
const ys = l1.concat(l2);
```

`xs` and `ys` are the original datasets that contained the class 1 and class 2 data. `input` specifies the vectors, including the constant 1 value as the `bias` parameter. This tensor will be used as input for the training process.

Logistic regression model with the Core API

The space of the input vector is a two-dimensional space, the weight parameter is defined as the two-element variable, the variable is initialized with the random values from the Gaussian distribution, and the range is [-0.5, 0.5]. By marking these as variables, the optimizer can recognize them as trainable parameters. Since the input vector has three elements, including the bias term, the weight parameter should have three elements as well:

```
// Initialize the weight parameters
const w = tf.randomNormal([3, 1]).sub(-0.5).variable();

// f(x) = sigmoid(w*x)
```

```
const f_x = x => {
  return tf.sigmoid(x.matMul(w));
}
```

The model's output is the sigmoid function of the multiplication between the input vector and the weight parameter. Check that the function matches the mathematical equation we introduced previously:

$$p(C_1|\mathbf{x}) = \sigma(\mathbf{w}^T\mathbf{x})$$

Now, we need to find the optimal value of w through the optimization process of our loss function.

Optimizing with the cross-entropy loss function

The last thing we need to do is define the loss function and set up the optimizer. We already know that we can use the cross-entropy loss function for the binary classification problem. Fortunately, the major loss functions are already provided by TensorFlow.js. We are going to use the tf.losses.sigmoidCrossEntropy API to calculate the loss function this time:

```
// A function to return the loss value calculated from the given input and
prediction.
const loss = (pred, label) => {
  return tf.losses.sigmoidCrossEntropy(pred, label).asScalar();
}

// Adam optimizer
const optimizer = tf.train.adam(0.07);
```

As usual, we can iterate the optimization process. The following experiment iterates the optimization up to 100 times:

```
for (let i = 0; i < 100; i++) {
  const l = optimizer.minimize(() => loss(f_x(input), ys), true);
  losses.push(l.dataSync());
}
```

The following screenshot illustrates the result of the classification with the same input. As we can see, the model can classify the input vector correctly in most cases:

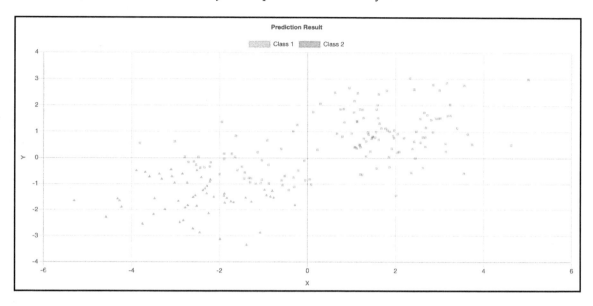

Since the loss value of each iteration also decreases constantly, the training process runs properly. The result doesn't look perfect, though:

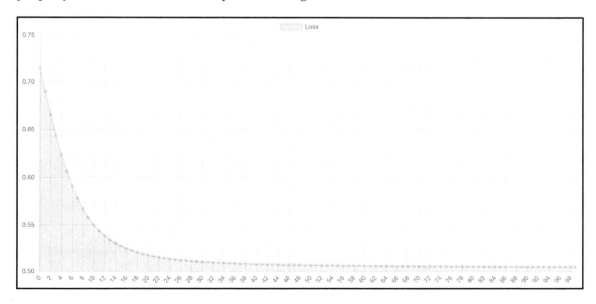

What will happen if we move the clusters? For instance, if we move two clusters close to each other, the performance will become worse. Since logistic regression highly depends on the linear relationship between the input vector and weight parameters, it can't classify the linearly separable clusters effectively:

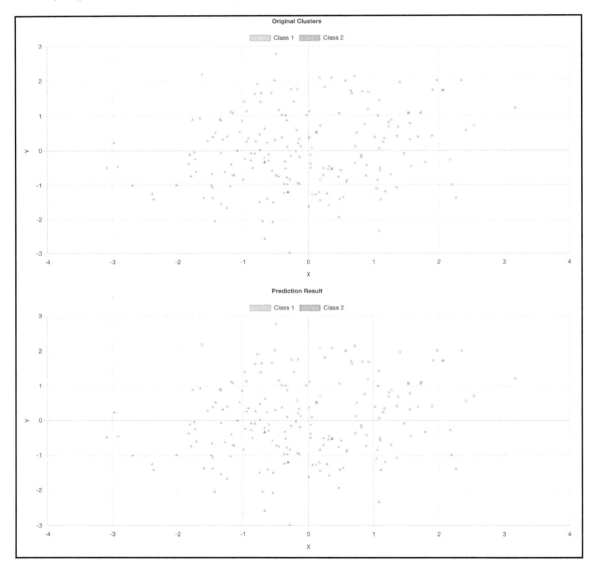

While we had a loss value of around 0.56 after 100 iterations in the previous case, we've only achieved 0.67 here:

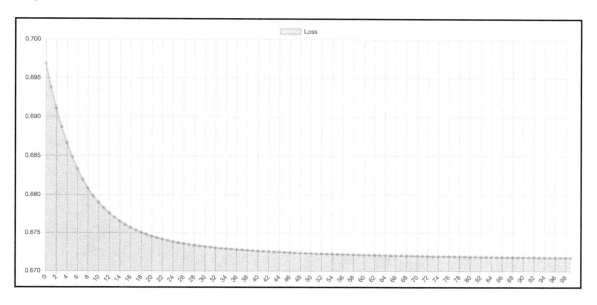

There are two possible ways to deal with this problem:

- Project an input vector into another space using a non-linear function
- Use a model that can classify a non-linear relationship

By mapping the original input vector to another space using a non-linear function, the input can be linearly separable. It is a common method to use the linear model on a complex dataset that cannot be classified by a linear classifier.

 Although we aren't going to do a deep dive into these methods, some references have been provided in the *Further reading* section, at the end of this chapter.

So far, we have seen how we can implement logistic regression with the low-level Core API, but there is another way we can do this. In the next section, we will use the Layers API to construct the logistic regression model.

Implementing a logistic regression model with the Layers API

Using the Core API allows you to construct the model in a flexible manner. Ideally, you can build any type of machine learning model that you like if you have a mathematical understanding of the model. However, in some cases, you may want to build a simple model such as logistic regression without writing much code.

The Layers API is an intuitive way to strike a good balance between flexibility and convenience. In this section, we are going to look into the implementation of logistic regression using the Layers API. The logistic regression model can be described as a single-layer neural network that has a single output connected to the input vector:

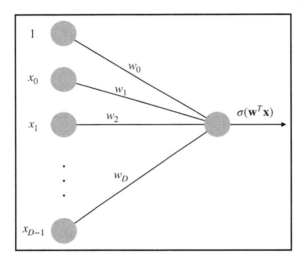

The input vector has (D+1) elements, and each element is connected to the output by the weight parameter. The raw output value is calculated as the inner product of w and x. The product is passed to the sigmoid function, which will be the output of the model. You can use the sequential model to build a multilayer neural network. The sequential model works if your model is a simple stack of multiple layers. All of the input of layers should be the output of the previous layers:

```
// Create a sequential model
const model = tf.sequential();

// Full connected layer
model.add(tf.layers.dense({units: 1, batchInputShape: [null, 2]}));
```

You can add each layer by using the `add` method. The dense layer is a layer whose input and output neurons are fully connected to each other. `units` is the size of the output, while `batchInputShape` specifies the shape of the input tensor that's aware of the batch size.

Like when we used the Core API, we can use the same loss function. To finalize the model's creation, it is necessary to call the `compile` method, along with the loss function and optimizer. In this case, the `adam` optimizer is being used. You can also pass the metric function in order to evaluate the model's accuracy in each iteration. `accuracy` counts the number of samples whose labels match the predicted label:

```
const loss = (pred, label) => {
  return tf.losses.sigmoidCrossEntropy(pred, label).asScalar();
}

model.compile({
  loss: loss,
  optimizer: 'adam',
  metrics: ['accuracy']
});
```

The function that's used to train the model needs to be called asynchronously so that we can get the training result by using the `await` keyword. We need to do this because the returned value from `fit` is Promise. `history`, which is returned by the `fit` method, contains information about the loss and metrics that were calculated in the iterative process. We train the model in 100 iterations, as we did previously. The `history` object contains the following properties:

- `epoch`: Indices of the iterations
- `history`:
    - `loss`: The history of loss values
    - `acc`: The history of accuracy metrics
- `params`: Parameter that's used for the optimization process (such as batch size)

This means that the loss value records for 100 iterations are contained in `history.history.loss`:

```
async function training() {
  console.log("start training...")
  const history = await model.fit(xs, ys, {
    epochs: 100
  });

  const ctx1 = document.getElementById('original');
```

```
        renderOriginal(ctx1, c1, c2);
        const ctx2 = document.getElementById('prediction');
        renderPrediction(ctx2, xs, model.predict(xs));
        const ctx3 = document.getElementById('loss');
        renderLoss(ctx3, history.epoch, history.history.loss);
    }

    training();
```

Since the training function doesn't block the main thread, it is possible to keep the application running without having to wait for the training process. TensorFlow.js implements the training process as an `async` function that returns a `Promise`. We can write the code so that we can render the result asynchronously, as shown in the following graph:

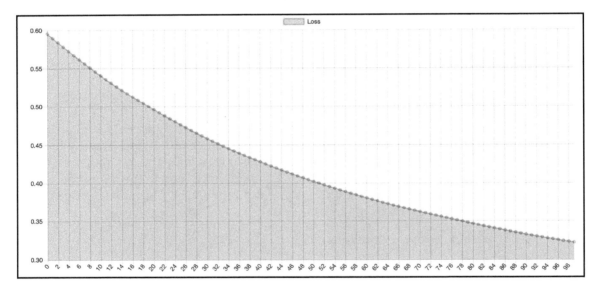

As you can see, the final loss value of the training process is around 0.33, which is lower than the previous case.

The logistic regression model can be easily illustrated as a single-layer neural network. You may not find any benefit in using the Layers API since it's not very different from the Core API in terms of the number of lines of code you need to write. However, if you want to implement a complicated neural network model (for example, a convolutional neural network), then the Layers API will help you save time implementing the model.

In the next section, we will look at one more example of implementing the logistic regression model by using a higher-level library, that is, `machinelearn.js`.

Implementing a logistic regression model with machinelearn.js

Software engineers don't always write applications from scratch. Often, we use an existing library or service if it meets our requirements as this saves on development time and allows us to focus on our application. This is often the case when developing machine learning applications.

`machinelearn.js` is a library that contains multiple implementations of popular machine learning algorithms. The library should be able to work like a Swiss Army knife in any machine learning implementation. First, you need to find an algorithm that you are comfortable using. Please add it to your dependencies in `package.json`:

```
{
  "name": "your-project",
  "version": "1.0.0",
  "description": "",
  "main": "index.js",
  "scripts": {
    "test": "echo \"Error: no test specified\" && exit 1"
  },
  "dependencies": {
    "@tensorflow/tfjs": "^1.1.2",
    "@types/chartjs": "^0.0.31",
    "chart.js": "^2.8.0",
    "machinelearn": "^2.1.3",
    "p5": "^0.8.0"
  }
}
```

You can use the logistic regression implementation of `machinelearn.js` without making too many modifications to the existing code:

```
async function training() {
  // Convert TypedArray to JavaScript array
  const xsData = tf.util.toNestedArray([N * 2, 2], xs.dataSync()) as
number[][];
  const ysData = tf.util.toNestedArray([N * 2], ys.dataSync()) as number[];

  console.log("start training...")
  await model.fit(xsData, ysData);
```

```
const ctx1 = document.getElementById('original');
renderOriginal(ctx1, c1, c2);
const ctx2 = document.getElementById('prediction');
renderPrediction(ctx2, xs, model.predict(xsData));
}
```

The model in `machinelearn.js` doesn't recognize the tensor data type from TensorFlow.js and TypedArray. It is necessary to convert tensors into JavaScript arrays so that they keep their original shape. TensorFlow.js provides a utility called `toNestedArray` so that we can make a TypedArray into a JavaScript array with a specified shape. For example, a `Float32Array` (original) with `[1, 2, 3, 4]` as its element can be squared by calling `tf.util.toNestedArray([2, 2], original)`. However, one thing to be careful of when using this method is typecasting. The returned type of the method will be `number` or `any[]`, which cannot be passed to the logistic regression model. Please ensure that you cast the type to the array of numbers appropriately.

You can dump the model in JSON format with the `toJSON` method:

```
start training...
▼ Object 🔲
    learning_rate: 0.001
  ▼ weights: Array(2)
      0: 1.6921625137329102
      1: 1.9352831840515137
      length: 2
    ▶ __proto__: Array(0)
  ▶ __proto__: Object
```

Other than containing weight parameters, it also contains the hyperparameters that are used by the optimizer. This allows us to restore the model from a JSON string, even though this isn't the standardized universal format that's shared with other libraries.

Summary

In this chapter, we looked at the theory behind the logistic regression model and how it solves the binary classification problem. Binary classification is a fundamental problem. You can naturally extend logistic regression to multiple class classification problems.

Ultimately, you learned about three ways in which you can implement a logistic regression model on the web. First, we looked at the TensorFlow.js Core API, which is suitable if we want to implement the algorithm in any way we like. It is capable of covering any kind of use case that can be solved by the operation graph. Then, we looked at the Layers API, which is useful if we want to construct a model that has a simple stack of neural layers. This API can help us build logistic regression but also proves its merit when it's used to create deep learning applications. Finally, we introduced machinelearn.js. A higher-level library such as machinelearn.js often helps us focus on the core of the application itself. Since it contains various kinds of implementations already, we won't lose anything from considering machinelearn.js in our application.

In the next chapter, we will learn about unsupervised learning.

Questions

1. Prove the linear relation of logistic regression by assuming that our Gaussian distributions share the same covariance matrix.
2. Change the learning rate of the optimizer and see how the loss value is increased/decreased in iterations.
3. Try to find the mapping function so that you can convert our non-linearly separable samples into linearly separable data points.
4. What will happen if the bias vector is not added to the input data?
5. What will happen if the loss function is changed? Change it to each of the following:
   - Mean squared error (`tf.losses.meanSquaredError`)
   - Absolute error (`tf.losses.absoluteDifference`)
   - Weighted loss (`tf.losses.computeWeightedLoss`)
6. Let's try to implement multiclass logistic regression that supports three-class predictions.
   - Hint: Combine two logistic regression models to do binary classification twice.
7. Save and load the logistic regression model in machinelearn.js.

Further reading

Refer to the following articles and links to learn more about the topics that we covered in this chapter:

- MNIST (http://yann.lecun.com/exdb/mnist/)
- Handwritten Digit Recognizer by TensorFlow.js (https://storage.googleapis.com/tfjs-examples/mnist/dist/index.html)
- linear_model.LogisticRegression from machinelearn.js: (https://www.machinelearnjs.com/api/linear_model.LogisticRegression.html)
- Loss functions in TensorFlow.js (https://js.tensorflow.org/api/latest/#Training-Losses)

Unsupervised Learning

6

So far, we've demonstrated how supervised learning works by looking at examples of regression and classification problems. In supervised learning, we already know the answer that will be predicted. In this chapter, the unsupervised learning problem will be introduced. This type of problem doesn't need the dataset to include the target value. We need to find the hidden pattern without any explicit target.

The clustering problem is a typical setting for unsupervised learning. It tries to make a group of samples in a natural manner. This chapter covers some ideas and algorithms that are useful for making groups of data points that focus on the implementation of the K-means algorithm.

The following topics will be covered in this chapter:

- What is unsupervised learning?
- Learning how K-means works
- Generalizing K-means with the EM algorithm
- Clustering two groups in a 2D space

Technical requirements

The following will be required in order to complete the tasks in this chapter:

- TypeScript/JavaScript
- A web browser (Chrome is recommended)
- A Node.js environment

Check out the following video to see the Code in Action:
http://bit.ly/37oGhlk

What is unsupervised learning?

As we mentioned previously, people often learn something without being given instructions to do so. They can find patterns by themselves and apply their own findings to the new observations naturally. This may be due to our creativity and our motivation to make meaningful progress in terms of the knowledge we seek. When we looked into machine learning algorithms, we learned that they need to be trained with a given target value. Due to this, you may have come to the assumption that computers don't learn anything unless they're provided with answers by a human.

Unsupervised learning is a type of machine learning problem that finds specific patterns spontaneously without getting the answers in the training phase. This sort of problem emerges not only when we don't have any clear answer to predict, but also when the purpose is not predicting the specific label in the first place. There are two typical use cases where unsupervised learning is utilized:

- Dimensionality reduction
- Cluster analysis

Dimensionality reduction is used to improve classification accuracy or make the prediction more efficient so that we can reduce the size of the samples without sacrificing accuracy. The goal of dimensionality reduction is to find the principal attribute of the data samples that make each piece of data unique. If we can find a feature that doesn't contribute to the classification result too much, reducing it can improve the performance of the classification model and even make it faster. As major examples of dimensionality reduction algorithms, **principal component analysis (PCA)** and **singular value decomposition (SVD)** are commonly used.

Cluster analysis is where we find a set of groups so that samples in the same group are more similar to each other than those of other groups. This problem description can be observed in various kinds of fields, such as pattern recognition, image processing, data compression, and machine learning. Let's think of a situation where each object in the world is grouped by certain criteria, but where the labels aren't specified. You can say that animals and fruits are different from each other even without knowing about the name of each category. The same goes for vehicles:

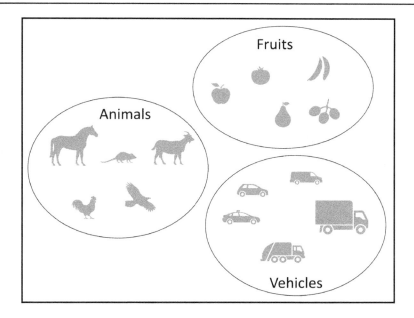

Therefore, the clustering algorithm allows us to find the implicit group structure of the given datasets. As you can see, it doesn't require the target value for the training process, which differs from supervised learning. The input of the model should only be the features of the samples. The K-means algorithm and other statistical cluster analysis algorithms often enforce us to convert the samples into a standardized numerical space for simplicity and efficiency. However, fundamentally, cluster analysis should be where we can define similarities between every data sample.

Next, we'll look at the famous K-means clustering algorithm. Then, we will discuss the EM algorithm, which is a general version of K-means and considers the probability of clusters.

Learning how K-means works

Now, we are going to illustrate how K-means works. This algorithm is the most famous clustering algorithm to be created and is widely used, regardless of the field. It is popular in both industry and academia due to its simplicity and efficiency. The purpose of this algorithm is to allocate a specific group to each sample in the dataset. Concretely, the task is to partition N samples into K clusters, in which each sample belongs to the nearest mean of the cluster.

The clustering problem is NP-hard in principle. K-means optimizes the loss function iteratively and converges the local minimum quickly. This means that it tries to minimize the given loss function step by step. In that sense, K-means is very similar to the supervised learning algorithms we introduced previously. The biggest difference is that the loss function can be calculated without any explicit target labels. It is also estimated by the algorithm.

A major well-known difficulty in K-means is that it is necessary to specify the number of clusters (which is often represented as K) in advance. This lets us seek the best *K*. To do so, we may need domain-specific knowledge about the data points or further computing power to explore the *K* value in a brute force manner. Although there are several methods we can use to find a good K value, we aren't going to look at them here. We are going to assume that the desired number of clusters has been provided.

Centroid

The representative point of a cluster is called a **centroid**. This is the center of the samples that belong to the cluster and works as a prototype of the cluster. Therefore, finding the appropriate centroids that partition samples in a good manner is the goal of the K-means algorithm:

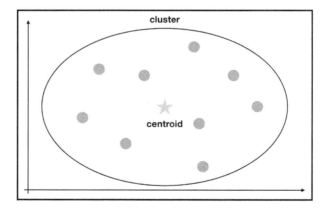

The centroid can be calculated as the mean of every point that belongs to the cluster. Assuming the sample points in the dataset are N vectors expressed as $X = \{\mathbf{x}_1, \mathbf{x}_2, \ldots, \mathbf{x}_n\}$, the centroid of the cluster, C_k, can be represented as follows:

$$\mu_k = \frac{1}{n_k} \sum_{i \in C_k} \mathbf{x}_i$$

This is just an equally weighted average of all the samples that belong to the cluster, C_k. The goal is to find the correct position of centroids. But how can we measure the *correctness* of centroids? As you may have guessed, the loss function acts as the measurement system for the centroids. In K-means, we measure the distance of each sample from the centroid of the cluster that the point belongs to. This is a simple and intuitive way to look at the definition of it:

$$\text{SSE} = \sum_i^n \sum_j^k w^{i,j} ||\mathbf{x}_i - \mu_j||^2$$

SSE represents the sum of the squared error. This error calculates the distance of the data points in the cluster from the centroid. Thus, $w^{i,j}$ represents the association of the data point to the cluster:

$$w^{i,j} = \begin{cases} 1 & \text{if } x_i \text{ belongs to the cluster } j \\ 0 & \text{otherwise} \end{cases}$$

In this sense, the right clustering is much better than the left. The total distance inside the cluster in the left clustering is much higher than the right. As you can see, the SSE loss function leads the result, which seems natural:

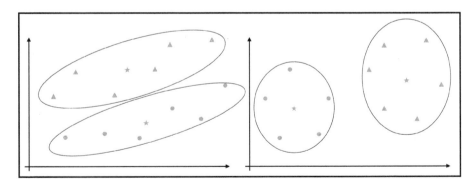

However, there is one problem with this loss function. There are two types of parameters that need to be optimized in the function: cluster assignment ($w^{i,j}$) and centroids (μ_j). These parameters are dependent on each other. Namely, the position of the centroids is given from the cluster assignments of each point. On the other hand, the cluster assignments depend on the distance between a point and the centroid that the point belongs to. Since we cannot optimize these two parameters in an iteration, we optimize them alternatively. That is what K-means does.

Algorithm

The K-means algorithm is so simple that we can quickly write it in 100 lines of code. The algorithm goes through the following steps to reach its goal:

1. First, it picks up data points from the samples as initial centroids.
2. Then, it assigns each sample to the closest centroid (μ_j) using the following formula:
   - $\mu_j, j \in \{1, \ldots, k\}$
3. Next, it updates the centroids so that they are at the center of the new clusters being led by the new cluster assignment.
4. Repeat steps 2-3 until the cluster assignment remains unchanged or reaches the maximum number of iterations.

First, we randomly pick up any centroids in the space. While it is possible to randomly generate centroids, it is also good to pick up k-points from the samples:

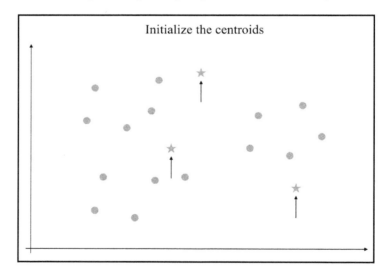

Then, we assign each sample to the closest centroid. This means that the sample is contained in the cluster represented by the centroid. In this step, each sample must belong to one cluster. Even if a point is close to multiple centroids in terms of distance, we only need to pick up one centroid. This is the most notable point of the K-means algorithm:

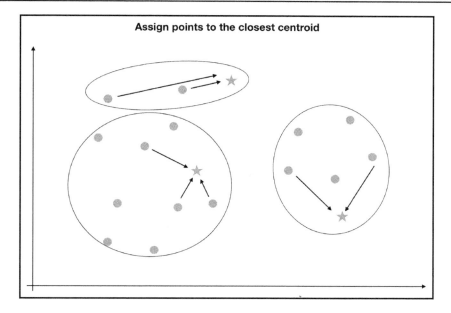

After that, we need to update the centroid's position based on the cluster assignment we calculated in the previous step. In this step, the centroid moves to the center of each cluster:

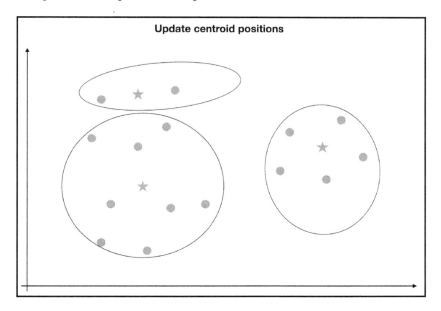

Then, we repeat steps 2-3 iteratively until it converges. The final cluster assignment may look like this:

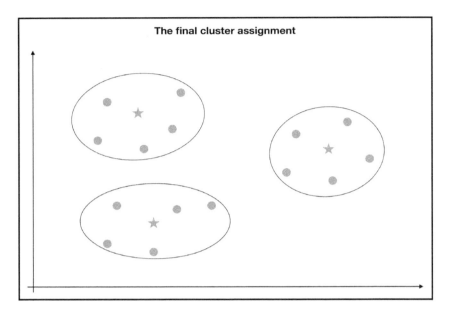

Each point belongs to the cluster naturally. When we can illustrate the result in a two-dimensional space, as shown here, it is easy to say that the clustering result is natural. But this isn't always true. What if the dataset is in higher dimensional space, which means we can't draw the result in a visible format? In this case, it is necessary to prepare the metrics so that we can evaluate the clustering result in a measurable manner.

Evaluation

There is nothing difficult about evaluating the results of the K-means algorithm. Simply using the loss function provides us with insight so that we can evaluate the clustering result. The loss function is the sum of the squared error:

$$\text{SSE} = \sum_{i}^{n} \sum_{j}^{k} w^{i,j} ||\mathbf{x}_i - \mu_j||^2$$

One challenge that the K-means algorithm usually faces is the decision of K. The desired number of clusters, K, must be provided as a hyperparameter. However, it is difficult to decide on the correct K parameter beforehand. Often, we don't have any information or knowledge on how many data points can be separated into clusters. In this case, the SSE metric is useful. Trying several patterns in a brute force manner should be helpful if we want to find the appropriate K value. This is called the **Elbow method**. The Elbow method illustrates the loss values by each K value and leads to the best value in a sufficiently generalized manner. The idea behind this method is to run K-means clustering on the dataset for a range of K values (the following example shows the losses for K values from 1 to 7). If the curve looks like an arm, the K value that has an "elbow" position is the best value:

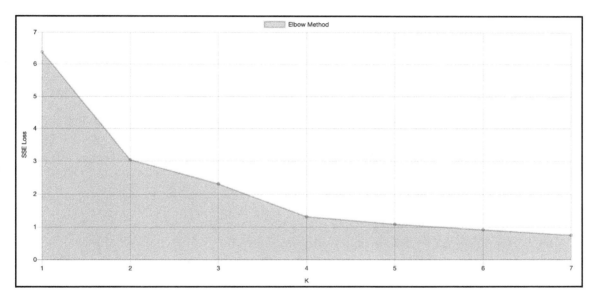

Technically, the SSE value decreases toward zero as we increase K because the SSE is zero when K is equal to the number of data points. Every data point belongs to its own cluster. But it is obvious that this cluster assignment hasn't been generalized intuitively. Therefore, our goal is to find the K value whose loss value is as small as the final values. The preceding chart indicates that the best K value is 3 or 4.

In this section, we demonstrated how K-means works. One notable thing about K-means is that each data point is assigned to one cluster exclusively. This is called a **hard cluster assignment**. However, as you can imagine, there are situations where it's difficult to decide on the cluster assignment distinctly. Let's take a brief look at a more general version of the clustering algorithm.

Generalizing K-means with the EM algorithm

The EM algorithm is a statistical algorithm that finds the maximum likelihood parameter. Since it supports **soft cluster assignment**, assuming that the mixed Gaussian distribution that generates samples and data can be assigned to multiple clusters at the same time with some degree of confidence, you will find that the algorithm is a general version of K-means clustering. The mixed Gaussian distribution that's generating the data is a weighted sum of the Gaussian distribution function:

$$p(\mathbf{x}) = \sum_{k=1}^{K} \pi_k \mathcal{N}(\mathbf{x}|\mu_k, \Sigma_k)$$

Each Gaussian distribution has μ_k as its mean and Σ_k as its covariance matrix. π_k represents the weight on the kth distribution for this sample. Now, let's introduce a hidden parameter to express the cluster assignment. Here, we will use π_k. z is a one-k-encoded vector. The data is assigned to the kth cluster, the kth element has a z of 1, while the other elements have a z of 0. The marginal distribution of z is given by π_k. Once the data has been observed, the posterior distribution of z is calculated by the third equation:

$$\mathbf{z} = \begin{pmatrix} z_1 \\ z_2 \\ \vdots \\ z_K \end{pmatrix}$$

$$p(z_k = 1) = \pi_k, \text{ prior distribution}$$

$$p(z_k = 1|\mathbf{x}) = \frac{\pi_k \mathcal{N}(\mathbf{x}|\mu_k, \Sigma_k)}{\sum_{j=1}^{K} \pi_j \mathcal{N}(\mathbf{x}|\mu_j, \Sigma_j)}, \text{posterior distribution}$$

Thus, our goal is to estimate the hidden parameter, z (true cluster assignment), of each data point so that we can know the true cluster label attached to the point. The posterior distribution can be regarded as the degree of how much the kth distribution "explains" the observation. This is often called the "**responsibility**" of the observation. In the EM algorithm, we aim to find the optimal responsibility with the given datasets.

It differs from K-means in that the hidden parameter representing the cluster assignment gives us the probability that the data belongs to the cluster. It indicates that each $z_1 \sim z_k$ can be 0~1. In this sense, the EM algorithm can solve the clustering problem in a more general way. The parameters that will be optimized by this EM algorithm are the position of the Gaussian distribution, μ_k, as well as K-means. The soft cluster assignment parameter, z, is optimized too. Please take care that each element shares the same covariance matrix to keep the discussion simple.

The algorithm

The algorithm for EM is pretty similar to the K-means algorithm. It keeps optimizing both parameters in an iterative manner. Let's go over these steps:

1. First, it initializes the Gaussian distribution's positions and prior distribution parameter, π_k.
2. **Expectation**: Then, it estimates the expected value of z by estimating π_k.
3. **Maximization**: Next, it updates the mean of the Gaussian distribution to the center of the new clusters that are led by the new cluster assignment.
4. Repeat steps 2-3 until the cluster assignment remains unchanged or reaches the maximum number of iterations.

Step 2 is called the expectation step since it estimates the expected value of responsibility. Although we've omitted the derivation of the estimation here, the responsibility is expressed as the ratio of how many data points are assigned to the kth cluster effectively (please note that N_k can be illustrated as a probability in the context of soft cluster assignment):

$$p(z_k = 1 | \mathbf{x}) = \frac{\pi_k \mathcal{N}(\mathbf{x}|\mu_k, \Sigma_k)}{\sum_{j=1}^{K} \pi_j \mathcal{N}(\mathbf{x}|\mu_j, \Sigma_j)}$$

$$N_k = \sum_{n=1}^{N} p(z_k = 1 | \mathbf{x}_n)$$

$$\pi_k = \frac{N_k}{N}$$

Once the responsibility has been estimated, we can maximize the target value by moving each element. This time, the mean of the Gaussian distribution can be estimated as the expected center of whole data points:

$$\mu_k = \frac{\sum_{n=1}^{N} p(z_k = 1|\mathbf{x}_n)\mathbf{x}_n}{\sum_{n=1}^{N} p(z_k = 1|\mathbf{x}_n)}$$

Overall, the EM algorithm keeps running the expectation step and maximization step alternatively.

Relationship with K-means

As we can infer, the estimation phase corresponds to cluster assignment in K-means, while the maximization phase corresponds to the phase where we calculate the next centroid. K-means is a hard clustering algorithm where each data point can belong to only one cluster. K-means is a special case of the EM algorithm that we described previously.

First, let's assume that each Gaussian distribution shares the same covariance matrix, expressed as ϵ. I, as an identity matrix:

$$\mathcal{N}(\mathbf{x}|\mu_k, \Sigma_k) = \frac{1}{2\pi\epsilon}\exp\{-\frac{1}{2}||\mathbf{x} - \mu_k||^2\}$$

By using this, the responsibility of the kth element for the data point, $\mathbf{x}_n$, is described as follows:

$$p(z_k = 1|\mathbf{x}) = \frac{\pi_k \exp(-||\mathbf{x}_n - \mu_k||^2/2\epsilon)}{\sum_j \pi_j \exp(-||\mathbf{x}_n - \mu_j||^2/2\epsilon)}$$

Although we aren't going to deep dive into a mathematical explanation, the responsibility converges to 1 with k so that $||\mathbf{x}_n - \mu_k||^2$ is minimal for $\epsilon \to 0$. This indicates that if the distribution does not spread, a data point is assigned to the cluster whose center point is closest. This matches what K-means aims to do.

On the other hand, the mean of each Gaussian distribution can be reformated so that it's compatible with the centroid definition of K-means clustering. It shows that the mean of the Gaussian distribution is the average of the points in the kth cluster. This is also exactly the same thing that K-means does:

$$\mu_k = \frac{\sum_{n=1}^{N} p(z_k = 1|\mathbf{x}_n)\mathbf{x}_n}{\sum_{n=1}^{N} p(z_k = 1|\mathbf{x}_n)}$$
$$= \frac{\sum_{n=1}^{N} w_{n,k}\mathbf{x}_n}{\sum_{n=1}^{N} w_{n,k}}$$
$$= \frac{\sum_{n=1}^{N} w_{n,k}\mathbf{x}_n}{N_k}$$

From this, we can conclude that K-means is a special version of the EM algorithm and takes on the responsibility of hard cluster assignment. Practically, not only K-means but also the EM algorithm with mixed Gaussian distribution is used since it is a powerful way to seek the optimal values of the hidden parameters. Implementing this algorithm is something you can try out by yourself as an exercise.

Clustering two groups in a 2D space

Understanding the theory behind the algorithm is still important. Let's try to run K-means clustering in order to separate three clusters in a two-dimensional space.

The three clusters

Three clusters are generated from the Gaussian distribution. Like we did in the previous chapter, we can use `tf.randomNormal` in TensorFlow.js to sample data points from the Gaussian distribution. The mean of the distribution is [0, 0] in a two-dimensional space. It is necessary to move the center by adding constants:

```
const N = 30;

const c1 = tf.randomNormal([N, 2]).add([2.0, 1.0]);
const c2 = tf.randomNormal([N, 2]).add([-2.0, -1.0]);
const c3 = tf.randomNormal([N, 2]).add([-2.0, 2.0]);

const xs = c1.concat(c2).concat(c3);
```

The three clusters can be illustrated as follows:

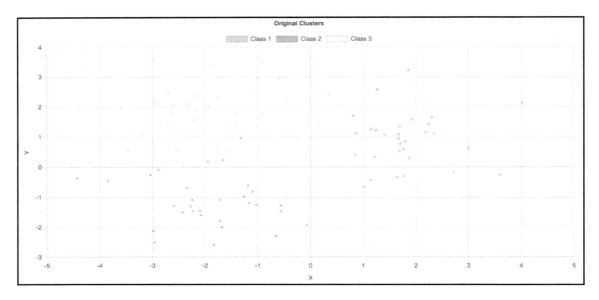

Since the clustering problem is a form of unsupervised learning, there are no target values to be predicted. The K-means algorithm only needs xs. In addition, K-means requires the number of desired clusters as a hyperparameter. When we have the data and the hyperparameters, the optimization process can be run iteratively:

```
// Initialize the model implementation.
const model = new KMeans(xs, 3);

const losses = [];
for (let i = 0; i < 10; i++) {
  const loss = model.update();
  losses.push(loss.dataSync());
}
```

In each iteration, KMeans finds the optimal cluster assignment and updates the position of the centroids. They correspond to steps 2 and 3 in the algorithm we introduced previously.

K-means implementation

The KMeans implementation has the following properties. The shape of the input data is assumed to be [batch size, dimension]. This would be [90, 2] in this case:

```
export class KMeans {
  // The desired number of clusters
  k: number;
  // The dimension of data points.
  dim: number;
  centroids: tf.Tensor;
  // Given data points
  xs: tf.Tensor;
  clusterAssignment: tf.Tensor;

  constructor(xs: tf.Tensor, k: number) {
    this.dim = xs.shape[1];
    this.k = k;
    // Initialize centroids by picking up K random points.
    this.centroids = tf.randomNormal([this.k, this.dim]);
    this.xs = xs;
  }
}
```

clusterAssignment is a tensor that stores the index of the cluster that each data point is assigned to. Thus, its shape will be [N, 1]. N is the number of data points. Now, we've completed the initialization of the algorithm. Next, we'll look at the method we'll be using for iterative optimization.

closestCentroids is a method that allocates the closest centroid to each point:

```
closestCentroids() {
  const expandedXs = tf.expandDims(this.xs, 0);
  const expandedCentroids = tf.expandDims(this.centroids, 1);

  const d = expandedXs.sub(expandedCentroids).square().sum(2);

  this.clusterAssignment = d.argMin(0);
  return d.min(0).mean();
}
```

expandDims adds the dimension to the given tensor with the specified position. Let's assume that we have the input tensor, xs, whose shape is [N, 2].tf.expandDims(this.xs, 0) will return the new tensor with the shape [1, N, 2]. The first dimension is added by the operation. In the same way, expandedCentroids will have the shape [3, 1, 2] because a new dimension is added to the first element. How is subtraction calculated with these two tensors? The sub method supports broadcasting, which replicates the value so that it matches the higher dimension:

```
expandedXs.sub(expandedCentroids)
```

This tensor has a shape of [3, N, 2], which specifies the difference in each element between the data points and the centroids. We can get the Euclidean distance by using square().sum(2). sum(2) specifies the summation by the second element so that the final shape is [3, N, 1]:

$$\mathbf{x} = \begin{pmatrix} x_1 \\ y_1 \end{pmatrix}$$

$$\mathbf{y} = \begin{pmatrix} x_2 \\ y_2 \end{pmatrix}$$

$$d = \sqrt{(x_1 - x_2)^2 + (y_1 - y_2)^2}$$

We will find the closest cluster index by calculating argMin(0). A zero is necessary for picking up the index of the cluster that gives us the minimum distance because the index of clusters is stored in the first dimension of the given tensor. The returned value of the method corresponds to SSE, which can be used as the loss function of the algorithm.

The next step in the iteration is to update the positions of the centroids:

```
updateCentroids() {
    const centers = [];
    for (let i = 0; i < this.k; i++) {
        // Get the data points assigned to the ith cluster.
        const cond = this.clusterAssignment.equal(i).dataSync();
        let index = [];
        for (let j = 0; j < cond.length; j++) {
            if (cond[j] == 1) {
                index.push(j);
            }
        }
    }
    const cluster = tf.gather(this.xs, index);
    const center = cluster.mean(0);
    centers.push(center);
}
```

```
        this.centroids = tf.concat(centers).reshape([this.k, this.dim]);
    }
```

What we are doing here is collecting the data point that was assigned to the cluster by the `gather` operation with the specified index. The mean of the collected data points is exactly the center of the cluster, that is, the centroid. Finally, we call `concat` to assemble multiple tensors into one tensor with a space of `[3, dimension]`.

The K-means algorithm keeps calling `closestCentroids` and `updateCentroids` alternatively:

```
update() {
    this.updateCentroids();
    return this.closestCentroids();
}
```

Since `closestCentroids` can return SSE, it directly returns it so that the caller can make use of it to illustrate the optimization progress. The following chart illustrates how the loss value of SSE is changed by the iterations:

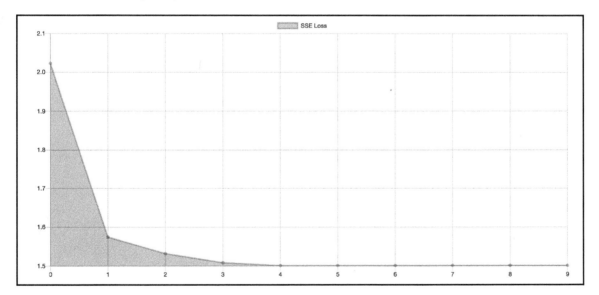

As you can see, the loss value is sufficiently decreased by iteration 3 or 4. The final result of the clustering is as follows. The big round dots are the centroids of each cluster:

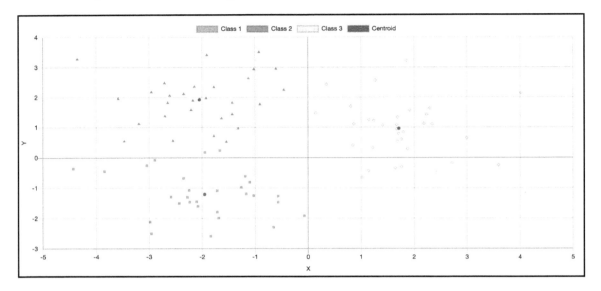

Clusters can be well visualized with these three centroids. This demonstrates how K-means works with TensorFlow.js.

Summary

In this chapter, we learned that the clustering algorithm is a type of unsupervised learning and how the K-means and EM algorithms work. Since the EM algorithm is a general version of K-means, we are now capable of applying the EM algorithm to more extensive use cases. Practically, the EM algorithm requires intensive computation power, and so we tend to use K-means to estimate the structure of the data points roughly first and run the EM algorithm later. Combining these two algorithms is a common pattern to follow when we want to complete any clustering task.

We also demonstrated how K-means can be implemented using TensorFlow.js. We did this by showing a clustering example in a two-dimensional space. This example illustrated that data points from multiple Gaussian distributions can be segmented into clusters that are represented by centroids. While we implemented a K-means algorithm from scratch, it may be more natural to use the existing library to run the clustering algorithm. `machinelearn.js` has a K-means implementation. Trying out the library is also a good opportunity to learn the algorithm practically. In the next chapter, we will look at sequential data analysis and use it for ML applications.

Exercise

1. Prove that the SSE converges with zero when we increase the number of desired clusters, K.
2. Using the example in this chapter, change the number of centroids and see how the final result varies.
3. What will happen if we move each cluster closer together?
4. There are multiple enhanced initialization methods of K-means. Let's try out the following initial centroids:
   - **Forgy method**: Choose K observations from the data points as centroids.
   - **Random partition**: Assign each data point to a cluster randomly.
5. Replace the naive K-means implementation that we used with the implementation in `machinelearn.js`.
6. It's not guaranteed that the K-means algorithm can be converged with the global optima. Illustrate where K-means only returns poor results.

Further reading

- K-means clustering: https://en.wikipedia.org/wiki/K-means_clustering
- Expectation-maximization algorithm: https://en.wikipedia.org/wiki/Expectation%E2%80%93maximization_algorithm
- tf.expandDims: https://js.tensorflow.org/api/latest/#expandDims
- cluster.KMeans – machinelearn.js: https://www.machinelearnjs.com/api/cluster.KMeans.html

Sequential Data Analysis 7

The data that we've looked at so far is known as static data. It doesn't contain information that can be varied through the time frame dynamically. However, it is also necessary for us to deal with the data changing. Examples of this include audio data and natural language. Their major characteristic is the fact that each point depends on the previous points in the sequence. While there are supervised learning techniques that predict labels by considering the dependencies within the sequence, we are going to focus on the underlying structure of the sequence.

In this chapter, we are going to take a look at techniques we can use to analyze sequential data. Specifically, we will cover Fourier transformation and its implementation in TensorFlow.js.

The following topics will be covered in this chapter:

- What is Fourier transformation?
- Cosine curve decomposition

Technical requirements

The following will be required in order to complete the tasks in this chapter:

- TypeScript/JavaScript
- A web browser (Chrome is recommended)
- Parcel

Check out the following video to see the Code in Action:
http://bit.ly/2OtsG3H

What is Fourier transformation?

Fourier transformation is a technique that decomposes a given sequence into multiple elements that correspond to a specific frequency. The given input is a time series signal such as audio data. Fourier transformation calculates the magnitude of each component corresponding to the frequency. The basic assumption behind Fourier transformation is that every periodic function can be represented as the weighted summation of simple curves, such as sine or cosine functions. While we can decompose any function by multiple polynomial terms with Taylor expansion, Fourier transformation allows us to disintegrate the periodic function with multiple cosines or sine components. Although this is a pretty plain assumption, it is powerful enough to allow us to perform mathematical analysis for any kind of signal value that shows a periodic pattern.

For example, the following visually complicated signal is expressed as a sum of only four sine curves:

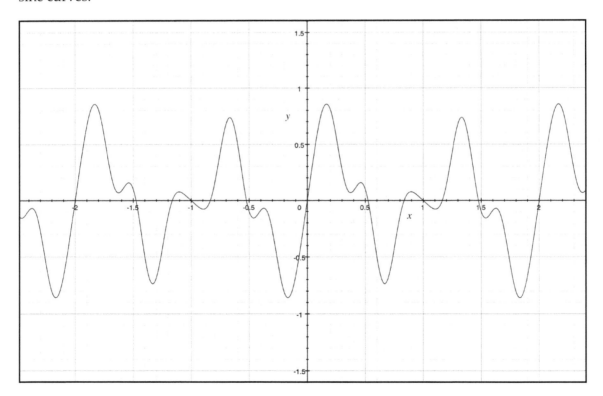

Its mathematical representation is given as follows:

$$y = 0.5\sin(2\pi x) + 0.25\sin(3\pi x) + 0.25\sin(5\pi x) - 0.1\sin(7\pi x)$$

It is composed of four sine curves with different phases and magnitudes. In short, Fourier transformation is a process that decides on the magnitude (coefficient) of each element of frequencies. When given a signal wave, the process finds the weight that's been allocated to each component. In this case, the targets are 0.5, 0.25, 0.25, and -0.1:

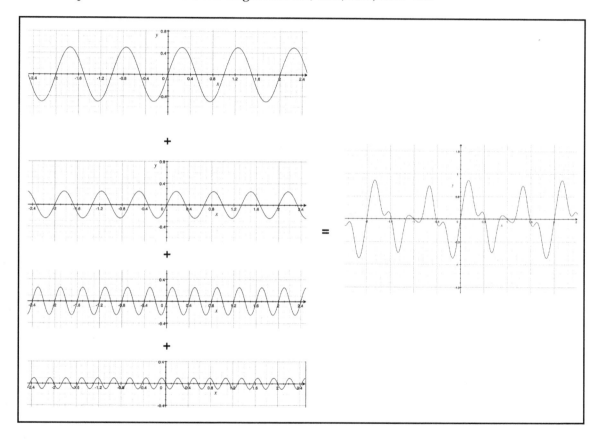

The important thing about Fourier transformation is that we can apply the process to any type of function once it meets the specific mathematical requirements. Although we haven't provided a detailed explanation about this here, note that most of the signals that we see in the machine learning field can be the target of Fourier transformation. Moreover, even if a periodic function isn't found, the function that has been found can be decomposed by multiple sines or cosine curves. This can be classed as infinite summation.

Constituent frequencies as a feature

In general, the original signal isn't suitable for machine learning algorithms because it is difficult to extract meaningful features from sequential data points. The component of each frequency can represent the original signal. Once the original sequence has been converted into the constituent frequencies, it is handled as a normal vector of features.

There are mainly two advantages to using components as features:

- We can use more tangible elements by converting the time domain into a feature space with a fixed size. This format allows us to provide traditional machine learning algorithms such as decision trees.
- Fourier transformation is a reversible operation. It is possible to construct the original signal from the transformed components. This shows that the terms of frequencies contain information that describes the original data.

The process of reconstructing the original signal is called **inverse Fourier transform**, which tends to be introduced as a sibling of Fourier transformation. As illustrated in the DeepSense algorithm (refer to the *Further reading* section at the end of this chapter for more detail), which has been developed to analyze time series mobile sensing data, Fourier transformation is used to extract features from the original signal for more advanced algorithms such as recurrent neural networks.

Fourier transformation is generally able to handle continuous values mathematically. However, we are mainly interested in the analysis of discrete values because the computer cannot recognize these continuous values fundamentally and the machine learning algorithm also expects the input to be in finite-length vectors. Thus, we need to use a special form of Fourier transformation called **discrete Fourier transform** (**DFT**). This algorithm aims to give us finite magnitudes of each frequency from the given finite samples in a sequence. The implementation of Fourier transformation in TensorFlow.js uses DFT, as well as major arithmetic libraries such as NumPy.

Now, let's illustrate how DFT works.

Discrete Fourier transform

DFT is a type of Fourier transformation that was specially designed for discrete values. The goal of the algorithm is to find the components in each frequency from the finite samples. Let's assume that the input samples are illustrated as a sequence of complex numbers, $\{\mathbf{x}_n\} = \{x_0, x_1, \ldots, x_{N-1}\}$. The magnitude corresponding to the frequency, $\omega_k = 2\pi k/N$, is calculated as follows:

$$F(\omega_k) = \sum_{n=0}^{N-1} x_n e^{-\frac{2\pi k}{N} ni} = \sum_{n=0}^{N-1} x_n e^{-\omega_k ni}$$

Considering the result of Euler's formula ($e^{ix} = \cos(x) + i\sin(x)$), this equation indicates that the sequence composed of $\{x_n\}$ is decomposed by multiple sine or cosine curves. In short, the original samples can be represented as follows:

$$x_n = \frac{1}{N}\sum_{k=0}^{N-1} F(\omega_k)e^{i2\pi kn/N}$$
$$= \frac{1}{N}\sum_{k=0}^{N-1} F(\omega_k)(\cos(2\pi kn/N) + i\sin(2\pi kn/N)$$

For example, each element of the next sequence is calculated by DFT. x is a sequence of samples with four elements:

$$\mathbf{x} = \begin{pmatrix} 2 \\ 2+i \\ -i \\ -1+3i \end{pmatrix} = \begin{pmatrix} x_0 \\ x_1 \\ x_2 \\ x_3 \end{pmatrix}$$

$$F(\omega_0) = 2e^{-i2\pi\cdot0\cdot0/4} + (2+i)e^{-i2\pi\cdot0\cdot1/4} + (-i)e^{-i2\pi\cdot0\cdot2/4} + (-1+3i)e^{-i2\pi\cdot0\cdot3/4}$$
$$= 3 + 3i$$
$$F(\omega_1) = 2e^{-i2\pi\cdot1\cdot0/4} + (2+i)e^{-i2\pi\cdot1\cdot1/4} + (-i)e^{-i2\pi\cdot1\cdot2/4} + (-1+3i)e^{-i2\pi\cdot3\cdot1/4}$$
$$= -2i$$
$$F(\omega_2) = 2e^{-i2\pi\cdot2\cdot0/4} + (2+i)e^{-i2\pi\cdot2\cdot1/4} + (-i)e^{-i2\pi\cdot2\cdot2/4} + (-1+3i)e^{-i2\pi\cdot2\cdot3/4}$$
$$= 1 - 5i$$
$$F(\omega_3) = 2e^{-i2\pi\cdot3\cdot0/4} + (2+i)e^{-i2\pi\cdot3\cdot1/4} + (-i)e^{-i2\pi\cdot3\cdot2/4} + (-1+3i)e^{-i2\pi\cdot3\cdot3/4}$$
$$= 4 + 4i$$

As you can see, DFT is simply implemented as a form of matrix multiplication. Each element, $F(\omega_k)$, is a form of linear multiplication that includes coefficients and input samples. If we were to assume that $\omega = e^{-i2\pi/4}$, the calculation for DFT can be expressed as the multiplication of matrices:

$$\begin{pmatrix} F(\omega_0) \\ F(\omega_1) \\ F(\omega_2) \\ F(\omega_3) \end{pmatrix} = \begin{pmatrix} \omega^{0 \cdot 0} & \omega^{0 \cdot 1} & \omega^{0 \cdot 2} & \omega^{0 \cdot 3} \\ \omega^{1 \cdot 0} & \omega^{1 \cdot 1} & \omega^{1 \cdot 2} & \omega^{1 \cdot 3} \\ \omega^{2 \cdot 0} & \omega^{2 \cdot 1} & \omega^{2 \cdot 2} & \omega^{2 \cdot 3} \\ \omega^{3 \cdot 0} & \omega^{3 \cdot 1} & \omega^{3 \cdot 2} & \omega^{3 \cdot 3} \end{pmatrix} \begin{pmatrix} x_0 \\ x_1 \\ x_2 \\ x_3 \end{pmatrix}$$

This is good news for developers because we can make use of existing linear algebra frameworks that have been optimized for the computation of matrix manipulation. You can easily implement the DFT algorithm once you come up with the matrix to be multiplied.

However, it is well-known that there is a faster algorithm we can use to compute the DFT. Most implementations, including TensorFlow.js, run Fourier transformation according to the **fast Fourier transform (FFT)** algorithm.

Fast Fourier transform

The implementation that TensorFlow.js uses for Fourier transform is known as **FFT**. Since the naive implementation of DFT is slow in general use cases, FFT is popularly used in the practical field. The time complexity of DFT in terms of matrix multiplication is $O(N^2)$, where N is the data size. FFT reduces the order of the computation to $O(N \log N)$. This is a huge difference, especially for long sequences. The benefit of FFT is not only its speed but also its accuracy since it removes rounded-off errors. There are many derived family implementations of the FFT algorithm. FFT is widely used for applications that process audio and look at music, science, and much more.

Although we aren't going to explain the FFT algorithm in depth, the basic idea behind the algorithm is to divide and conquer. It breaks down a sequence that's N in size into a smaller problem that's N_1 and N_2 such that $N = N_1 N_2$ in size and applies DFT to many smaller sequences. It is similar to other divide-and-conquer algorithms, such as QuickSort:

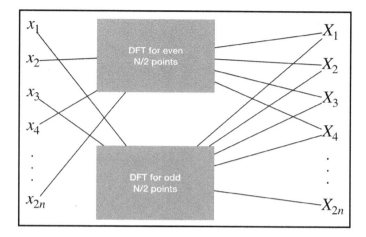

As this high-level overview shows, after we compute the DFT for half of the original sequence, we combine the result with the final magnitude in terms of frequency. By repeating this process recursively, we can achieve $O(N \log N)$.

Let's review the goal of FFT again. FFT is an algorithm that's been designed to find the magnitude of periodical components from their respective frequencies using a finite number of data samples. Thanks to the nature of the divide-and-conquer approach, it achieves an $O(N \log N)$ order of complexity.

Cosine curve decomposition

In this section, we are going to actually use the TensorFlow.js API to run the FFT program. TensorFlow.js provides several derived implementations for FFT:

- `tf.spectral.fft`
- `tf.spectral.ifft`
- `tf.spectral.rfft`
- `tf.spectral.irfft`

TensorFlow.js also supports short-term Fourier transforms, which are a type of Fourier transformation that takes in a windowed sequence of the original samples:

- `tf.singal.stft`

By showing the output of these APIs with samples from cosine or sine waves, we will learn how this algorithm behaves.

Complex number type

Fourier transformation is fully generalized in the space of complex numbers. A complex number is a number that's expressed as a pair of real and imaginary numbers. The imaginary number is a number whose squared value can be negative and is commonly represented by i. This number is usually illustrated as a point in the complex plane. Thus, we can express the complex number as a pair of values when we describe the point in a two-dimensional coordination system:

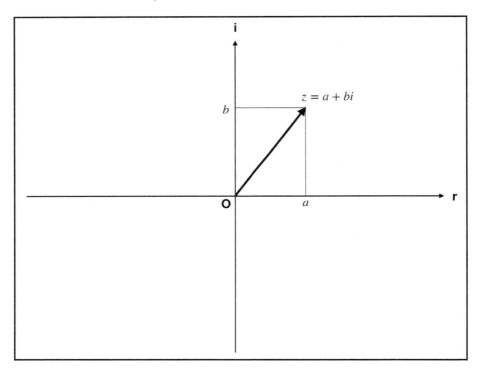

To fully utilize the FFT implementation of the library, it is essential to support complex numerical types. Actually, TensorFlow.js started supporting complex data types for the purpose of FFT-related operations.

To create tensors with a complex number, we can use the tf.complex API:

```
const c1 = tf.complex([1.0, 2.0], [3.0, 4.0]);
```

This represents the list of complex values, $[1 + 3i, 2 + 4i]$. The first argument is the tensor of the real number, while the second argument corresponds to the imaginary part. The shape of the constructed tensor is exactly the same as the shape of the input. Thus, the shape of the real part and the imaginary part should match.

To extract the value of each part, we can use `tf.real` and `tf.imag` separately:

```
const r1 = tf.real(c1);
// -> [1.0, 2.0]
const i1 = tf.imag(c1);
// -> [3.0, 4.0]
```

These complex values need to be treated differently from the real numbers. For example, the addition of complex values can be done element-wise, and the norm of the complex value is calculated as the square root of each element:

$$z_1 = a + bi$$
$$z_2 = c + di$$
$$z_1 + z_2 = (a + c) + (b + d)i$$
$$\|z_1\| = \sqrt{z_1 \overline{z_1}} = \sqrt{(a + bi)(a - bi)} = \sqrt{a^2 + b^2}$$

The operations that support complex types recognize these specific operations. FFT operations also recognize the nature of complex numbers internally.

Thus, the tensors that FFT can receive or return have a `dtype = complex64`. We can check the `dtype` of the tensor by printing it in verbose mode:

```
const c1 = tf.complex([1, 2], [3, 4]);
c1.print(true); // verbose = true

// It shows
//
// Tensor
//   dtype: complex64
//   rank: 1
//   shape: [2]
//   values:
//      [1 + 3j, 2 + 4j]

console.log(c1.dataSync());
// Float32Array(4) [1, 3, 2, 4]
```

The layout of the underlying data is presented as a list of each element that has been formed into real and imaginary values.

The cosine curve

The dataset that's going to be transformed by FFT is a single cosine curve. The phase of the wave is illustrated as xs, which is pi multiplied by the continuous range. The cosine and sine curve return 2π:

```
const doublePi = tf.scalar(2.0 * Math.PI);
const xs = tf.mul(doublePi, tf.range(-1.5, 1.5, 0.1));

const ys = tf.cos(xs);
```

The original curve is drawn as follows. The number of samples in the dataset is 30, which is decided by the number of points that are generated by tf.range:

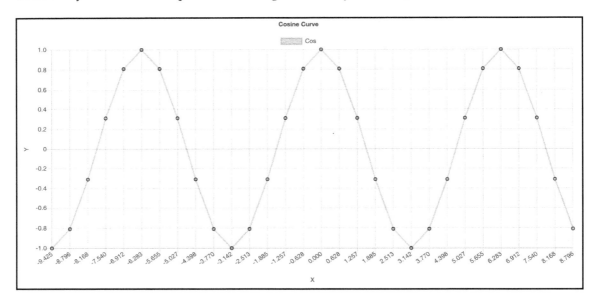

Fourier transformation for cosine curves

tf.fft requires complex data types for its arguments. However, the cosine curve we are discussing here only has real values in its sequence. We aren't interested in the imaginary part of the input this time because we aim to draw the curve in the real 2D space.

The best way to deal with this situation is by padding the imaginary part with zero. `tf.zerosLike` gives us a tensor whose shape is exactly the same as the input tensor, with all zero values:

```
const input = tf.complex(ys, ys.zerosLike());
```

Thus, we get the input tensor with an imaginary part, zero. This will be the N-dimensional vector whose length is 30:

$$\text{input} = \begin{pmatrix} -1.0 + 0i \\ -0.8 + 0i \\ -0.3 + 0i \\ \vdots \\ -0.8 + 0i \end{pmatrix}$$

The usage of FFT is simple. All we need to do is pass the vector to `tf.fft`:

```
const transformed = tf.fft(tf.complex(ys, ys.zerosLike()));
```

As we saw previously, DFT generates the same length sequence as the input. Therefore, `transformed` is a 30-element vector with `complex64` as its `dtype`. Each element represents the magnitude corresponding to the specific frequency. We can see how the original wave can be decomposed by FFT by looking at its magnitude.

Let's illustrate which of the frequencies constructs the original wave. To do so, we need to calculate the norm of the magnitude because the size of the complex value is evaluated by the norm of the value. Previously, we explained that the norm of the complex value is the square root of the summation of the square. The following code shows the norm of each element in the tensor:

```
const real = tf.real(transformed);
const imag = tf.imag(transformed);

const norm = tf.sqrt(real.square().add(imag.square()));
```

The real part and the imaginary part can be extracted by `tf.real` and `tf.imag`. Since tensors can call the operation in a chainable manner, the square of the real part can be written as `real.square()` and so on.

Now that we know how much each factor contributes to the original wave, let's illustrate this:

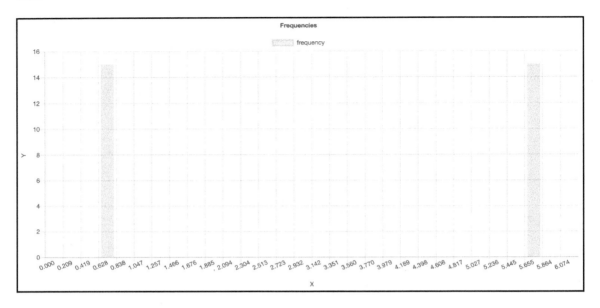

There are two frequencies in the chart. The original curve is composed of one single cosine curve. Why can we see two frequencies?

Recall the DFT matrix. This is the DFT matrix where the number of samples is four (=N):

$$\begin{pmatrix} \omega^{0\cdot0} & \omega^{0\cdot1} & \omega^{0\cdot2} & \omega^{0\cdot3} \\ \omega^{1\cdot0} & \omega^{1\cdot1} & \omega^{1\cdot2} & \omega^{1\cdot3} \\ \omega^{2\cdot0} & \omega^{2\cdot1} & \omega^{2\cdot2} & \omega^{2\cdot3} \\ \omega^{3\cdot0} & \omega^{3\cdot1} & \omega^{3\cdot2} & \omega^{3\cdot3} \end{pmatrix} = \begin{pmatrix} 1 & 1 & 1 & 1 \\ 1 & -i & -1 & i \\ 1 & -1 & 1 & -1 \\ 1 & i & -1 & -i \end{pmatrix}$$

Considering the fact that $\omega^x \equiv \omega^x \bmod N$, the sequence of FFT can be interpreted as follows:

- The first element measures the mean of the magnitude of each factor.
- The second element corresponds to the frequency of $2\pi i/N$, while the last element (fourth element) corresponds to the frequency that is a conjugate of the second element.

In general, the first element is called the **DC bias** of the original wave, while $F(\omega_k)$ and $F(\omega_{N-k})$ are the magnitudes of the positive part and the negative part, respectively. If the input is a real number sequence, their frequencies can be a conjugate. Although we won't go over them here, note that there are components that correspond to roughly N/2 frequencies for the positive and negative parts of the input size N:

```
const pi = tf.scalar(4.0 * Math.PI);
const xs = tf.mul(pi, tf.range(-1.5, 1.5, 0.05));
```

This results in the following graph:

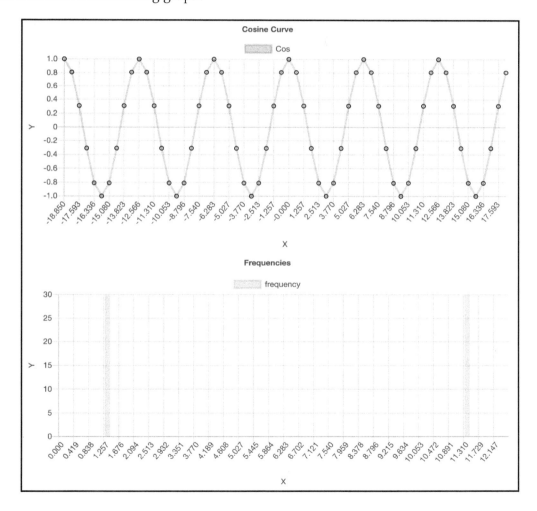

Here, we doubled the frequency of the original sequence. Due to this, the FFT value is also doubled.

Fourier transformation for composite curves

Let's try to decompose a curve that has been constructed from multiple cosine curves. The curve is formed by the addition of two cosine curves:

$$f(x) = \cos(2\pi x) + 0.3\cos(4\pi x)$$

The first one is an original curve, while the second one is a doubled frequency that's been multiplied by a smaller weight value, 0.3:

```
const pi = tf.scalar(2.0 * Math.PI);

// Original Frequency
const xs = tf.mul(pi, tf.range(-1.5, 1.5, 0.05));
// For double Frequency
const xs2 = tf.mul(pi, tf.range(-1.5, 1.5, 0.05)).mul(2.0);

const ys = tf.cos(xs).add(tf.cos(xs2).mul(0.2));
```

We expect there to be two peaked frequencies, where one is smaller than the other if we decompose with FFT.

Take a look at the following graph:

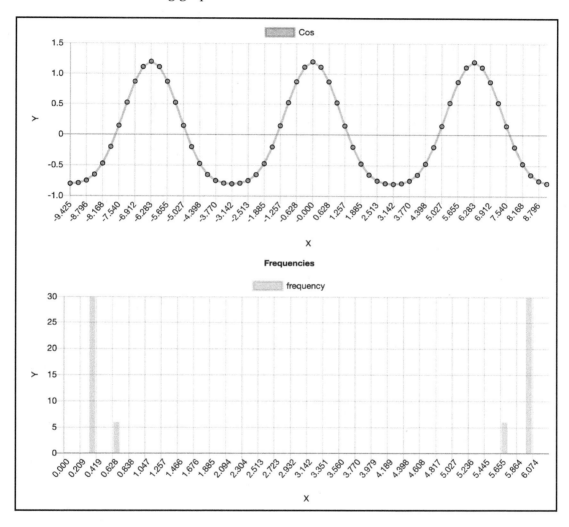

This is exactly what we anticipated. FFT seems to correctly decompose the given curve into the factors by each frequency. Take some time to construct more complicated periodic functions by combining multiple cosine and sine curves so that you can understand the capability of FFT to unveil the hidden characteristics of a periodic function.

Inversed Fourier transform

In this section, we are going to try to recover the original curve by running the inversed Fourier transform, that is, `tf.ifft`. Fourier transformation has an inverted operation, as we mentioned at the beginning of this chapter. By running a similar computation, we can recover the original function from the magnitudes of the frequencies. TensorFlow.js has an API that does this for us. Since the input and output are interchangeable, the output of `tf.fft` can be directly passed to `tf.ifft`:

```
const pi = tf.scalar(2.0 * Math.PI);
const xs = tf.mul(pi, tf.range(-1.5, 1.5, 0.05));
const xs2 = tf.mul(pi, tf.range(-1.5, 1.5, 0.05)).mul(2.0);
const ys = tf.cos(xs).add(tf.cos(xs2).mul(0.2));

const transformed = tf.fft(tf.complex(ys, ys.zerosLike()));
const inversed = tf.ifft(transformed);
```

We will get the same result that we received initially:

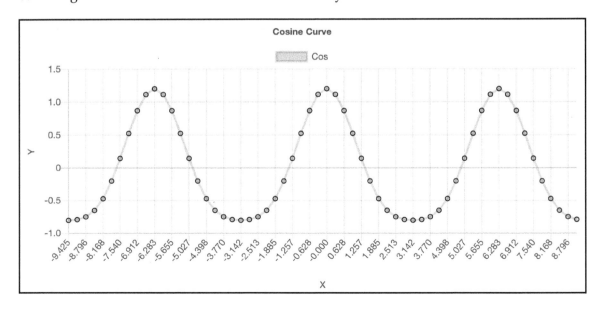

Summary

In this chapter, we introduced the traditional way of analyzing sequential data. Fourier transformation is an established method of unfolding data into multiple factors, just like Taylor expansion does. The most important thing about Fourier transformation is that it is able to find the fundamental building blocks of the periodic sequential data, which is the frequency in a complex numerical space.

TensorFlow.js allows us to access the fast implementation of Fourier transformation. Due to this, we looked into how to use FFT and inversed FFT for compound cosine curves and observed the results. In the next chapter, we will look at dimensionality reduction and t-SNE.

Exercise

1. Execute DFT manually for the following input sample:

$$\mathbf{x} = \begin{pmatrix} 1 \\ 1+i \\ 2-i \\ 4i \end{pmatrix}$$

2. What will happen if we apply DFT to non-periodic functions such as $y = x^2 + 1$?
3. Construct the complex type tensor with the shape [2, 3].
4. How will the DFT result change if we increase the number of samples?
5. Illustrate the curve and magnitude of each frequency in the following function:
   1. $y = 0.25\cos(3\pi x) + 1.25\cos(\pi x) - 0.5\sin(4\pi x)$

6. What will happen to the result in the frequency domain if the input samples have an imaginary part?

Further reading

- DeepSense: https://arxiv.org/abs/1611.01942
- Discrete Fourier transform: https://en.wikipedia.org/wiki/Discrete_Fourier_transform
- tf.complex: https://js.tensorflow.org/api/latest/#complex
- DFT Matrix: https://en.wikipedia.org/wiki/DFT_matrix

8
Dimensionality Reduction

One of the most important processes that we can apply machine learning to is the preprocessing of feature vectors. Data in the real world is undoubtedly dirty and noisy in general. We need to pick the most useful features when it comes to prediction. Due to this, it is important to clean the data. This contributes not only to improving the accuracy of the prediction, but also reducing the time it takes for training by saving the size of the input data. In this chapter, we are going to introduce two popular ways to extract meaningful features from the original data. The first approach we will look at is **principal component analysis** (**PCA**), an unsupervised learning technique that projects the original data into a low-dimensional space. The other is an embedding technique that's typically used by NLP problems with t-SNE, which is a more advanced dimensionality reduction algorithm.

In this chapter, we will cover the following topics:

- Why dimensionality reduction?
- Understanding principal component analysis
- Projecting 3D points into a 2D space using PCA
- Word embedding

Technical requirements

The following will be required in order to complete the tasks in this chapter:

- JavaScript
- TypeScript
- A web browser (Chrome is recommended)

Check out the following video to see the Code in Action:
http://bit.ly/2Xx1XtS

Why dimensionality reduction?

By using the feature selection algorithm, we can reduce the number of features that will be used for training. We can achieve this by simply picking up features that seem to be useful to predict the target value efficiently. This is assumed to contribute to improving the accuracy, as well as the efficiency, of the computation as it remediates the **curse of dimensionality**.

Curse of dimensionality

The curse of dimensionality is a common problem where the number of necessary data points is exponentially increased when the dimension is increased. Let's say we have two datasets: one in a one-dimensional space and one in a three-dimensional space. If we want to achieve sufficient accuracy with 10 data points in the one-dimensional space, then we need to collect around 1,000 bits of data. The following diagram illustrates a situation where the curse of dimensionality can happen:

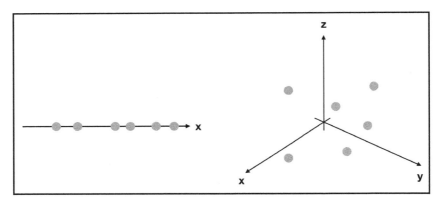

In the left low-dimensional space, the data points cover the one-dimensional space pretty well. However, the same number of data points show the sparsity in the three-dimensional space. This indicates that the dataset may not be able to achieve a result that's as good as the one we achieved in the one-dimensional space. It is necessary for us to collect more data.

Variance maximization

Let's assume that the data is N points represented as a set of D dimensional vectors, $\{\mathbf{x}_n\}$. We are going to project the data into an M-dimensional space so that M < D. M is given in advance as a hyperparameter. We will find the first principal component first.

The first principal component is considered to be the direction where the variance of the original data is max. After we find it, we can pick up the second principal component, whose variance follows the first one. This leads the linear projection to the two-dimensional space that was defined with the first and second principal components. Finding the arbitrary number of principal components allows us to map the observations into any dimensional space.

Another assumption we have is that the length of the vector of the principal component is 1. We can make $|\mathbf{u}_1| = 1$ without losing generality. This means that the inner product of the vector is 1:

$$\mathbf{u}_1^T \mathbf{u}_1 = 1$$

The new data points that have been projected onto the principal component based on this assumption can be represented by the multiplication of the principal component vector and the sample vector:

$$y_n = \mathbf{u}_1^T \mathbf{x}_n$$

y_n is regarded as the position in the space that's coordinated by the vector u_1. Although y_n is just a scalar that's projected by one component, it is immediately generalized to the n-dimensional space using multiple principal components.

Now, we can calculate the variance of the data points in the new space:

$$\frac{1}{N} \sum_{n=1}^{N} (\mathbf{u}_1^T \mathbf{x}_n - \mathbf{u}_1^T \overline{\mathbf{x}}) = \mathbf{u}_1^T \mathbf{S} \mathbf{u}_1$$

$\bar{\mathbf{x}}$ is the mean of the set of samples, while $\mathbf{S}$ is a covariance matrix:

$$\bar{\mathbf{x}} = \frac{1}{N} \sum_{n=1}^{N} \mathbf{x}_n$$

$$\mathbf{S} = \frac{1}{N} \sum_{n=1}^{N} (\mathbf{x}_n - \bar{\mathbf{x}})(\mathbf{x}_n - \bar{\mathbf{x}})^T$$

As we explained previously, our goal is to maximize the variance in the projected space, $\mathbf{u}_1^T \mathbf{S} \mathbf{u}_1$. By using Lagrange multipliers, the problem can be formulated as follows:

$$\mathbf{u}_1^T \mathbf{S} \mathbf{u}_1 + \lambda_1 (1 - \mathbf{u}_1^T \mathbf{u}_1)$$

The second term is induced by the size of the principal component vector, $\mathbf{u}_1^T \mathbf{u}_1 = 1$. Since the method asks us to maximize the value, the derivative next to $\mathbf{u}_1$ is zero. We can find the local maxima at $\mathbf{u}_1$ as follows:

$$\mathbf{S} \mathbf{u}_1 = \lambda_1 \mathbf{u}_1$$

This proves that u_1 is an **eigenvector** of the covariance matrix, S. Therefore, the principal component is given as an eigenvector and is the corresponding eigenvalue of the covariance matrix of the original data. It is easy to calculate the eigenvector of the given matrix mathematically. Taking care of the fact that the length of u_1 is 1, the variance on the new projected space is given as an eigenvalue:

$$\begin{aligned} \mathbf{u}_1^T \mathbf{S} \mathbf{u}_1 &= \mathbf{u}_1^T \lambda_1 \mathbf{u}_1 \\ &= \lambda_1 \mathbf{u}_1^T \mathbf{u}_1 \\ &= \lambda_1 \end{aligned}$$

The variance is maximized when we pick up the eigenvector whose corresponding eigenvalue is max. By doing this, we can select several eigenvectors from the top eigenvalues. Let's assume these are $\mathbf{u}_1, \mathbf{u}_2, \cdots, \mathbf{u}_M$. Here, the projection matrix can provide us with a linear transformation that achieves the maximum variance on the new space:

$$U = (\mathbf{u}_1 \quad \mathbf{u}_2 \quad \ldots \quad \mathbf{u}_M)$$

The shape of the matrix is (D, M). The original data in the D-dimensional space can be converted into the M-dimensional space:

$$X = (\mathbf{x}_1 \quad \mathbf{x}_2 \quad \ldots \quad \mathbf{x}_n)^T$$
$$X' = XU$$

Here, we need to confirm that the shape of the projected dataset, X', is (N, M), since this illustrates that the dimension is reduced from D to M for each data point. Now, we understand the process of the preprocessing method, which reduces the dimensions of the original data. It is capable of maximizing the variance in the projected space. The structure that's mapped by PCA is useful for any machine learning process.

Let's try to run the PCA process using TensorFlow.js. Unfortunately, there is no direct implementation for PCA in TensorFlow.js. We're going to need to combine several libraries to get the desired result.

Projecting 3D points into a 2D space with PCA

In this section, we are going to experiment on the dataset in a 3D space. The data points that will be generated in the 3D space cannot be rendered in the two-coordinate system.

Three-dimensional clusters

We have already seen how we can generate the dataset from a normal distribution. To reduce the dimensionality of the original dataset, we will need to use the shape (Batch, 3):

```
const N = 30;
const D = 3;

// tf.randomNormal generates the tensor with the given shape from the
normal distribution.
const c1 = tf.randomNormal([N, D]).add([1.0, 0.0, 0.0]);
const c2 = tf.randomNormal([N, D]).add([-1.0, 0.0, 0.0]);
const c3 = tf.randomNormal([N, D]).add([0.0, 1.0, 1.0]);


const xs = c1.concat(c2).concat(c3);
```

Each cluster contains 30 points. Concatenation packs them into the original dataset with a shape of (90, 3). To visualize the points in two-dimensional coordinates, we need to project each piece of data onto the plane space. We can use the gather operator to pick up the specific elements of the data points:

```
// Pick up 1st, 2nd elements of each point
const xs1 = xs.gather([0, 1], 1);

// Pick up 1st, 3rd elements of each point
const xs2 = xs.gather([0, 2], 1);

// Pick up 2nd, 3rd elements of each point
const xs3 = xs.gather([1, 2], 1);
```

The following is a visualization of xs1, which is picking up the first two elements:

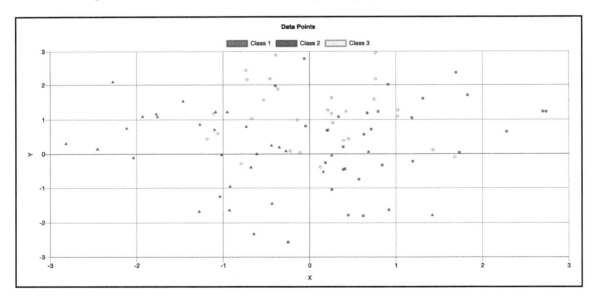

Next, we are going to find the principal components of the original three-dimensional data.

Principal component calculation

As we have already seen, the PCA process can be described in two steps:

1. Calculate the covariance matrix of the original data.
2. Choose the eigenvalues to construct the projection matrix.

Let's remind ourselves how the covariance matrix is expressed. It is the multiplication of the difference between the data points and their mean value:

$$\mathbf{S} = \frac{1}{N} \sum_{n=1}^{N} (\mathbf{x}_n - \overline{\mathbf{x}})(\mathbf{x}_n - \overline{\mathbf{x}})^T$$

The mean of each dimension of the original data is provided by the `mean` operation:

```
const batch = xs.shape[0];
const meanValues = xs.mean(0);
```

The argument of reduction operations, such as mean = **axis**, specifies the dimensions where the reduction happens. Axis=0 means the row-wise operation, while axis=1 means the column-wise operation. This illustrates what the result looks like after the reduce operation is used with the axis argument. Since we want to know the mean value of each column, we can pass 0 as the axis parameter. The dataset with a shape of (N, D) will be converted into a matrix with a shape of (1, D):

$$
\begin{pmatrix}
x_1^1 & x_2^1 & \cdots & x_d^1 \\
x_1^2 & x_2^2 & \cdots & x_d^2 \\
x_1^3 & x_2^3 & \cdots & x_d^3 \\
\vdots & \vdots & \ddots & \vdots \\
x_1^n & x_2^n & \cdots & x_d^n
\end{pmatrix}
\xrightarrow{\text{axis=1}}
\begin{pmatrix}
\overline{x^1} \\
\overline{x^2} \\
\overline{x^3} \\
\vdots \\
\overline{x^n}
\end{pmatrix}
$$

$$\downarrow \text{axis=0}$$

$$\left(\overline{x_1} \quad \overline{x_2} \quad \cdots \quad \overline{x_d}\right)$$

For example, `xs.mean(0)` gives us a matrix with a shape of (1, 3). As we can see, each element of the result is the mean of the corresponding feature in the original dataset:

```
const x = tf.randomNormal([5, 3]);
x.print();

// Tensor
//      [[-1.4045854, 0.7128999 , -0.0510314],
//       [-0.3591872, 0.7678196 , -0.7086825],
//       [0.891787  , -0.2265666, -0.9310723],
//       [1.079685  , 0.5257578 , 0.9313632 ],
//       [0.1935443 , -0.1113114, -1.0499427]]

x.mean(0).print();
// Tensor
//      [0.0802487, 0.3337199, -0.3618731]
```

The difference between the data points and the mean vector can be calculated using the `sub` operation. The `meanValues` vector is automatically broadcasted:

```
const sub = tf.sub(xs, meanValues);
```

A covariance matrix is expressed as the multiplication of `sub` and `sub`, transposed. It has a shape of (N, D), which means that the transposed matrix has a shape of (D, N). The final result of the `matMul` operation will be (D, D). This will match the expected shape, thereby showing how it correlates with every feature:

```
tf.matMul(sub.transpose(), sub)
```

Now that we have finished building the covariance matrix, the eigenvectors should be found in that matrix. Unfortunately, TensorFlow.js doesn't provide any implementation for us to find the eigenvectors in the given tensor. However, the community has a plan to extend this functionality around linear algebra. We will use a library called `numeric` to perform linear algebraic calculation. Please add it to the list of dependencies in the `package.json` file of our project:

```
{
  "dependencies": {
    // ...
    "numeric": "^1.2.6",
    // ...
  }
}
```

Since `numeric` doesn't recognize the tensor type of TensorFlow.js, we need to convert a tensor into a JavaScript array. However, this comes with a bit of overhead. `tf.util.toNestedArray` has the capability to convert the tensor into a JavaScript array without losing any shape information. The array for the covariance matrix should have (D, D) as its shape:

```
// Make the tensor to same shaped JavaScript array.
const covarianceData = tf.util.toNestedArray([D, D], covariance.dataSync())
as number[][];

// Compute the eigen vectors
const eig = numeric.eig(covarianceData);
```

`numeric.eig` returns the eigenvalues and eigenvectors of the input tensor. We can get the eigenvectors by accessing `eig.E`:

```
eig(A: Matrix, maxiter?: number): { lambda: Tensor; E: Tensor };
```

Note that the data type that's returned by `numeric` is not compatible with TensorFlow.js. We need to construct the tensor again so that it works with TensorFlow.js. The raw array of eigenvectors can be accessed via `eig.E.x`. Slicing the first nth vectors means picking up the eigenvectors that correspond to the eigenvalues that are nth large values. Linearly projecting the sliced matrix will give the data in a space a new appearance, which achieves the large variance we want:

```
const eigenvectors = tf.tensor(eig.E.x).slice([0, 0], [-1, nComponents]);
const newXs = tf.matMul(sub, eigenvectors);
```

Overall, the function that we need to use to complete the PCA process is as follows. It gets the tensor containing the original data and the number of components the new feature space should have:

```
async function pca(xs: tf.Tensor, nComponents: number) {
  const batch = xs.shape[0];
  const meanValues = xs.mean(0);
  const sub = tf.sub(xs, meanValues);
  const covariance = tf.matMul(sub.transpose(), sub);
  const covarianceData = tf.util.toNestedArray([D, D],
covariance.dataSync()) as number[][];
  const eig = numeric.eig(xsData);
  const eigenvectors = tf.tensor(eig.E.x).slice([0, 0], [-1, nComponents]);
  return tf.matMul(sub, eigenvectors);
}
```

The variance of projected datasets

Comparing the variance of the data can demonstrate that PCA is able to achieve the most variance if we convert it into a low-dimensional space. The variance of the data is the Euclidean distance of the difference between the data points and the mean of the feature. As we saw previously, the mean of each feature is calculated by `xs.mean(0)`:

```
function variance(xs: tf.Tensor) {
  const v = xs.sub(xs.mean(0)).pow(2).mean();
  console.log(v.dataSync());
}
```

Let's see how the variance can be changed by projecting the data in four ways:

- Projection with 0, 1st features
- Projection with 0, 2nd features
- Projection with 1, 2nd features
- Projection with PCA

This can be done using the following code:

```
console.log("Variance of xs1");
variance(xs1);

console.log("Variance of xs2");
const xs2 = xs.gather([0, 2], 1);
variance(xs2);

console.log("Variance of xs3");
const xs3 = xs.gather([0, 2], 1);
variance(xs3);

console.log("Variance by pca");
const pcaXs = await pca(xs, 2);
variance(pcaXs);
```

The result shows that the variance PCA provides is the largest value (1.762). Feel free to construct your own projection matrix and see what the variance looks like. As we can see, PCA always results in the largest variance value:

```
Variance of xs1
▶ Float32Array [1.652011513710022]
Variance of xs2
▶ Float32Array [1.509261131286621]
Variance of xs3
▶ Float32Array [1.509261131286621]
Variance of pca
▶ Float32Array [1.7624872922897339]
```

The following graph illustrates how each point is rendered in a two-dimensional space with PCA. Although there's not much difference between the other projections, it maximizes the variance of the data:

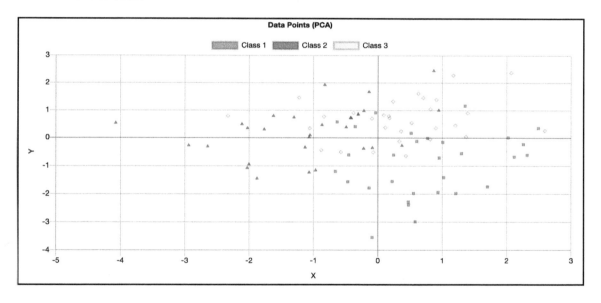

Word embedding

PCA is used to reduce the dimension of features for structured data. However, it is not designed to be aware of the target labels and application-specific metrics due to the nature of unsupervised learning. Note that traditional methods such as PCA often don't work as expected in more complicated examples such as natural language processing.

In this section, we are going to introduce a technique that embeds higher dimensional data, such as natural language or audio, into a fixed dimensional space, while keeping some semantics for processing.

What is word embedding?

Word embedding is a feature engineering technique that's used in the context of NLP. In short, each vocabulary is mapped to the fixed-length vector of real numbers. A word is traditionally treated as a discrete atomic value in NLP processing. This type of encoding can be arbitrary and lacks useful information representing the relationships among vocabularies. It raises the issue of sparse data, which tends to require more data to train the statistical model successfully. Here, we would use word embedding by using vector space models to convert the discrete values into a continuous vector space while keeping its semantics. For example, a five-dimensional embedding of English word vocabulary can be seen in the following dataset:

```
yellow: [0.13412, 0.12412, 0.53312, -0.51343, 0.72346]
dog: [0.62351, 0.72341, -0.12451, 0.13451, 0.13623]
green: [0.67234, 0.62341, 0.72454, -0.72511, -0.41352]
cat: [0.72141, -0.41341, -0.71121, -0.11412, -0.61124]
```

None of the dimensions have any inherent meaning. The overall relative pattern shows the structure of the semantics of words. Embedding is more and more important, not only as the input, but also as the output of the model. Thanks to its ability to measure the similarity between objects, applications can use the results of the embedding to find the nearest neighbors. By using this tool for visualization, it is much easier to explore datasets in a discrete space. In the upcoming subsections, we are going to learn how to visualize embeddings.

Word2vec is the most popular algorithm for word embeddings and is similar to neural networks in terms of their contexts. The embedding algorithms that are implemented by TensorFlow libraries are also based on this algorithm.

Now, let's embed the IMDb dataset into a fixed continuous value space.

Loading the IMDb dataset

The IMDb sentiment dataset is the most famous movie review dataset. It contains text that can be used to evaluate movies with a positive/negative sentiment.

We are going to use the preprocessed dataset and the code in `tfjs-examples` to load the IMDb dataset since it contains several util libraries that we can use to convert the IMDb dataset into a TensorFlow.js-compatible format. Please see the original code to find out how to load the IMDb dataset.

Here, we will load sentences that are a maximum of 100 words in length. The vocabulary size for this dataset is 10,000. This is the same as the sentiment analysis example in `tfjs-examples`:

```
const numWords = 10000;
const maxLen = 100;
const embeddingSize = 8;

console.log('Loading data...');
const {xTrain, xTest, yTrain, yTest} = await loadData(numWords, maxLen);
```

Although the preceding code returns the test datasets (`xTest`, `yTest`), we don't use them here. `embeddingSize` specifies the output of the embedded space. All of the words in the vocabulary will be mapped into an eight-dimensional space.

Embedding the model

The embedding model is constructed using the Layers API. `tf.layers.embedding` allows us to train the mapping in order to embed words into fixed-length vectors. The size of the input dimension is the vocabulary size, and each output should have an embeddingSize-length vector. Please note that `inputLength` is the maximum length of the sentence in the dataset, which is different from `inputDim`. Since the target label is a positive/negative flag, the `sigmoid` activation function is used after the output of the embedding is flattened. One interesting thing about this is that this embedding can take labels into consideration. These are set in terms of the application's purpose. This indicates the flexibility in customizing the embedded space so that it fits the purpose of the application:

```
function buildModel(numWords: number, maxLen: number, embeddingSize:
number) {
  const model = tf.sequential();
  model.add(tf.layers.embedding({
    inputDim: numWords,
    outputDim: embeddingSize,
```

```
      inputLength: maxLen
  }));

  model.add(tf.layers.flatten());

  model.add(tf.layers.dense({units: 1, activation: 'sigmoid'}));
  return model;
}
```

For the loss function, we use `binaryCrossEntropy` in order to minimize the difference between the positive/negative sentiment. We're going to use the Adam optimizer for this. We start the training process by running the `fit` method of the sequential model of the Layers API:

```
const model = buildModel(numWords, maxLen, embeddingSize);

model.compile({
  loss: 'binaryCrossentropy',
  optimizer: 'adam',
  metrics: ['acc']
});
model.summary();

console.log('Training model...');
await model.fit(xTrain, yTrain, {
  epochs: 3,
  batchSize: 64,
  validationSplit: 0.2
});
```

Tuning hyperparameters such as `batchSize` and `metrics` has been left as an exercise.

Visualization of embeddings

This is the most exciting part of the word embedding experiment. Seeing is believing, and visualizing the embedded space should be able to provide us with an intuitive understanding of what embedding results look like. The TensorFlow community has provided a tool that we can use to visualize the embedded space. This is called **Embedding Projector**:

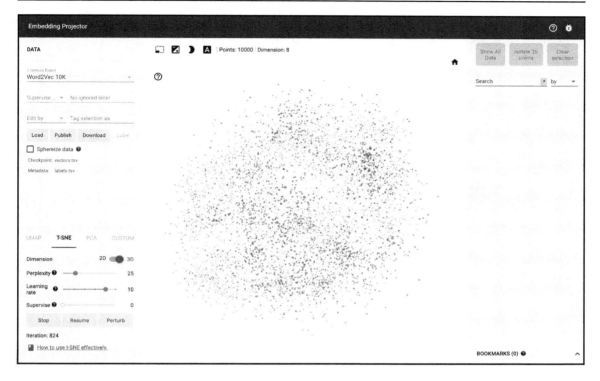

With this tool, we can create visual information about the embedded space in a 2D or 3D manner. The algorithms we can use here are PCA and t-SNE. t-SNE is another dimensionality reduction algorithm that is quickly gaining popularity in the deep learning community.

We can use this tool by uploading the dataset containing the embedding vectors and the corresponding labels. The labels will be in TSV format. Since TSV strings are printed in the console of the sample application, we can simply copy and paste the data. These strings are called `vectors.tsv` and `labels.tsv`, respectively. Please upload them from the dialog that appears after you click the **Load** button:

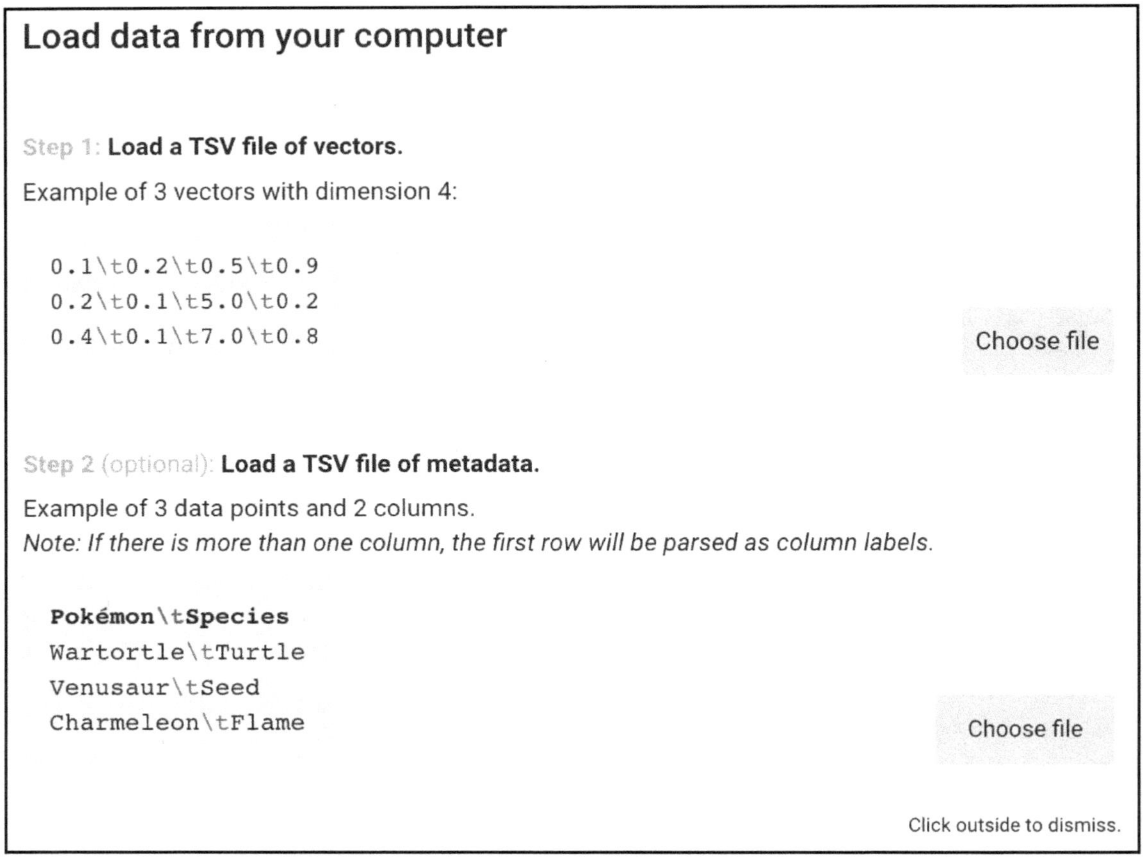

Load data from your computer

Step 1: **Load a TSV file of vectors.**

Example of 3 vectors with dimension 4:

```
0.1\t0.2\t0.5\t0.9
0.2\t0.1\t5.0\t0.2
0.4\t0.1\t7.0\t0.8
```

Choose file

Step 2 (optional): **Load a TSV file of metadata.**

Example of 3 data points and 2 columns.
Note: If there is more than one column, the first row will be parsed as column labels.

```
Pokémon\tSpecies
Wartortle\tTurtle
Venusaur\tSeed
Charmeleon\tFlame
```

Choose file

Click outside to dismiss.

The points that are rendered by the projector express their similarity in terms of their distance in the three-dimensional space. The projector also attaches the labels of each point to the point itself so that we know which point corresponds to every other point:

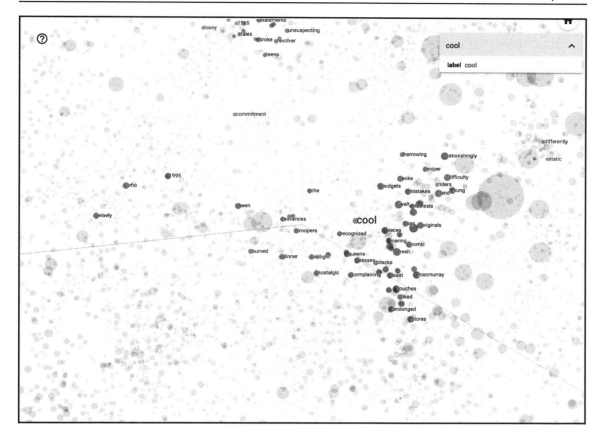

The preceding screenshot shows the points that are close to the word `cool`. Some of the words around `cool` seem to have the same sentiment, such as `nostalgic` or `liked`, but there are still words that aren't related to each other. This may have been caused by a lack of training. This leaves room for hyperparameter tuning.

Summary

In this chapter, we covered the techniques and algorithms we can use for dimensionality reduction. Here, we learned how the data points in a high dimensional space are distributed into a low dimensional space to make the machine learning process more efficient and accurate. One widely used approach is PCA. PCA is an algorithm that's designed to maximize the variance in the projected data space. Due to its simplicity and efficiency, it is the most popular dimensionality reduction algorithm.

Another algorithm that we looked at in this chapter was word embedding. This allows us to map data that's been placed in a discrete value into the vectors of real numbers. The pattern that's projected by embedding is similar to the context machine learning applications take advantage of. Moreover, the embedded space can be used for visual analysis.

Then, we looked at an example of how to create a picture showing the similarities between each point in a three-dimensional space using the Embedding Projector tool. It is possible to apply this approach in order to envision discrete objects in the spaces we recognize intuitively. In the next chapter, we will look at implementing Bellman equation to solve the Markov decision process problems, and how it can be used in reinforcement learning.

Exercise

1. Try to use PCA to reduce the size of the dimension to 1 and compare the result with the projected data in the x, y, and z axes, respectively.
2. Compare the results of PCA and t-SNE that are shown by the **Embedding Projector** tool. Which is better in terms of visibility?
3. Implement the PCA algorithm without using the `numeric` library (Hint: the operator for the eigenvalue is necessary).
4. Tune the hyperparameters of the embedding layer in order to visualize the embedding dataset to reflect the semantics of the data.
5. Try to embed MNIST data into a three-dimensional space.

Further reading

- Planning for Linear Algebra in TensorFlow.js: `https://github.com/tensorflow/tfjs/issues/1516`
- Numeric in npm: `https://www.npmjs.com/package/numeric`
- Vector Representations of Words: `https://www.tensorflow.org/tutorials/representation/word2vec`
- tfjs-examples/sentiment: `https://github.com/tensorflow/tfjs-examples/tree/18cc9ce0c4c7b625f961f0e685243cae1790677c/sentiment`
- Embedding Projector: `https://projector.tensorflow.org`

9
Solving the Markov Decision Process

Reinforcement learning is one of the most exciting fields in machine learning. There are many machine learning systems leveraged by reinforcement learning algorithms. AlphaGo is the famous example for this type of application. So far, we have seen applications using supervised learning and unsupervised learning techniques. While they are powerful in specific fields, they do not provide a distinct solution where even a human does not know the correct answer. In this chapter, we are going to introduce reinforcement learning, which has become one of the most prominent fields recently. This technology has shown outstanding performance when there is no complete knowledge about the target, such as in TV games. We will also learn how to implement the Bellman equation for solving **Markov decision process** (**MDP**) problems and how it relates to reinforcement learning.

This chapter covers the following basics of reinforcement learning:

- What is reinforcement learning?
  - MDP
  - Discounted total reward
  - State-value function
  - Bellman equation
  - Q-learning
- Solving the four-states environment

Technical requirements

The following will be required in order to complete the tasks in this chapter:

- TypeScript
- Web browser (Chrome is recommended)

Check out the following video to see the Code in Action:
`http://bit.ly/2rWjjSs`

Reinforcement learning

A problem that reinforcement learning can solve is a type of situation where there is no complete knowledge about the target assumption and the situation is likely to change based on the action toward the target. A subject to pursue the correct goal is called an **agent**. The agent tries to achieve the goal under the given **environment**. Imagine a situation where a person is drifting in an uninhabited island. Although the person tries to escape from the island and get back home, they do not have the complete knowledge to do so. It is necessary for them to seek the solution alongside exploring the environment, such as collecting food and building a temporary house on the island. The following diagram is an example of the problem reinforcement learning attempts to solve. The person is an agent and the environment is the island in this case:

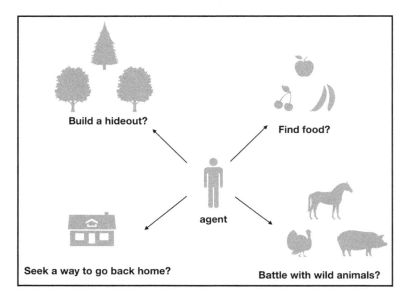

What should an agent do? All possible options can be a trade-off. Some of them contribute to improving the situation (for example, lock their home); others do not (for example, injured). The value to measure the goodness of the situation is called a **reward**. Additionally, these results are not given deterministically, as you may infer. The same action does not always lead us to the same situation. The probability of how the state is transitioned is not provided explicitly. The purpose of the agent is to maximize the total reward obtained through the process of the exploration and find the policy taking the appropriate action to achieve the goal.

This type of problem is mathematically defined as the MDP.

MDP

The problem of reinforcement learning can be formulated as the MDP. The MDP is the mathematical notion to define the mutual interaction between states, actions, and rewards in the environment. It contains the following factors:

- Set of states S
- Space of actions A(s)
- Initial states P_0
- State transition function $P(s'|s, a)$
- Reward function $r(s, a, s')$

The MDP is a probabilistic process described by these factors. *S* contains all possible states in the process. *A(s)* is a set including all possible actions decided by each set. As possible actions depend on the current state, the set of actions is fixed with the given state. The process is started with the initial state contained in P_0. Through each action, the state that the agent is facing changes. The probability in which state it is picked up by each action is defined by the state transition function. This is a conditional probability defined with the given state and action. The reward function returns the reward decided by the combination of the current state, the action taken, and the next state.

The possible states are *N*-types of states:

$$\mathbf{S} = \{s_1, s_2, \ldots, s_N\}$$

As each state is a probability variable, the sequence of the states in the process is described as follows:

$$S_0, S_1, \ldots, S_t, \ldots$$

Generally, the possible actions can be different from each current state. But we are going to use the same set of actions for simplicity this time:

$$\mathbf{A} = \{a_1, a_2, \ldots, a_M\}$$

The initial state is sampled from the probability distribution, P_0:

$$S_0 \sim P_0$$

Now, we have defined the three basic factors of the MDP: state, action, and reward. States are described as the probability variables sampled from the initial distribution and transition distribution functions. Now, let's look at how the MDP is expanded along with the time steps.

After an agent observes the initial step, it chooses the specific action based on its own policy. The next step is probabilistically decided with the current state, S_0, and the action, A_0:

$$P(S_1 | S_0, A_0)$$

The reward given in the step is specified as follows:

$$R_1 = r(S_0, A_0, S_1)$$

We can do the same steps continuously until reaching the end state. Although the MDP is theoretically defined with an infinite number of sequences of states, we will treat only the MDP as having a finite number of states for simplicity.

The following diagram is an illustration of how the MDP can be visualized by using the example of tic-tac-toe. An agent needs to choose where to put the first circle in the given initial state. The next state is given after the state is changed by the action of an opponent. The states combining ones from agent actions and opponent actions construct the tree structure:

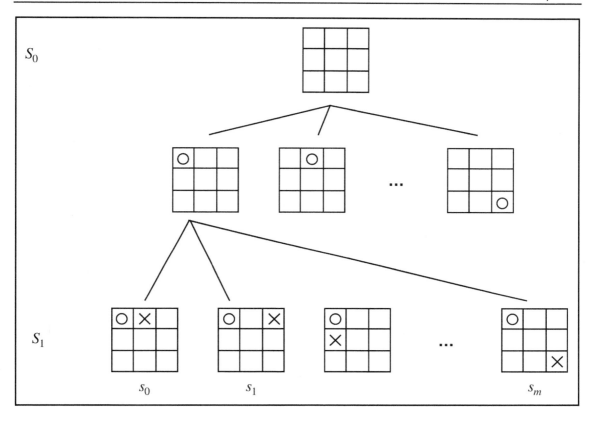

It is possible to find the best solution if an agent can traverse all nodes in the tree. But we cannot expect such a perfect situation in general because of the high computational cost of searching a vast amount of space of the game (for example, Go, Mahjong). The goal of reinforcement learning is to find the policy to achieve the maximized reward without knowing the entire structure of the game.

Before introducing the algorithms for solving the MDP problem, it is necessary to touch on the concept of discounted total reward first.

Discounted total reward

The simple sum of the reward can be defined as follows:

$$G_t = \sum_{r=0}^{T-1} R_{t+1+r}$$

This is just a total of the rewards obtained from the current state in relation to a specific range of future steps.

In reality, the simple metric is not appropriate as a target to be maximized because it can diverge to infinity when the time step increases. The infinity reward is not working well with the mathematical algorithms. To deal with the situation, it is common to use a **discounted total reward** instead of reinforcement learning. This type of reward is a formulation aimed to express the uncertainty by using the discounted reward. Specifically, it is described as follows:

$$G_t = \sum_{r=0}^{T-1} \gamma^r R_{t+1+r} = R_{t+1} + \gamma R_{t+2} + \cdots + \gamma^{T-1} R_{t+T}$$

The discount value, γ, takes between 0 and 1 ($0 \leq \gamma \leq 1$), which expresses how much the future reward is discounted. It indicates that the gamma close to 1 views the long-term benefit more. On the other hand, a value close to 0 means it puts more weight on the short-term reward in the process. It evaluates the actions that bring immediate benefit. Thus, the gamma can be thought of as a hyperparameter of this problem's settings.

Thanks to the discounted total reward, we can treat the process that continues infinitely as well as the finite process. That assumption is also compatible with our natural thought processes. We tend to get the immediate benefit rather than waiting for the long-term benefit if the value amount is the same. This indicates that we also naturally do the calculation discounting the reward obtained in the future. Therefore, the consideration around the discounted total reward results in an agent that behaves as we expect.

However, do please recall that the sequence of states is composed of the probability variables. The reward is not given deterministically conditioned by the current state and the actions an agent takes. It is not a desirable format to evaluate the state or action the agent should take. From now on, we are going to use the expected value of the total discounted reward starting from the current state. This is used as a measurable indicator to evaluate each state in the process.

State-value function

The state-value function measures the expected worth of each state in the process. As was suggested, the value can be described as the expected discounted total reward. Here is the mathematical formulation of the state value from the given state, *s*, at step *t*:

$$V^\pi(s) = \mathbb{E}^\pi[G_{t+1}|S_t = s]$$

π is a policy function that defines which action is taken by the agent. While our goal is to find a good policy function, the state-value function is fixed by the policy function. Thus, the state value is a scalar number that is a sum of discounted reward from the given state:

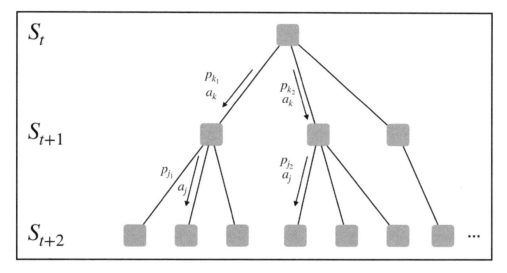

This diagram illustrates the situation of how the state value is calculated. As described previously, the same action does not lead us to the same state deterministically. The next state is decided based on the conditional probability described as the transition function. An action, a_k, brings us the left state with the probability p_{k1} and the right state with the probability p_{k2}. Therefore, the state value is a mean of possible reward resulted from the actions taken by the given policy. As you may already find, we can define the order of the policies by using the state value.

We can say that the policy π is better than π' if they satisfy the following condition:

$$\forall s \in S, \ V^{\pi'}(s) \leq V^{\pi}(s)$$
$$\exists s \in S, \ V^{\pi'}(s) \leq V^{\pi}(s)$$

If we can find the best policy according to the criteria, we can call it the **optimal policy**. The state value given by the optimal policy is the optimal state value, which can be described as follows:

$$\forall s \in S, \ V^{*}(s) = \max_{\pi} V^{\pi}(s)$$

Although the state-value function gets only the state as its parameter, it is much more useful if we have actions so that we can evaluate practically the pair of the given state and the action the agent should take. From now on, we use the **action-value function**, which is derived from the state-value function naturally:

$$Q^{\pi}(s, a) = \mathbb{E}[S_{t+1} | S_t = s, A_t = a]$$

It is a mean reward of all possible paths starting from the state, s, and action, a. It enables us to evaluate the goodness of actions taken by the agent. As well as the optimal policy for state value function, we can find the optimal policy by using the action value function:

$$Q^{*}(s, a) = \max_{\pi} Q^{\pi}(s, a)$$

We have learned the way to find the optimal policy by using the maximum state value or action-value. But these functions depend on the transition function and possible reward. It is unusual to explicitly know these factors in the MDP in advance. Since the action-value function is not expected to be given, it is necessary to estimate it from our observation.

We took a long way to come here. By way of a final step in explaining the basis of reinforcement learning algorithms, the Bellman equation and Q-learning are discussed to estimate the action-value function.

Bellman equation

As the calculation of expected value is a linear operation, the action-value function is rewritten as follows:

$$Q^\pi(s,a) = \mathbb{E}^\pi[G_{t+1}|S_t = s, A_t = a]$$
$$= \mathbb{E}^\pi[R_{t+1}|S_t = s, A_t = a] + \mathbb{E}^\pi[\gamma R_{t+2} + \gamma^2 Rt + 3 + \ldots |S_t = s, A_t = a]$$
$$= \mathbb{E}^\pi[R_{t+1}|S_t = s, A_t = a] + \gamma\mathbb{E}^\pi[R_{t+2} + \gamma Rt + 3 + \ldots |S_t = s, A_t = a]$$

Although we omit the detail of the calculation here, the **Bellman equation** regarding the action-value function is derived from the following calculation:

$$Q^\pi(s,a) = \sum_{s' \in S} P(s'|s,a)\left(r(s,a,s') + \sum_{a \in A(s')} \gamma P(a'|s')Q^\pi(s',a')\right)$$

This expression indicates that we can compute the action value of every pair of state and action recursively. This makes things much simpler. However, it does not resolve the essential problem because the Bellman equation still depends on the transition function, P. We need to come up with the algorithm estimating action value without using the transition function.

Q-learning

Q-learning is the most widely used reinforcement learning algorithm to construct the best policy by estimating the action-value function. Q-learning is an iterative optimization process that updates the initial action-value function with each observation:

$$Q(S_t, A_t) \leftarrow (1-\alpha)Q(S_t, A_t) + \alpha(R_{t+1} + \gamma \max_{a' \in A(s')} Q(S_{t+1}, a'))$$

Alpha is a learning rate specifying how much the function is updated in one iteration. As you can see, it does not contain the transition function. The action-value function can be estimated from only observations.

But how can we make sure to converge to the optimal value by this iterative process? Let's rewrite the equation as follows:

$$Q(S_t, A_t) \leftarrow Q(S_t, A_t) + \alpha(R_{t+1} + \gamma \max_{a' \in A(s')} Q(S_{t+1}, a') - Q(S_t, A_t))$$

If the process converges, the second term must be 0. For example, it should look like this at the first iteration:

$$r(s_1, a_1, s_2) + \gamma \max_{a' \in A(s')} Q(s_2, a') - Q(s_1, a_1) = 0$$

This result is completely consistent with the Bellman equation for the action-value function when the policy always chooses the action whose action value is the maximum:

$$Q(s_1, a_1) = r(s_1, a_1, s_2) + \gamma \max_{a' \in A(s')} Q(s_2, a')$$

It illustrates the fact that if Q-learning converges, we can get the action-value function by using a policy of always selecting the action whose action-value function is maximized. Therefore, Q-learning is an algorithm to find the action-value function under the specific policy that keeps taking the action whose value is the maximum.

We can now stop here and take a look at how Q-learning works under the simple MDP problem.

Solving the four-states environment

We assume that the simple environment has four global states. In every state, there are two possible actions. For simplicity, the transition can be settled deterministically, which means the next state is decided only by the current state and action taken by the agent. Here is the diagram illustrating the MDP we are discussing:

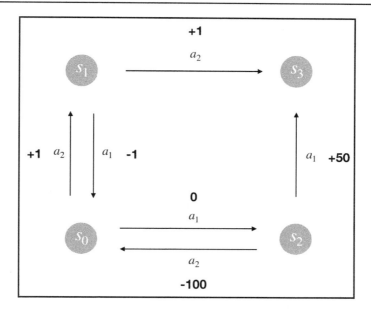

s_0 is the initial state, and s_3 is the goal. There are two possible actions, a_1 and a_2 for every state other than the goal. The number represents the reward obtained by the specific transition. We are going to construct the agent updating the action-value function by using the Q-learning algorithm.

Designing the environment

The environment containing four states can be designed as follows. The environment has a list of states and actions at first and also rewards corresponding to the pair of state and action. The reward is decided deterministically based on the current state and action an agent takes:

```
class Environment {
  private states = [0, 1, 2, 3];
  private actions = [
    [2, 1],
    [0, 3],
    [3, 0],
    [3, 3], // End state
  ];
  // Reward is decided based on the current state and action an agent
takes.
  private rewards = [
    [0, 1],
```

```
    [-1, 1],
    [50, -100],
    [0, 0],
];

// Other methods...
}
```

The environment, in this case, has several utility methods to provide internal states:

```
private currentState: number;
constructor() {
  this.currentState = 0;
}

getCurrentState(): number {
  return this.currentState;
}

getStates(): number[] {
  return this.states;
}

getNumStates(): number {
  return this.states.length;
}

getNumActions(): number {
  return this.actions[0].length;
}

isEnd(): boolean {
  if (this.currentState === 3) {
   return true;
  } else {
    return false;
  }
}
```

To update the internal states with the action taken by an agent, the environment class provides the following methods. The `update` method returns the reward after changing the current state:

```
update(action: number): number {
  const reward = this.rewards[this.currentState][action];
  this.currentState = this.actions[this.currentState][action];
  return reward;
}
```

```
reset() {
  this.currentState = 0;
}
```

The agent keeps taking action until it reaches the end state and gets the reward corresponding to each transition. One iteration starting from the initial state and the goal state is called an **episode**. In Q-learning, an agent tries to converge the action-value function by running several episodes.

The Q-learning process

In this experiment, we use 0.01 as a learning rate and 0.8 as a discount value. This is the code to initialize the environment and hyperparameters for the training:

```
async function qlearning() {
  const episodes = [];
  for (let i = 0; i < 1000; i++) {
    episodes.push(i);
  }

  // Initialize Environment
  const env = new Environment();

  // Initialize the action-value function as the 2-dim tensor
  // with the shape [numState, numActions]
  let actionValue = tf.fill([env.getNumStates(), env.getNumActions()], 10);

  // Learning Rate
  const alpha = 0.01;

  // Discount Value
  const discount = 0.8;

  // Optimization with Q-learning
  // ...
}
```

We can update the action-value function by observing the result from the environment in episodes (1,000 episodes run in this training phase):

```
  // Optimization with Q-learning

  const xs = [];
  actionValue.print();

  // Iterations for every episode
```

```
for (let i of episodes) {
  let isEnd = false;

  while (!isEnd) {
    // Play the game until the episode is finished.
    // Pick up the next action...
  }
  env.reset();
}
```

An agent picks up the next action as follows:

```
// Policy picks the action randomly
const action = policy();
```

Based on the action taken by the agent, we update the action-value function for the following iterations:

```
const prevState = env.getCurrentState();
const reward = env.update(action);
const currentState = env.getCurrentState();

// Initialize the update value with zero.
const array = new Float32Array(env.getNumStates() *
env.getNumActions());
  array.fill(1.0);
  const buffer = tf.buffer([env.getNumStates(), env.getNumActions()],
'float32', array);

// Set the maximum action-value expected from the currentState.
const maxValue = tf.util.toNestedArray(
    [env.getNumStates(), 1],
actionValue.max(1).dataSync())[currentState];
  buffer.set(reward + discount * maxValue, prevState, action);

// Update action-value function.
actionValue = tf.mul((1 - alpha), actionValue).add(tf.mul(alpha,
buffer.toTensor()));

// If it reaches the end state, the episode is completed.
isEnd = env.isEnd();
```

In order to implement the following algorithm, we use a tensor buffer to update the part of the value:

$$Q(S_t, A_t) \leftarrow (1 - \alpha)Q(S_t, A_t) + \alpha(R_{t+1} + \gamma \max_{a' \in A(s')} Q(S_{t+1}, a'))$$

A tensor buffer is a useful data structure to construct the tensor iteratively. It is suitable for random access. By initializing the buffer with 1, it only updates the value corresponding to the current state and action. A reward is returned by the environment as a result of an action. To construct the final tensor, `buffer.toTensor()` needs to be called. The one iteration is repeated specific times. In this case, 1,000 episodes are experienced for the agent.

The policy is a function to pick up either action probabilistically. The following policy function selects both actions with exactly the same probability so that the agent can explore every action as many times as possible. The integer 0 means action 1, while 1 means action 2 in this code:

```
function policy() {
    if (Math.random() < 0.5) {
        return 0;
    } else {
        return 1;
    }
}
```

Let's see how the action value of $s0$ is converged. The initial action values for all states are initialized with 10:

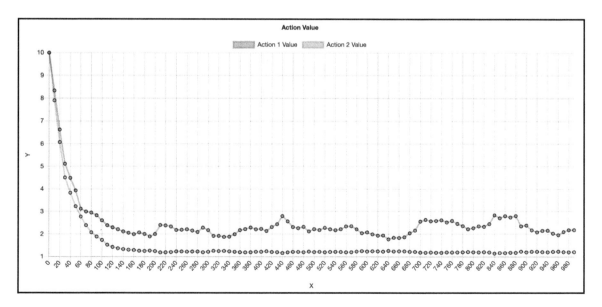

In the long term, taking action 1 brings more total discount reward because it makes the reward +50 higher possible even if there is some chance to get -100 reward by taking action 2. We will see how the final reward is changed after we updated the policy function as follows:

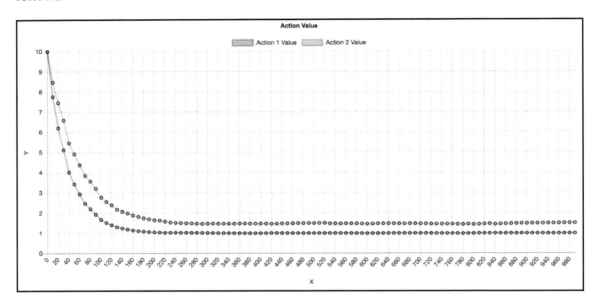

As you can see, the action value for action 2 is increased. It is considered due to the lower probability to select action 1 which brings the higher reward +50. Taking action 1 in state 1 is more likely to achieve lower a total reward on average. With this policy function, the action value for state 2 has shown a slightly different result:

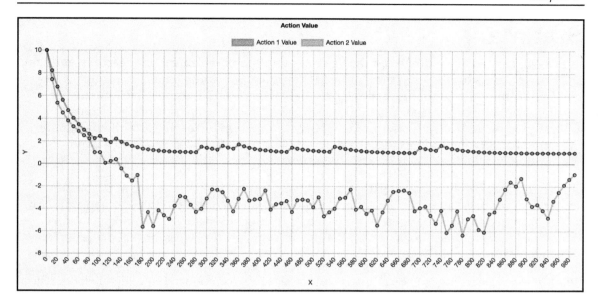

Even with a much lower probability to pick up action 1, the action value for it is significantly higher than the other one. This indicates that action 1 is definitely the best choice in the case of state 2 because action 1 reaches the goal with a reward of +50 deterministically. Action 1 gives us -100 and needs to keep working the game further. That is the reason why the action value for action 2 is fluctuating more.

In this experiment, the policy function keeps exploring to see how the action-value function converges. But it is not so difficult to achieve the best result just after convergence by taking the actions that always give us the maximum action value. That is the basic assumption behind the Q-learning algorithm.

Summary

In this chapter, we have discussed the basic assumption of reinforcement learning and how Q-learning works by showing the simple MDP problem. Reinforcement learning is a powerful technique for solving a situation where we do not have complete knowledge of the environment itself. This leads to the desired result with a few sets of definitions naturally modeled from the environment observation. While we still carefully design the transition function between states, the deterministic transition also provides a good assumption of MDP as shown in our experiment.

Q-learning is a widely used algorithm to resolve the reinforcement learning problem. It is an iterative process to update the action-value function according to the Bellman equation. It is guaranteed to be converged, and gives us a result consistent with our expectations. While the algorithm itself looks pretty simple, it is powerful enough to beat a human in a TV game or traditional Go game.

Reinforcement learning is an exciting development because the way in which it solves the MDP process is very similar to what we do. In that sense, reinforcement learning is regarded as a typical field where artificial intelligence is applied. The behavior of the algorithm gives the impression that it has intelligence. Since there are many examples and implementations to solve more complicated problems, you may want to try to run the program to achieve more human-like results.

In the next chapter, we will learn how to deploy machine learning applications.

Exercise

1. Come up with a situation around you that can be defined as an MDP problem.
2. Do you think we can use the state-value function to solve the MDP problem in the same way as we use the action-value function?
3. Explore the active-function result by changing the following hyperparameters for the four-states MDP introduced here:
    1. Discount ratio
    2. Learning rate
    3. Reward in the transition from state 2 to 3

4. Use the following policy for the four-states MDP introduced in the chapter:
    1. Always choose action 1.
    2. Always choose action 2.
    3. Choosing the action maximizing the action value.
5. Try to run the CartPole example in the example code and see how the behavior is changed.

Further reading

- Reinforcement learning: `https://en.wikipedia.org/wiki/Reinforcement_learning`
- The Bellman equation: `https://en.wikipedia.org/wiki/Bellman_equation`
- tf.buffer: `https://js.tensorflow.org/api/0.11.2/#buffer`
- Q-learning: `https://en.wikipedia.org/wiki/Q-learning`
- CartPole game: `https://gym.openai.com/envs/CartPole-v0/`

3
Section 3: Productionizing Machine Learning Applications with TensorFlow.js

This section of the book focuses on deploying machine learning applications, generating high performance from hardware-accelerated backends, and training your model with TensorFlow Core. Moving ahead, we will discuss tips and tricks to improve the performance of TensorFlow.js.

This section contains the following chapters:

- Chapter 10, *Deploying Machine Learning Applications*
- Chapter 11, *Tuning Applications to Achieve High Performance*
- Chapter 12, *Future Work Around TensorFlow.js*

10
Deploying Machine Learning Applications

There are several ways in which we can deploy web applications. We need to be familiar with the common frameworks that pack up our artifacts and machine learning models. In this chapter, we are going to learn how to create a package of TensorFlow.js applications. In the previous chapters, we have written various kinds of machine learning applications using TensorFlow.js. These applications are so simple that it would be great to learn about the basic building blocks that we use when we write an application with TensorFlow.js. But this is just the beginning.

From this chapter onward, more advanced topics will be covered. Therefore, it would be useful to make our applications production-ready in terms of performance and portability.

In this chapter, we will cover the following topics:

- The ecosystem around the JavaScript platform
- Module bundler
- Deploying modules with GitHub Pages

Technical requirements

The following will be required in order to complete the tasks in this chapter:

- A web browser (Chrome is recommended)
- Node.js
- TypeScript
- A GitHub account

Check out the following video to see the Code in Action:
http://bit.ly/2qu43Mj

The ecosystem around the JavaScript platform

JavaScript is the central building block of web applications. The purpose of this book is to show you how to run an interesting machine learning application on the web. However, so far, we haven't talked about this much. In this section, we are going to learn how JavaScript works in modern web browsers and the developer tools that support the platform.

JavaScript in modern web browsers

Most modern web browsers have their own JavaScript runtime so that the client-side application can easily and securely run the JavaScript program. The JavaScript runtime in web browsers is fundamentally isolated from the underlying operating system and is strictly managed by the browser. Even if we were to run a resource-intensive machine learning application, it shouldn't affect applications that are running in the same machine:

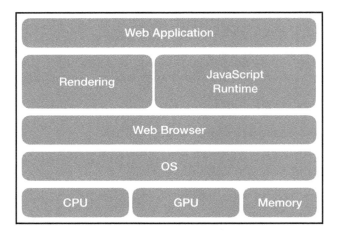

JavaScript is a language that obeys the standards of ECMAScript. Therefore, JavaScript is just one implementation of ECMAScript. There is little difference between browsers in terms of the ECMAScript versions supported. At the time of writing, the most widely supported version is version 6, officially known as ECMAScript 2015, which has numerous features, all of which are provided by modern programming languages such as object-oriented systems. There should be no incompatible differences in terms of JavaScript implementation, but each browser is slightly different, especially when it comes to experimental APIs such as WebGPU. That is why we recommend using Chrome to run TensorFlow.js; it's been thoroughly tested on the Chrome platform.

The good thing about web browsers is that you don't need to care about managing the runtime. Once we've installed the browser on our machine, it will work correctly. It is unnecessary to think too much about troublesome things that are dependent on the type of platform you're using, such as security and resource management. Browser vendors should be responsible for keeping any kind of machine or operating system safe and performant. Although there are some exceptions, we can generally ensure that we can run our application, which is written in JavaScript, in any kind of client environment.

While web browsers are the primary JavaScript runtime environment, there is another platform we can use to run server-side JavaScript.

Node.js

Node.js is a JavaScript runtime built on the V8 JavaScript engine. Since V8 is the engine contained in Chrome, we can achieve the same performance and functionality with this platform. Node.js also supports major operating systems such as macOS, Windows, and Linux. As well as web browsers, it provides us with a platform-agnostic runtime that we can retrieve just by running Node.js.

There are some features of ECMAScript 2015 that aren't supported or not enabled by Node.js by default; for example, tail recursion optimization is not fully enabled. We can find information on all the supported features at `https://node.green`.

However, rest assured that this isn't an issue. The TypeScript compiler takes care of the differences in terms of syntax and features based on the specified target.

So far, we've built our project for browsers, but it is also possible to build it with Node.js. The following command will generate the compiled code in the `dist` directory:

```
# Compile the project for the Node.js target
$ npx parcel build --target node src/ch10/hello.ts

# Run the code
$ node dist/hello.js
```

One significant difference from the browser environment is that we can use TensorFlow as a backend through the C extension of Node.js. It provides faster implementation for every supported kernel. We can use the following dedicated binding so that we can use TensorFlow in a Node.js environment:

```
$ npm install @tensorflow/tfjs-node
```

This is shown in the following code:

```
import * as tf from '@tensorflow/tfjs-node';

// Construct your model as normal
tf.xxx
```

Just changing the referred namespace makes it possible for us to change the backend implementation from Node.js to JavaScript to TensorFlow C through C extensions.

We can see how much faster the `tfjs-node` backend is by running a simple benchmark. `tf.time` is an API that measures the elapsed time it takes to run a given function:

```
import * as tf from '@tensorflow/tfjs';

// Run matrix multiplication for 100 times
function benchmark(size: number) {
    for (let i = 0; i < 100; i++) {
        const t1 = tf.randomNormal([size, size]);
        const t2 = tf.randomNormal([size, size]);
        const result = t1.matMul(t2);
    }
}

async function runBenchmark() {
    console.log('size,kernelMs,wallMs');
    for (let s = 1; s < 100; s++) {
        const time = await tf.time(() => benchmark(s));
        console.log(`${s},${time.kernelMs},${time.wallMs}`);
    }
}

runBenchmark();
```

The following chart shows the elapsed time it took to run the benchmark with the `tfjs` backend and the `tfjs-node` backend. The larger the matrix, the slower it becomes compared to the `tfjs-node` backend. When the size of the tensor is small, the `tfjs` backend is faster. This difference is mainly caused by the overhead of the C extension of Node.js. But thanks to the highly efficient implementation of TensorFlow kernels, `tfjs-node` achieves much better performance, even with the overhead of calling the TensorFlow C API through extension:

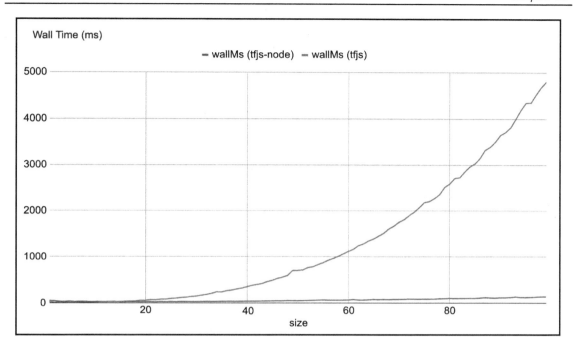

Moreover, Node.js allows us to run the program with more advanced hardware acceleration than the browser environment. Since TensorFlow.js has a Node.js dedicated backend, it is possible to run kernels using CUDA and NVIDIA GPU drivers if our machine supports it. To enable NVIDIA GPU support, it is necessary to install the following libraries:

- NVIDIA GPU Drivers > 410.x
- CUDA Toolkit 10.0
- cuDNN SDK >= 7.4.1

We also need to install the special binding for Node.js GPU support:

```
$ npm install @tensorflow/tfjs-node-gpu
```

Now, we should be able to use the GPU support kernel:

```
import * as tf from '@tensorflow/tfjs-node-gpu';
```

Please try to compare the CUDA backend with other backends by yourself.

In this section, we have learned that we can easily change the backend implementation in the Node.js runtime just by changing the reference to the package. The fact that we can use TensorFlow C++ implementation through the `tfjs-node` backend indicates that we can make use of the same TensorFlow.js code in every TensorFlow runtime where the C API can be one. Once your machine learning application has been written in TensorFlow.js, we can use all of the capabilities of TensorFlow.

Node package manager

As we have already seen, TensorFlow.js and its backend implementations are distributed as a **node package manager** (**npm**) package. npm is the Node.js ecosystem's package manager. Over 1 million packages have been uploaded to npm. Everything that's written in JavaScript or AltJS is uploaded to npm. Since npm is the built-in package manager of Node.js, we don't need to install it again.

The following is a list of packages that have been distributed by the TensorFlow.js community. These packages are managed under the `@tensorflow` namespace:

Name	Usage
`@tensorflow/tfjs`	TensorFlow.js core implementation
`@tensorflow/tfjs-layers`	Layers API
`@tensorflow/tfjs-node`	CPU backend of the Node.js runtime
`@tensorflow/tfjs-node-gpu`	GPU backend of the Node.js runtime
`@tensorflow/tfjs-data`	Data Loader API and its implementations
`@tensorflow/tfjs-vis`	Visualization tool intended for use in browsers
`@tensorflow/tfjs-converter`	Converter for TensorFlow and TensorFlow.js models
`@tensorflow/tfjs-react-native`	Backend for React native (experimental)
`@tensorflow/tfjs-backend-webgpu`	Backend for WebGPU (experimental)
`@tensorflow/tfjs-automl`	APIs that load models using AutoML edge

These are categorized into two groups: one group is used for the backend implementation of kernels, while the other group is used utility libraries in order to provide useful APIs that make it easy for us to construct a machine learning pipeline on the web. Keep in mind that some backend implementations are still experimental and their APIs may be changed drastically through their development lifetime. It isn't recommended to use them in a production application.

We are going to cover these advanced libraries in more detail in Chapter 12, *Future Work Around TensorFlow.js*.

Benefits of TypeScript in ML applications

TypeScript is a superset programming language of JavaScript that has a static type system. This allows us to write programs efficiently and safely thanks to its type system. Although there are dozens of AltJS languages in the world, TypeScript has a good balance between the programmer's productivity and the novelty of the design. Since TypeScript is just a superset of JavaScript, all JavaScript code can be executed as a TypeScript program, which doesn't prevent us from using the existing resources written in JavaScript. TypeScript is designed to be kept as just a *Typed JavaScript* so that we can learn the language loosely.

We can configure the TypeScript compiler in various ways. The compiler will find a file named `tsconfig.json` at the root of the project to get the specified configuration. It is a little cumbersome to write the `tsconfig.json` file from scratch, so `tsc --init` creates the file for us. Changing the target of the ECMAScript version allows us to support multiple target versions once it's written in TypeScript. This means that TypeScript provides us with an abstraction on the target platform as long as TypeScript supports the underlying target language.

TensorFlow.js and its libraries are also written in TypeScript. We can use TensorFlow.js from JavaScript code, but it's better to write our machine learning application with TypeScript to get the benefit of the type system. The tensors that are used in machine learning applications can have any kind of shape and rank. To apply mathematical operations to tensors of specific shapes correctly, we need to see the type of tensor statistically. For instance, `tf.conv2d` is a convolution operation that computes 2D convolution over the input tensor. It requires three or more ranked tensors as input. The signature of the operations is written as follows:

```
function conv2d_<T extends Tensor3D|Tensor4D>(
    x: T|TensorLike, filter: Tensor4D|TensorLike,
    strides: [number, number]|number, pad: 'valid'|'same'|number,
    dataFormat: 'NHWC'|'NCHW' = 'NHWC',
    dilations: [number, number]|number = [1, 1],
    dimRoundingMode?: 'floor'|'round'|'ceil'): T {

    //...
}
```

Thanks to the static type system, we can ensure that the input has a `Tensor3D` or `Tensor4D` type whose rank is over three. If we pass the less ranked tensor, it will be detected at compile-time, not runtime. This provides huge practical benefits because finding a bug at runtime is generally challenging, especially for client-side applications. We want to resolve any potential errors beforehand. The shape of the tensor can be transitioned by the chain of operations. The static type system helps us write the operational graph that transforms tensors one by one.

Module bundler

A module bundler is a tool that bundles all the resources that are needed to run the application in a deployable format. Web applications depend on various kinds of resources and assets, such as HTML, stylesheets, JavaScript code, and images. They are essentially separate files. We need to build an artifact that contains all the necessary resources in order to deploy the application. The JavaScript community develops many bundle tools for this purpose. Naturally, we can make use of them when building machine learning applications on the web.

In this section, we are going to use some bundle tools to create packages for our machine learning application.

Parcel

We have already used Parcel in this book. The code in this book assumes that Parcel runs the application as a bundle tool. We have chosen it for its ease of use and simplicity.

Parcel is a relatively newer tool in the module bundler field. Just by running one command, it builds the artifact that contains all the resources in an optimized format for a web application. Thanks to its ability to use multicore sources, it is fast to compile and build the artifact in our machine. It also supports various kinds of asset types, including TypeScript, so that we can quickly compile them in a format that can be run in browsers. Some of these assets are as follows:

- **Normal Resources**: HTML, CSS, JavaScript
- **Alternative Stylesheets**: SCSS, LESS, Stylus
- **AltJS**: TypeScript, CoffeeScript
- **UI Framework**: Vue.js

- **Data Format**: JSON, YAML, TOML
- **API DSL**: GraphQL
- **Low-Level Language**: WebAssembly

Parcel automatically detects the types of these resources and compiles them. Parcel is able to recognize that the resource is written in TypeScript. TypeScript compilation is an out of the box feature of Parcel. Even without installing the TypeScript compiler and writing `tsconfig.json` explicitly, we are able to build the project because Parcel knows how to build a TypeScript project just by looking at our source code. Note that the default TypeScript compilation of Parcel doesn't do type checking, but this isn't crucial for small projects. If you do need to execute type checking, `tsc --noEmit` will run through this process for you.

Installing Parcel can be completed with `npm`:

```
$ npm install parcel --save
```

The `npx` command allows us to run the local executable package so that we don't need to install Parcel in the global environment. The `parcel` command is run as a subcommand of `npx`:

```
$ npx parcel --help
Usage: parcel [options] [command]

Options:
  -V, --version output the version number
  -h, --help output usage information

Commands:
  serve [options] [input...] starts a development server
  watch [options] [input...] starts the bundler in watch mode
  build [options] [input...] bundles for production
  help [command] display help information for a command

  Run `parcel help <command>` for more information on specific commands
```

Parcel automatically resolves the dependencies between files and modules. All we need to do is write a TypeScript program. Let's say we want to build a single-page web application just showing *Hello, World*. This is the top page of `index.html`:

```
<html>
<head>
  <title>HelloWorld App</title>
</head>
<body>
```

```
    <div id='message'></div>
    <script src="./index.ts"></script>
  </body>
</html>
```

Since web browsers aren't capable of recognizing TypeScript source code, `<script src="./index.ts"></script>` is an invalid expression. However, Parcel discovers which files need to be compiled by traversing *language-specific anchors*. In the case of the TypeScript module system, `import`/`export` are also properly recognized by Parcel:

`index.ts`:

```
import {Message} from './message';

const message = new Message();
const p = document.getElementById("message");
p.innerText = message.say();
```

`message.ts`:

```
class Message {
  private message: string = "Hello, World";

  public say() {
    return this.message;
  }
}

export { Message };
```

The structure of the project is as follows. All of the source files are contained under the `root` directory:

```
$ tree ch10/
ch10/parcel-demo
├── index.html
├── index.ts
└── message.ts
```

The following command builds the project and launches a server that hosts the resources in your local machine. As expected, `http://localhost:1234` will show you a simple web page:

```
$ npx parcel ch10/parcel-demo/index.html --open
```

To help us develop the project faster, we can use hot module replacement and live reloading. It is unnecessary to restart the server whenever the code is changed. But for the purpose of fast development, the compiled code is not fully optimized for production usage. To enable full minification and optimized assets, we can use `build`:

```
$ npx parcel build ch10/parcel-demo/index.html
```

Since it can take a long time to complete compilation with the optimization process, run it at the end of development. It shouldn't be used in the middle of the development process. Putting all the resources that are accessible from the root of the server will productionize the application:

```
$ cd dist
$ python -m http.server

# http://localhost:8000 will show the application
```

Webpack

Webpack has a longer history than Parcel and is the most widely used module bundler. Webpack is more customizable and flexible than Parcel, which means we can do anything to build the project if we can write the proper build configuration. While Parcel is easy to start, Webpack is suitable for projects that are complicated.

We need to have a dedicated configuration file named `webpack.config.js`. By writing the configuration file, we can perform asset management, code splitting, and code generation. The huge amount of plugins Webpack provides also gives it substantial flexibility.

Unlike Parcel, Webpack generates one large file that combines all the necessary resources. The entry point of the application needs to load only one file—main.js. Thanks to the ease in moving files, Webpack generates a more portable format than Parcel does:

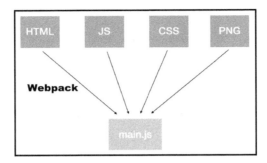

We need to write a little more before we're done building the TypeScript project using Webpack. Ensure that you include ts-loader in addition to the TypeScript compiler:

```
{
  "name": "webpack-demo",
  "version": "1.0.0",
  "description": "",
  "private": true,
  "scripts": {
    "build": "webpack",
    "watch": "webpack -w"
  },
  "devDependencies": {
    "ts-loader": "^6.1.1",
    "typescript": "^3.6.3",
    "webpack": "^4.40.2",
    "webpack-cli": "^3.3.9"
  }
}
```

The structure of the Webpack project should look as follows:

```
$ tree ch10/webpack-demo
├── dist
│   └── index.html
├── package.json
├── src
│   ├── index.ts
│   └── message.ts
├── tsconfig.json
└── webpack.config.js
```

To distinguish between the source code under `src` and the built artifact under `dist`, it is necessary to create these directories by hand.

`dist/index.html`:

```
<!doctype html>
<html>
 <head>
 <title>HelloWorld App</title>
 </head>
 <body>
 <p id='message'></p>
 <script src="./main.js"></script>
 </body>
</html>
```

Unlike Parcel, Webpack doesn't recognize the original source code that's included on the page. Add the link to the compiled file in `main.js`. The file is expected to be put in the `dist` directory.

The original source code is written in TypeScript. These files are similar to the files that are used by Parcel.

The following is the `src/index.ts` file:

```
import {Message} from './message';

const message = new Message();
const p = document.getElementById("message");
p.innerText = message.say();
```

The following is the `src/message.ts` file:

```
class Message {
  private message: string = "Hello, World";

  public say() {
    return this.message;
  }
}

export { Message };
```

Giving Webpack `tsconfig.json` explicitly is required. This is a minimal file that specifies ECMAScript 2015 as a target version and module system:

```
{
  "compilerOptions": {
    "target": "es6",
    "module": "commonjs"
  }
}
```

The last thing we need to do is write the `webpack.config.js` file. This is just a JavaScript file containing an object that has configuration properties inside it. The root of the file is `module.exports` so that we can expose the object externally:

```
module.exports = {
  // Adjust the built-in optimization process
  mode: "development",

  // Entry point of the program
  entry: "./src/index.ts",

  // Specification of how to load and compile source codes
  module: {
    rules: [
      {
        test: /\.ts$/,
        use: "ts-loader"
      }
    ]
  },
  resolve: {
    extensions: [".ts"]
  }
};
```

`yarn build` or `npx webpack` generates the `main.js` file, which contains the build artifacts. An HTTP server embedded in Python will show this page:

```
$ cd dist
$ python -m http.server
# See http://localhost:8000
```

While we need to write more configuration and code to build the Webpack project, a well-written `webpack.config.js` file brings us more fine-grained control over the project's settings.

Deploying modules with GitHub Pages

Running an application in the local machine only exposes it to yourself. The benefit of using web platforms to run the application is the easiness of publishing it to the world. Typically, we buy the web server ourselves and maintain it so that it can host the web page by running an HTTP server. However, this takes a long time and we have to do an array of things to complete the setup.

There is a better way to publish a website quickly. **GitHub Pages** is a service that hosts static pages stored in the GitHub repository. This service is used for publishing the websites, portfolios, blogs, and so on. The simplicity and capability of this service is attracting many developers. Just editing and pushing the code will make these changes public.

In this section, we will publish the machine learning application we have created so far.

GitHub Pages use a specially named repository to host the site. Create a repository named (username).github.io in your account. The service automatically maps the content in the repository to http://(username).github.io. The username is the name of your GitHub account:

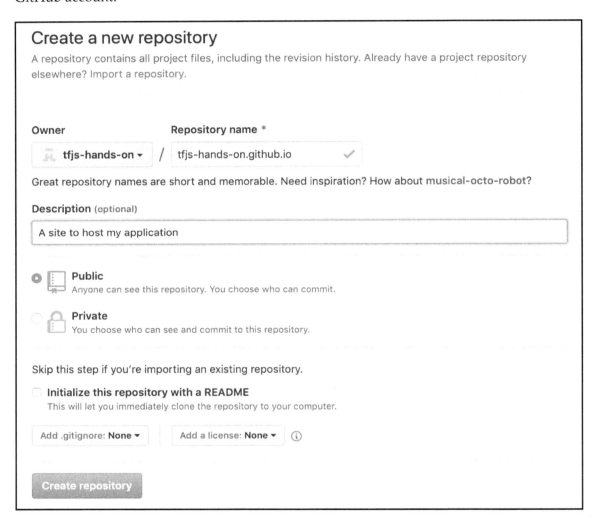

Ensure that you make the repository public so that you can publish the site with a free account. Move the generated content to the cloned repository. The root of the repository is directed to the root path of the page. This means that the `index.html` file in the root can be accessed via `http://tfjs-hands-on.github.io/index.html`:

```
$ git clone git@github.com:tfjs-hands-on/tfjs-hands-on.github.io.git
```

Build the project in optimization mode with Parcel. The site's contents are generated in the `dist` directory:

```
$ npx parcel build src/ch10/parcel-demo/index.html

$ cp dist/* /path/to/tfjs-hands-on.github.io

$ ls /path/to/tfjs-hands-on.github.io
index.html parcel-demo.088532f7.js parcel-demo.088532f7.js.map
```

This contains the top page file and the JavaScript file that was compiled from the original TypeScript code. Create the initial commit:

```
$ git add -A
$ git commit -m 'Initial commit'

# The site is rendered from the contents in the master branch
$ git push origin master
```

Once the build action has been completed, the application can be accessed from the internet:

After a while (it takes some time to discard the cache), the site will be available at `https://tfjs-hands-on.github.io`:

What we've created so far is too simple to attract users. However, what we've learned here is that GitHub Pages has the ability to publish any type of static resource to the web because it just works as a file hosting server. Machine learning applications with TensorFlow.js can also be published. However, you may feel that writing HTML files every time is cumbersome. **Jekyll** is a tool that transforms plain text written in markdown or any other language into HTML files. Jekyll supports template engine and variables so that it can achieve consistent design. It is flexible and powerful so that you can create websites as you see fit. The great thing about Jekyll is that GitHub Pages supports it by default. Once you've written your documentation in plain text with the Jekyll system, GitHub Pages is able to render the HTML pages on our behalf. If you want to create a more complicated site, Jekyll is the best tool for that.

Summary

In this chapter, we covered the basic tools and software that support web platforms. Web platforms are supported by numerous kinds of ecosystems, including programming languages that alternate between the *de facto* standard and package managers. While JavaScript is the primary language that's used in web applications, TypeScript is gaining popularity rapidly because of its safety and scalability.

Due to the way web platforms work, bundling all the resources into a portable format is required if we wish to publish the application. For machine learning applications in particular, it is common to have multiple types of resources in an application, such as images, audio, and movies, that can be used for training and prediction. Module bundlers can help us build the final artifacts. We looked at Parcel and Webpack so that we can use them to build a publishable format for machine learning applications on the web.

To make these applications public to the internet, we can use GitHub Pages. GitHub Pages is a simple static page hosting service that pushes HTML files and stylesheets. We need to be familiar with `git` and GitHub if we want to publish our applications using `git push`.

The web is a great platform that you can use to attract people to your applications. Try to distribute a machine learning application through the internet so that people around the world can look at what you've created. In the next chapter, we will look at how we can tune our TensorFlow.js applications to achieve the best performance possible.

Questions

1. Which TensorFlow.js backend is faster?
    - tfjs-node
    - tfjs-node-gpu
2. Which GPU environment is supported by tfjs-node-gpu?
    - CUDA
    - OpenCL
3. Which is the most widely used programming language on the web?
    - JavaScript
    - TypeScript
    - CoffeeScript
4. Does JavaScript have a static type system?
5. What is the name of the file that provides build configuration for Webpack?
6. Create your own site with GitHub Pages under your GitHub account.

Further reading

For more information on the topics that were covered in this chapter, please take a look at the following links:

- ECMAScript 2015 (ES6) and beyond: https://nodejs.org/en/docs/es6/
- npm: https://www.npmjs.com/
- TypeScript: https://www.typescriptlang.org
- tsconfig.json—TypeScript: https://www.typescriptlang.org/docs/handbook/tsconfig-json.html
- Parcel: https://parceljs.org
- WebPack: https://webpack.js.org
- GitHub Pages: https://pages.github.com
- Jekyll: https://jekyllrb.com

Tuning Applications to Achieve High Performance

11

TensorFlow.js was originally designed to achieve the high performance that's required for us to run machine learning applications while using hardware acceleration mechanisms such as WebGL. Having said that, there are several points to take note of so that we can make the most of these mechanisms and gain higher efficiency. One of the biggest advantages of TensorFlow.js over other frontend machine learning frameworks is the performance acceleration that's leveraged by several of its backend implementations. Thanks to these accelerators, applying TensorFlow.js can help us achieve competitive performance. We will learn how we can make use of these backend implementations to pursue high performance, as well as some useful tips we can use to tune the application we've written in TensorFlow.js.

In this chapter, we'll cover the following topics:

- The backend API of TensorFlow.js
- Tensor management
- Asynchronous data access
- Profiling
- Model visualization

Technical requirements

In this chapter, you will need the following technical requirements:

- TypeScript
- A web browser (Chrome is recommended)

Check out the following video to see the Code in Action: http://bit.ly/2KEedAL

The backend API of TensorFlow.js

There are multiple backends in TensorFlow.js. The **backend** is an underlying platform where we can execute operations in the graph. Every backend has the same interface so that the application running on top of it doesn't need to take care of the backend in most cases. TensorFlow.js operations are designed to be sufficiently abstract to hide the low-level implementation in the background.

But if our primary interest is performance, then things are different. Each backend implementation has different performance characteristics. Some make use of the available hardware acceleration properties as much as possible, but others don't. To maximize the performance of our application, we need to be familiar with the details of the backend implementation.

TensorFlow.js supports the following backend implementations:

- CPU (pure JavaScript)
- WebGL
- WebGPU
- WebAssembly
- Node.js
- Node.js with a GPU

It is possible to change the backend implementation explicitly. We can check the current default backend by using the `getBackend` method:

```
import * as tf from '@tensorflow/tfjs';

window.onload = async (e) => {
  const element = document.getElementById('backend_name');
  // Ensure to complete the initialization of the backend.
  await tf.ready();

  // Return the name of backend like 'cpu', 'webgl'.
  const backendName = tf.getBackend();

  // You will see 'webgl' if the browser supports WebGL API.
  console.log(backendName);
  element.innerText = backendName;
}
```

If you prefer the other backend, the `tf.setBackend` API changes the backend manually. Since this method initializes the backend in the background, there is no need to call `tf.ready` explicitly:

```
import * as tf from '@tensorflow/tfjs';

window.onload = async (e) => {
  const element = document.getElementById('backend_name');
  tf.setBackend('cpu');
  // Return the name of backend like 'cpu', 'webgl'.
  const backendName = tf.getBackend();

  // This case 'cpu' should be returned.
 console.log(backendName);
  element.innerText = backendName;
}
```

TensorFlow.js automatically chooses the best backend if applicable. For example, TensorFlow.js checks the availability of WebGL in the browser platform and uses the WebGL backend when possible, without a specific configuration. Some backends, such as the Node.js backend, still require us to take special care when making use of it.

In this section, we are going to discuss how each backend implements an operation and how much performance is improved.

Operations that use the CPU backend

The CPU backend is the most basic backend because of its colossal availability and universality. Kernel operations are implemented in the JavaScript program so that it can be executed wherever TensorFlow.js can be run. It is simple and easy to create a new kernel operation in this backend. However, as a tradeoff, the performance of this implementation cannot be said to be competitive by any standard. The whole execution runs on a single thread. There is no benefit of hardware acceleration. The available resource is limited by the runtime of JavaScript. In general, the CPU backend should not be used in a production-level application.

Before we talk about CPU backend implementation, let's take a look at the interface of the backend. The backend is applied to implement the same interface so that it can hide the details of the backend from the application on top of it:

```
export class KernelBackend implements TensorStorage, Backend, BackendTimer
{
  time(f: () => void): Promise<BackendTimingInfo> {
    throw new Error('Not yet implemented.');
```

```
  }
  // ...

  add(a: Tensor, b: Tensor): Tensor {
    throw new Error('Not yet implemented');
  }
}
```

`KernelBackend` is the superclass that all the backend implementations should inherit. Moreover, three interfaces need to be implemented in the backend:

- `TensorStorage`: Used for managing the mapping of tensor metadata and actual data
- `Backend`: Used to mimic classes to avoid circular dependencies
- `BackendTimer`: A timer class that uses a backend-specific measurement

Each kernel operation is added as a method of the `KernelBackend` class. In the preceding case, the `add` operation is shown but not implemented. The subclasses need to have the actual implementation.

The backend for the pure JavaScript kernels is called `MathBackendCPU`. For example, the add operation is written as follows. Since it supports the complex type, there are two implementations we can use to achieve the addition operation:

- `broadcastedBinaryComplexOp`
- `broadcastedBinaryOp`

In this method, an abstract implementation that supports broadcast semantics is built. Any binary operation can make use of it.

Broadcast is a common notion when it comes to tensor calculations. It is an operation that makes the inputs of different shapes compatible with each other for a specific arithmetic operation. Let's think about a situation where we want to add a tensor with the shape of (2,2) and a scalar value. Here, we assume that the second argument is added to the first one elementwise. In this case, the second argument is broadcasted to make its shape compatible:

$$10 \begin{pmatrix} 1 & 2 \\ 3 & 4 \end{pmatrix} = \begin{pmatrix} 10 & 10 \\ 10 & 10 \end{pmatrix} \odot \begin{pmatrix} 1 & 2 \\ 3 & 4 \end{pmatrix}$$
$$= \begin{pmatrix} 10 & 20 \\ 30 & 40 \end{pmatrix}$$

As we can see, element-wise multiplication is executed after we broadcast the given value. Basically, the tensor with a small shape is replicated to fit the larger tensor. We can use the following code to do the same thing with TensorFlow.js:

```
const a = tf.tensor2d([1, 2, 3, 4], [2, 2]);
const b = tf.scalar(10);

a.add(b).print();

// The result has a shape (2, 2).
//
// Tensor
//     [[11, 12],
//      [13, 14]]
```

Not every operation supports broadcasting due to its nature. It can also have a significant impact on performance because it may require the original data in the memory to be replicated. But for the vanilla CPU backend, the broadcast operation is implemented by us reusing the same reference for the values. This happens because they are always available in the runtime memory.

As we can see, the vanilla CPU backend doesn't introduce any additional complexity to the runtime environment. We can run it as a simple JavaScript application, just like we run web applications in modern browsers. This fact leads us to two significant benefits of using the CPU backend: low overhead and memory management.

Low overhead

Due to the nature of the CPU backend, there is no additional overhead to save and load the tensor data. All the data in the tensors exist in the memory of the JavaScript runtime. The underlying data can be quickly accessed with a few CPU cycles. The main memory that's connected to the CPU is the fastest resource that's universally available.

The benefit of the low overhead of using a CPU backend emerges when the size of the tensor is relatively small. For extensive data, the impact of the overhead of copying and loading the data between specific hardware or remote resources can be ignored compared to the performance gain of acceleration. But for smaller data, the overhead is a dominant factor of the whole performance measurement. The time that's taken to process the operation on the small data is relatively short. Therefore, copying and loading the data takes up a large percentage of the execution time.

There are no clear criteria regarding when to choose the CPU backend. It highly depends on your use case and the size of the data at hand. But if your data is only a few KB in size, it is worth considering using a CPU backend by specifying it explicitly with the `setBackend` method.

Memory management

Another benefit of the CPU backend is its lack of manual memory management. The JavaScript runtime has a garbage collection mechanism that frees us from managing troublesome memory management. All of the objects that are created in JavaScript are tracked by the garbage collector. They are safely released once they're no longer used. Low-level programming languages such as C require us to allocate and free the memory carefully and not cause any leaks.

The CPU backend can benefit from the garbage collection of the JavaScript runtime because the data of tensors simply exists as an array of the `TypedArray` object of JavaScript. `TypedArray` is a binary buffer object in the JavaScript world. It gives us a way to access the underlying sequence of values efficiently. The CPU backend is well balanced in terms of the efficiency and the safety that's offered by the garbage collection mechanism. As we will see later in this chapter, other backends often ask us to control our memory by hand. This can be considered a trade-off problem between efficiency and safety.

There are some reasons to use the CPU backend, but for production use and higher scalability, using another backend is generally recommended due to performance efficiency. Next, we are going to discuss the WebGL backend, which is actively developed by the community.

Implementing higher parallelism using the WebGL backend

WebGL is a backend implementation that uses the WebGL API. WebGL is a standard API that's used for graphical processing on the web. Most web browser vendors implement this API in their web browsers. The WebGL backend implements kernel operations by using shader programs so that we can make use of the capabilities of higher parallelism. The WebGL backend stores tensors as textures that can be uploaded to GPU memory. Each element in the tensor is treated as a point of the texture. Shader programs execute these operations by the point in the texture in parallel. In general, we can get up to 100 x faster performance than a CPU backend.

The kernel operation in the WebGL backend is written as a plain string in TensorFlow.js. For example, an add operation, which is a binary operation, is written as follows:

```
// Code snippet for add operation
export const ADD = 'return a + b;';

// The snippet is given as a op string.
// It is embedded in the userCode string by interpolation.
constructor(op: string, aShape: number[], bShape: number[]) {
    this.outputShape =
        broadcast_util.assertAndGetBroadcastShape(aShape, bShape);
    this.userCode = `
      float binaryOperation(float a, float b) {
        ${op}
      }

      void main() {
        float a = getAAtOutCoords();
        float b = getBAtOutCoords();
        setOutput(binaryOperation(a, b));
      }
    `;
}
```

The WebGL shader program is a string that's compiled by the WebGL compiler before its execution. Since this compilation can have a significant overhead against the whole execution process, the WebGL backend caches the precompiled shader code so that we can reuse it in the application.

The classes of the WebGL backend have utilities in the shader program. The accessor functions for the input and output data are part of them.
The getAAtOutCoords() function gets the value that exists at the position that corresponds to the output data. The add operation is an element-wise execution operation. Therefore, the output is computed by adding two elements that are in the same position as the input tensors, as shown in the following diagram:

$$\begin{pmatrix} 1 & 2 \\ 3 & 4 \end{pmatrix} + \begin{pmatrix} 1 & 2 \\ 3 & 4 \end{pmatrix} = \begin{pmatrix} 2 & 4 \\ 6 & 8 \end{pmatrix}$$

The high performance of the WebGL backend is achieved by its high parallelism. The main method of the shader program is executed in the thread system of the GPU so that the computation on the huge tensor can be completed in a shorter time than the sequential execution that's completed by the CPU backend.

Here is a simple benchmark that measures how fast the WebGL backend is:

```
import * as tf from '@tensorflow/tfjs';

function benchmark(size: number) {
    for (let i = 0; i < 10; i++) {
        const t1 = tf.randomNormal([size, size]);
        const t2 = tf.randomNormal([size, size]);
        t1.matMul(t2).dataSync();
    }
}

async function runBenchmark() {
    const backend = 'cpu';
    // Or const backend = 'webgl';
    tf.setBackend(backend);
    let resultStr = "";
    resultStr += `size,kernelMs(${backend}),wallMs(${backend})\n`;
    for (let s = 10; s < 600; s += 10) {
        const time = await tf.time(() => benchmark(s));
        resultStr += `${s},${time.kernelMs},${time.wallMs}\n`;
    }
    console.log(resultStr);
}

runBenchmark();
```

It multiplies two matrices of a given size and measures the time the computation took. The following chart shows the result of this benchmark on the CPU backend and the WebGL backend:

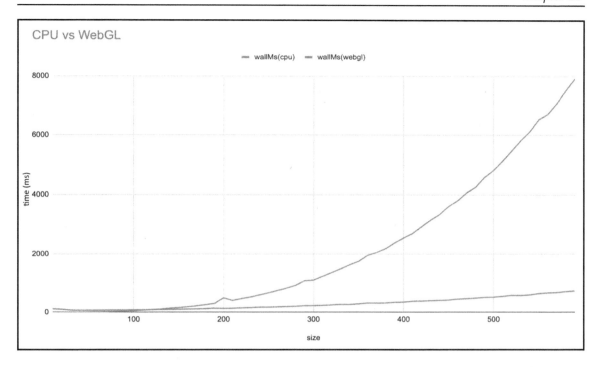

As we suggested in the previous section, the CPU backend beats the WebGL backend in terms of smaller input due to its lighter overhead. But when it comes to bigger tensors, the performance of the WebGL backend is significantly better. While the time the computation took on the CPU backend increases exponentially, the WebGL backend keeps it relatively linear.

Each thread on the GPU is executed independently. As you may have noticed, it is a little challenging to implement an operation whose output is dependent on another operation. No thread has information about what is done in the other threads. It is difficult to implement an operation that generates a tensor whose elements are random values that have been conditioned by the previous value. Therefore, implementing a kernel operation in the WebGL backend correctly requires a little bit of care.

There are a few tips we need to take into account so that we can maximize the benefits of using the WebGL backend. Otherwise, using the WebGL backend can make the performance and usability of our application worse.

Avoid blocking the main thread

The operation of calling TensorFlow.js is performed synchronously. This means that none of the operations can block the main thread of the application. This ensures that the interactive interface of the application can work smoothly. However, this does not indicate that the result is immediately ready because the actual computation is deferred by the backend of TensorFlow.js. The returned tensor is just a pointer to the tensor. The underlying data is prepared by the backend asynchronously.

Thanks to the asynchronous design of TensorFlow.js, programmers don't need to care about the asynchronous side of things as much. But to ensure that you don't block the main application thread and user interface interaction, avoid using synchronous APIs such as dataSync and araySync, which force the thread to wait for the computation of the result. The user experience will deteriorate, especially if the operation is computationally heavy and slow to complete.

The synchronous method is primarily used for testing code or debugging because it gets values quickly. Make sure that you don't infuse the code with the production code accidentally as this would contribute to making the code performant.

Prefer tf.tidy to be free from memory management

Memory management is another pitfall when we use the WebGL backend. The data that's allocated in the GPU memory buffer is outside of the memory management capabilities of the JavaScript runtime. Garbage collection does not free the memory that exists in the GPU buffer automatically, even if there is no reference to the data. The textures that are stored in the GPU buffer are managed by WebGLTexture, which is the final store of the tensor data. This class is not deallocated by the browser automatically. This means that we need to manage the memory of each tensor manually and explicitly.

To explicitly free the memory that's been allocated by the tensor, we can use the dispose method. tf.memory provides information about how much memory is used by tensors. In the latest version of TensorFlow.js, although the information does not contain numBytesInGPU, it gives us general information about the memory's arrangement:

```
import * as tf from '@tensorflow/tfjs';

const t1 = tf.tensor1d([1, 2, 3, 4]);

console.log("Before Dispose");
console.log(tf.memory());
// {unreliable: false, numBytesInGPU: 0, numTensors: 1, numDataBuffers: 1,
numBytes: 16}
```

```
t1.dispose();

console.log("After Dispose");
console.log(tf.memory());
// {unreliable: false, numBytesInGPU: 0, numTensors: 0, numDataBuffers: 0,
numBytes: 0}
```

While `numTensors` is the number of tensors managed by TensorFlow.js, `numDataBuffers` is the real data that's allocated in the buffer memory. It can be less than `numTensors` if an operation creates a new tensor without copying the data. For example, `t1.reshape([1, 4])` will create a new tensor but shares the original data in memory.

The `dispose` method deallocates the unnecessary memory buffer. However, it is still messy to manually write the code to dispose of all the unnecessary memory buffers and is also prone to memory leaks if it forgets to call the dispose method. Manual memory management still leads to problems in terms of the debugging process, as well as the readability of code. TensorFlow.js allows us to chain multiple operations together, but it is impossible to destroy all of the tensors that are created in the chain of operations since we'd need to hold every reference to every tensor:

```
import * as tf from '@tensorflow/tfjs';

const t1 = tf.tensor1d([1, 2, 3, 4]);
const t2 = tf.tensor1d([1, 2, 3, 4]);

console.log("Before Dispose");
console.log(tf.memory());
// {unreliable: false, numBytesInGPU: 0, numTensors: 2, numDataBuffers: 2,
numBytes: 32}

const t3 = t1.add(t2).square().log().neg();

// Ensure to run the computation synchronously.
t3.dataSync();
t3.dispose();

console.log("After Executed");
console.log(tf.memory());
// {unreliable: false, numBytesInGPU: 48, numTensors: 5, numDataBuffers: 5,
numBytes: 80}
```

The preceding code shows that four additional tensors are created by chaining the operations. Even after the last one is disposed of, the others remain in the buffer. Since the tensors that are created in the chain of the methods aren't referenced, it is impossible to destroy them afterward. However, TensorFlow.js has an API that we can use to manage memory more simply. tf.tidy tracks the intermediate tensors that are created in the given function. The add, square, and log tensors are the intermediate tensors and are destroyed after the computation is completed. Thus, the only returned tensor (t3, in this case) needs to be disposed of explicitly. Tensors that are created before the tidy execution are still there after the computation:

```
import * as tf from '@tensorflow/tfjs';

const t1 = tf.tensor1d([1, 2, 3, 4]);
const t2 = tf.tensor1d([1, 2, 3, 4]);

console.log("Before Dispose");
console.log(tf.memory());
// {unreliable: false, numBytesInGPU: 0, numTensors: 2, numDataBuffers: 2,
numBytes: 32}

const t3 = tf.tidy(() => {
  const result = t1.add(t2).square().log().neg();
  return result;
});

// Ensure to run the computation synchronously.
t3.dataSync();
t3.dispose();

console.log("After Dispose");
console.log(tf.memory());
// {unreliable: false, numBytesInGPU: 0, numTensors: 2, numDataBuffers: 2,
numBytes: 32}
```

Overall, using tf.tidy is highly recommended in terms of the WebGL backend as it makes memory management neat and free from memory leak problems. Note that even if we use tf.tidy, it is still necessary to dispose of the last result of the chain explicitly. There is no downside to using tf.tidy, even in the CPU backend, which has a garbage collection algorithm in the runtime. We can reuse the same code for the WebGL and CPU backends.

Floating number precision

Machine learning models generally need 32-bit floating point precision for the training phase. However, some WebGL implementations, such as mobile devices, only support 16-bit precision. This can cause precision problems when we port the model that we've trained on a higher precision machine to a lower precision machine. Considering the popularity of the quantization of machine learning models, this downgrade is not a major problem if the model is only used for inference. However, it is still necessary that we keep the range in-between [0.000000059605, 65504] to achieve full compatibility in terms of accuracy and performance.

Save the overhead of shader compilation

As we mentioned previously, the WebGL backend compiles the shader program to execute it. The compilation process runs in a lazy manner. It doesn't run at the time when the operation graph is defined; instead, it runs when the computation is requested (for example, with `data` or `dataSync`) because compiling the shader program is not a lightweight operation. To make full use of the shader resource, TensorFlow.js has a cache for the precompiled shader program. This is shown in the following diagram:

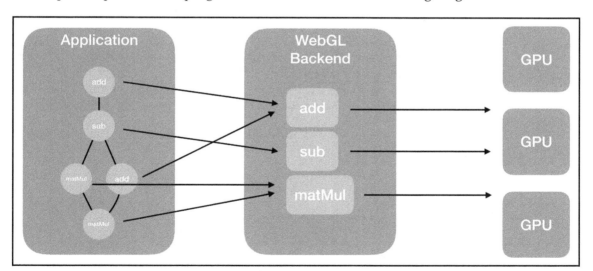

This technique can contribute to improving the performance of the application. Before running training or inference, the warming up process puts the compiled code into the cache. The code in the cache is reused in the execution that follows. Then, the hyperparameters of the operation are given to the shader program as uniform variables so that it doesn't trigger the recompilation process, even if one of the parameters changes. Typically, the machine learning application that's provided by TensorFlow.js runs the same operation again and again. Constructing the precompiled cache in advance is helpful in reducing the overhead of shader compilation.

Using TensorFlow with the Node.js backend

Node.js is the most popular server-side JavaScript platform and is widely used for creating web applications. Node.js uses V8 as a JavaScript runtime. It is also used by Chrome so that we can quickly run the existing code that's been written for web browsers. This indicates that once our application is written with TensorFlow.js, it can be run on the client side and the server side.

Node.js was initially designed to handle many network connections in a scalable manner by using event-driven I/O. Due to this concurrency model, Node.js is not the optimal choice when we're dealing with CPU-intensive workloads, such as machine learning. *So why do we use Node.js as a backend for TensorFlow.js?*

The Node.js backend is a C extension of Node.js. It allows us to use the C API of TensorFlow, which leads to more potential in terms of GPU and TPU. TensorFlow's C implementation is well optimized for hardware acceleration. This means we can achieve competitive performance with TensorFlow's core implementation by using the C API.

To use the Node.js backend, we need to load a special package, as shown in the following code:

```
// Load the binding for Node.js
import * as tf from '@tensorflow/tfjs-node';

// Running with GPU through Node.js C extension
import * as tf from '@tensorflow/tfjs-node-gpu';
```

We can use the Node.js backend transparently, just like the WebGL backend. Let's see how fast it is compared to other backends:

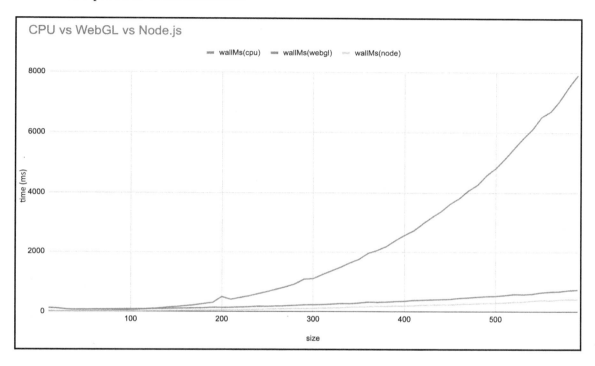

This is the result of running the same benchmark program that we ran previously. As we can see, the Node.js backend without GPU acceleration achieves slightly better performance than the WebGL backend. It indicates that the hardware acceleration via a web browser is competitive in terms of its low overhead since it directly uses CPU resources. If we want to pursue performance, using the Node.js backend for the training process is a pretty reasonable choice.

In this section, we have discussed the various kinds of backend implementations. The backend we choose mainly controls how our computation is executed. CPU-intensive workloads are affected by which backend is used. Typically, we should use a backend that supports lower overhead hardware acceleration if it is available. If we don't have such a backend available, then leaving the option as it is without specifying any backend is recommended because TensorFlow.js automatically chooses the best backend from the ones that are available.

Tensor management

When we talk about backend implementation, we mainly talk about the topic of computation. But there is another interesting topic the surrounds data transfer and buffer management. Data transfer provides a form of input and fetches the result from computational units such as GPUs. How can we access the underlying buffer of the tensor? When can we get the result? Tensor management answers these questions. By definition, tensors are the fundamental building blocks of TensorFlow.js. Mastering how to use tensors efficiently allows us to write performant machine learning applications with the platform.

Tensor construction

A **tensor** is a data structure that holds metadata such as shapes, data types, and pointers for the underlying buffer. To construct a tensor, we need to provide some data as parameters. `tf.tensor` allows us to create the arbitrary shape of the tensor:

```
tf.tensor([1, 2, 3, 4], [2, 2]).print();
    Tensor
    [[1, 2],
     [3, 4]]
```

The API recognizes the dimensions of the given JavaScript array, which allows us to specify the shape explicitly:

```
tf.tensor([[1, 2], [3, 4]]).print();
    Tensor
    [[1, 2],
     [3, 4]]
```

There are also several rank-specific APIs that we can use to create tensors:

- `tf.tensor1d`: Tensor1D
- `tf.tensor2d`: Tensor2D
- `tf.tensor3d`: Tensor3D
- `tf.tensor4d`: Tensor4D
- `tf.tensor5d`: Tensor5D
- `tf.tensor6d`: Tensor6D
- `tf.scalar`: Scalar

These APIs return the corresponding tensor data type that contains the rank information. For example, `tf.tensor4d` returns an object of the Tensor4D type. The benefit of using these special classes is that it makes it easy to find problems at compile time. Let's say we are writing a function that returns a tensor that's rank 4 and the tensor is passed to another function that expects the given tensor to be rank 4. We want to make sure that our function always returns the rank-4 tensor. If it creates a tensor that's rank 3 or rank 5, it causes problems since this creates a shape that's incompatible between two functions. Like functional programming languages, combining the rank-specific tensor type and the TypeScript compiler allows us to check the shape's compatibility at compile time, not runtime. If the rank that's being used for the tensor is clear, it is recommended that we use a specific data type.

The data of a tensor is fundamentally immutable. Operations in TensorFlow.js create new tensors to generate results. Immutable data structures have many advantages because they make it easy for us to optimize the execution graph and avoid any unexpected behavior that's caused by changes that have occurred in the underlying data. But what if we want to construct a tensor one element at a time? What if we only want to update one element of the tensor?

`TensorBuffer` is a class that updates the underlying data flexibly. Unlike tensors, `TensorBuffer` is a mutable data structure that we can convert into a tensor of a specific shape. To construct an empty `TensorBuffer`, we can use the `tf.buffer` API:

```
// Create a TensorBuffer with shape [2, 2]
const buffer = tf.buffer([2, 2]);
buffer.set(1, 0, 0);
buffer.set(2, 1, 0);

// Make a tensor from the TensorBuffer.
buffer.toTensor().print();

// Tensor
//    [[1, 0],
//     [2, 0]]
```

It is also possible to move back to `TensorBuffer` from the tensor. The `bufferSync` or `buffer` method of a tensor object returns a `TensorBuffer`, which has the same data as the original tensor:

```
const a = tf.tensor([[1, 2], [3, 4]]);

// buffetSync returns a TensorBuffer with the underlying data
const buf = a.bufferSync();

buf.set(0, 0, 1);
```

```
buf.set(0, 1, 1);

buf.toTensor().print();
// Tensor
//    [[1, 0],
//     [3, 0]]
```

Of course, there is some overhead to making a `TensorBuffer` from a tensor as it needs to get the underlying data and push it to the new `TensorBuffer`. It can block the thread with both `buffer` and `bufferSync`.

As we mentioned previously, a tensor is just a container for metadata. This makes it easy and efficient for us to change the shape of tensors without touching the underlying data. The shape is just a declaration of how we should treat the tensor in terms of its structure. While we can redefine the shape of a tensor by using the `reshape` method, there are other, more straightforward, methods that we can use to change the shape of tensors:

- `asScalar`
- `as1D`
- `as2D`
- `as3D`
- `as4D`
- `as5D`
- `as6D`

These are just wrappers of the `reshape` method, but the rank of the converted tensor is clear. We can change the data type of a tensor since the data type is also managed separately from the underlying data:

```
const a = tf.tensor([[1, 2], [3, 4]]);
a.print(true);

// Print with verbose option shows more detailed information
Tensor
  dtype: float32
  rank: 2
  shape: [2,2]
  values:
    [[1, 2],
     [3, 4]]
```

`asType` provides us with a cast operation in TensorFlow.js. As long as the new data type is compatible with the original data type, the cast succeeds:

```
const a = tf.tensor([[1, 2], [3, 4]]);
const b = a.asType('bool');
b.print(true);

Tensor
  dtype: bool
  rank: 2
  shape: [2,2]
  values:
    [[true, true],
     [true, true]]
```

Tensors as variables

Fundamentally, a tensor is an immutable data structure. Even if we use `TensorBuffer`, we just create another tensor with new data and a new shape. The design of a tensor can't help us fit the parameters of machine learning models through the training process. `tf.variable` is an API that we can use to generate a mutable container for the tensor:

```
const x = tf.variable(tf.tensor([[1, 2], [3, 4]]));

// Assign a new value to the variable
x.assign(tf.tensor([[4, 5], [6, 7]]));

x.print();

// Tensor
//    [[4, 5],
//     [6, 7]]
```

The merit of using a variable is that we can use it to validate the data type and shape of the tensor. It ensures the initial data type and shapes are correct, even after the new value has been assigned. Hence, the model can guarantee that the weight parameter has the same structure throughout the whole training process once `tf.variable` is used to keep the weight parameters in check:

```
const x = tf.variable(tf.tensor([[1, 2], [3, 4]]));
x.assign(tf.tensor([1, 2, 3]));

// An error occured on line: 2
// shape of the new value (3) and previous value (2,2) must match
```

We can also make a variable from an existing tensor by using the chainable method:

```
const a = tf.tensor([[1, 2], [3, 4]]);
const v = a.variable();
v.print();

// Tensor
//     [[1, 2],
//      [3, 4]]
```

One thing that is noteworthy is that `tf.variable` is not truly mutable because it needs to generate a new tensor every time the assignment happens. The `assign` method is given a tensor and replaces the internally managed tensor with it. This means that using variables does not release us from the overhead of creating tensors. Think about it as a way of improving the management of a mutable tensor in a solid manner, but not its performance.

Revisiting tensor destruction

Tensor destruction is important so that we can avoid resources being leaked from the tensor. As we mentioned previously, we can use the `dispose` method or `tf.tidy` to safely discard the resource that's allocated by the tensor. It is a neat way of managing memory for tensors. We should always make sure that we use them so that we can avoid any unexpected degradation that may occur in our application.

Unfortunately, variables are not deallocated by `tf.tidy`. Even if we write `tf.variable` inside the `tf.tidy` clause, the variable is not automatically cleaned up. There are two ways to dispose of variables in our application:

- Use the `dispose` method of the variable
- Use `tf.disposeVariables`

Since the variable is a subclass of the tensor, it also has a `dispose` method. This allows us to clean up the resource that's been allocated to the variable. If our application uses a lot of variables, it would be tedious to call the dispose method again and again. `tf.disposeVariables` discards all of the variables that are managed by the backend in one go. Apart from releasing the resource from the variable, it also removes the reference to it from the tensor manager.

The following diagram shows the overall structure of the variable as a wrap-up of the variable's life cycle. Tensors and variables are managed by `TensorManager`, which runs inside the backend implementation. It holds the references to the active tensors. Once a tensor is disposed of, `TensorManager` also removes the reference:

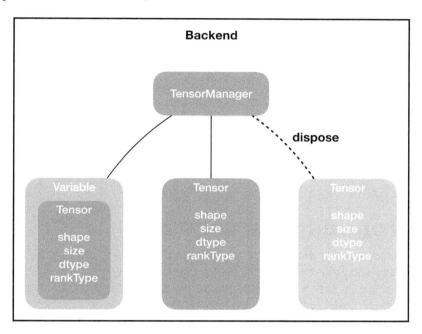

The `tf.tidy` method automatically dereferences the intermediate tensors when it goes out of the scope, and variables are kept in their default states. However, there are some situations where we may want to keep some specific tensors while using `tf.tidy`. In such cases, `tf.keep` allows us to mark certain variables so that they remain after the scope is tidied up:

```
let c;
const y = tf.tidy(() => {
    const a = tf.tensor([[1, 2], [3, 4]]);
    const b = tf.tensor([[5, 6], [7, 8]]);

    // c is not disposed automatically
    c = tf.keep(a.square());

    return c.add(b);
});

// It allows us to refer c even out of tf.tidy scope.
```

```
c.print();

// Tensor
   [[1,  4 ],
    [9, 16]]
```

Without `tf.keep` for the intermediate tensor, an error message such as the following would be thrown. Every operation checks the validity of each tensor when it is called:

```
tensor.ts:682 Uncaught (in promise) Error: Tensor is disposed.
    at t.throwIfDisposed (tensor.ts:682)
    at t.dataSync (tensor.ts:638)
    at t.toString (tensor.ts:796)
```

We often need intermediate tensors when we wish to inspect data for debug purposes or performance tuning. `tf.keep` will allow us to do so without having to rewrite the code in the application.

Asynchronous data access

As a natural consequence of the heavy computation of machine learning algorithms, asynchronous data access is inevitable if we wish to keep our application efficient and working interactively. In JavaScript, asynchronous execution is often implemented with a `Promise` object. A promise represents an asynchronous operation that ends in either success or failure. Most of the operations that download data from tensors return a `Promise` object, which ensures that the user fetches the data once it is ready.

To return a `Promise` object, we need to declare the function as an `async`. For instance, the `Tensor.data` method returns a `Promise` that computes `TypedArray`, which contains the data's results:

```
async data<D extends DataType = NumericDataType>(): Promise<DataTypeMap[D]>
{
  // Do something to return the value.
  // ...
  return data as Promise<DataTypeMap[D]>;
}
```

`DataTypeMap[D]` represents one of the expected `TypedArray` that corresponds to a given data type:

- float32: `Float32Array`
- int32: `Int32Array`

- bool: `Uint8Array`
- complex64: `Float32Array`
- string: `string[]`

There are two ways we can use the data that's stored in the `Promise`:

- Use chainable methods, such as `then` and `catch`
- Use `await`

`then` and `catch` are the chainable methods of `Promise`. They call the function once the result is ready or throw an exception if it isn't:

```
const p = new Promise(function(resolve, reject) {
  setTimeout(() => {
    // For success, resolve function is called with the result.
    resolve('It is ready');

    // For failure, error object is passed to reject function.
    // reject(new Error('An error happens'));
  }, 300);
});

p.then((value) => {
  console.log(value);
}).catch((err) => {
  console.log(err);
});
```

Although the preceding code is functional, it is still redundant and tedious to write methods such as `then` and `catch` for every `async` call – especially if we need to chain the method multiple times so that we can elaborate on the returned values.

JavaScript and TypeScript provide us with better syntax sugar that saves us from writing obvious function calls. `async` and `await` let us write code in a more synchronous style without losing the merit of asynchronous execution. The `async` keyword wraps our function and returns the `Promise` that contains the original value. The `await` keyword, on the other hand, allows us to wait for the result synchronously inside the async function. For instance, let's assume that we want to chain two `Promise` functions so that we can add the following values:

```
function add() {
    A().then(a => {
        B().then(b => {
            console.log(a + b);
        })
```

```
    })
}

function A() {
    return Promise.resolve(1)
}

function B() {
    return Promise.resolve(2)
}

add();
```

We can rewrite the preceding code in a simpler fashion using the async/await keyword:

```
async function add() {
  const a = await A();
  const b = await B();
  console.log(a + b);
}

async function A() {
    return 1;
}

async function B() {
    return 2;
}

add();
```

Assuming that we wish to manipulate multiple tensors without using operation nodes in the execution graph, the async/await keyword is the best way to do so. Let's say we want to double the element of the tensor that's been positioned by the given value of the first tensor. Since no operation has been prepared for this in TensorFlow.js, using async/await is the only way for us to manipulate the TypedArray variable that's been returned by the tensor:

```
// Index as a tensor
const index = tf.scalar(2);

const x = tf.tensor([[1, 2], [3, 4]]);

async function myDouble() {
  const xData = await x.data();
  const iData = await index.data();
  // Double the element specified by the given index
```

```
    xData[iData] = xData[iData] * 2;
    for (let i = 0; i < xData.length; i++) {
      console.log(xData[i]);
    }
  }

  myDouble();
```

Of course, the computation should be completed in the execution graph to avoid unnecessary overhead. However, bear in mind that there are some cases where it is quicker and more straightforward to manipulate the downloaded `TypedArray` variable directly due to a missing operation or a complicated execution flow. `async/await` allows us to construct a straightforward bridge between the backend environment and the JavaScript runtime.

Due to this, tensors provide wrapper methods that use the `async/await` function implicitly:

Purpose	The `async` method	The `sync` method
Gets a buffer that's been initialized the tensor	buffer	bufferSync
Gets a JavaScript array	array	arraySync
Gets a TypedArray	data	dataSync

These methods download the underlying data to the corresponding data type. Each method has a synchronous version that does the exact same thing as `await`:

```
const x = tf.tensor([[1, 2], [3, 4]]);

async function download() {
  const d1 = await x.data();
  const d2 = x.dataSync();
  console.log(d1 === d2);
}

download();
```

Using `async/await` or the data load APIs of tensors is the key to achieving a good balance between low overhead and the simplicity of code in our application. If you cannot find the proper operation in TensorFlow.js, then download the data from the backend environment and manipulate the data by sacrificing some efficiency.

Profiling

As the saying goes, *premature optimization is the root of all evil*. Without sufficient knowledge and understanding of the system, optimization is often rather harmful. It is important to get the data of the system's runtime and find out what bottlenecks need to be optimized. Profiling is a method that we can use to collect information or signals that measure how the system works. The following information is helpful if we wish to find problems that exist in our application:

- Performance bottlenecks (CPU, I/O, memory, and so on)
- Statistics regarding the code's execution
- How long the execution time took to complete

By knowing about such information, we can make our application more performant. There are several tools we can use to inspect and get insight into what happens in the TensorFlow.js runtime. In the last section of this chapter, we are going to take a look at the tools we can use to profile TensorFlow.js applications.

We have already looked at `tf.memory`, which allows us to gather information about the memory usage of the application. It returns data regarding how much memory is being used for tensor and buffers. This information is about the whole memory footprint of the backend environment. But sometimes, we want to know about the memory capacity that's being used by a specific execution graph. This kind of knowledge is especially beneficial when we are using multiple models in our application and we want to find out whether a certain model is using a lot of space in the main memory. TensorFlow.js provides `tf.profile` so that we can measure the memory that's being used by a certain execution graph:

```
async function profiling() {
  const profile = await tf.profile(() => {
    const x = tf.tensor([[1, 2], [3, 4]]);
    const a = x.neg();
    x.dispose();
    const b = a.log();
    return b;
  });

  console.log(`newBytes: ${profile.newBytes}`);
  console.log(`newTensors: ${profile.newTensors}`);
  console.log(`all kernels: ${profile.kernels.map(k =>
k.totalBytesSnapshot)}`);
}

profiling();
```

```
// newBytes: 32
// newTensors: 2
// all kernels: 32,48
```

The tf.profile function gathers closure information about the graph's construction, which we need to measure the memory footprint of the program. It tracks the tensors that have been created in the given function. We can find out how many tensors and how much memory is being used in the execution graph by using this profiling tool. We can gather the following information:

- newBytes: The bytes that have been allocated by the function
- newTensors: The number of tensors that have been created by the function
- peakBytes: The maximum number of bytes that have been allocated by the function
- kernels: Information about each kernel that's used in the function

If we want to find out the peak memory usage of the execution graph, we can use peakBytes. Kernel information is also useful if we wish to compare metrics in terms of the memory footprint of each kernel. This tells us which kernel should be optimized first. It chooses based on whether the kernel will have a significant impact on memory usage.

The semantics of tf.tidy and tf.keep are also recognized by this tool:

```
async function profiling() {
  const profile = await tf.profile(() => {
    tf.tidy(() => {
      const x = tf.tensor([[1, 2], [3, 4]]);
      const a = x.neg();
      const b = a.log();
      return b;
    });
  });

  console.log(`newBytes: ${profile.newBytes}`);
  console.log(`newTensors: ${profile.newTensors}`);
  console.log(`peakBytes: ${profile.peakBytes}`);
  console.log(`all kernels: ${profile.kernels.map(k =>
k.totalBytesSnapshot)}`);
}

profiling();

// newBytes: 16
// newTensors: 1
```

```
// peakBytes: 64
// all kernels: 32,64
```

The total number of tensors is the only piece of information that's returned by `tf.tidy`. The other intermediate tensors are properly disposed of. However, the kernel footprint is recorded by two operations: `neg` and `log`. The compiled code is kept in the backend cache so that it can be counted by the profiler.

Chrome profiler

Google Chrome also provides a powerful tool that we can use to inspect the performance of our web applications. Although it is designed for general web applications, we can use it to profile our machine learning application. After launching the window for the profiler, click on the **Performance** tab. This tool calculates the time each function call of the JavaScript runtime takes to complete. The following screenshot shows the call diagram of the benchmark we used previously:

As we can see, `tf.matMul` took 1.65 ms to complete. By zooming into the image, we can find out what `tf.matMul` does. As shown in the following screenshot, compiling the kernel code took 1.52 ms, which is 92% of the execution time of `tf.matMul`:

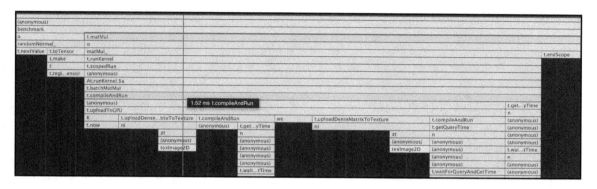

Therefore, the performance tool of the Chrome profiler lets us find out about the dominant factors of our program in terms of their execution time. If our machine learning application is slow, this tool tells us how to make it faster.

It is also possible to measure how much memory is used by the application by going to the **Memory** tab. There are three types of memory profiling available:

- Heap snapshot
- Using the allocation instrumentation on the timeline
- Allocation sampling

The heap snapshot is used to measure the static metrics of the application. It takes a snapshot of the application's state and records memory usage at a specific time. The other types of memory profiling record memory usage at a certain time. They keep track of the metrics that are concerned with the application's state and show us the number of objects that have been constructed in the JavaScript runtime and the size of the allocated memory:

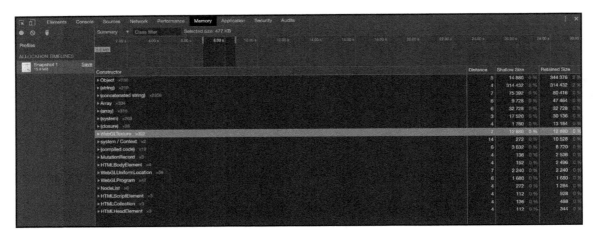

The performance profiler also tells us how we can reduce how much memory is consumed by the application.

Model visualization

Visualization is an efficient way of learning about what happens in the machine learning model. The progress of the training process can be tracked in terms of the accuracy or loss value of the target function. Seeing how the elements of a tensor are distributed can also provide us with some insight into how the machine learning algorithm runs. In this section, we are going to look at `tfjs-vis`, which is a visualization tool that's been designed especially for the TensorFlow.js framework.

As is often the case, `tfjs-vis` can be installed using `npm`. It provides UI components that can be easily and seamlessly rendered in our machine learning application. The tool has a pane on the right-hand side of the UI. Here, we can add any number of components to show the metrics of the machine learning model.

First, the layer inspection section provides information about the name and shape of a certain layer in the sequential model. The following code adds the new window, which shows the statistics of the first layer of the model.

`tfvis.show.layer` automatically creates the UI element and adds it to the current
window:

```
import * as tf from '@tensorflow/tfjs';
import * as tfvis from '@tensorflow/tfjs-vis';

const model = tf.sequential({
  layers: [
    tf.layers.dense({inputShape: [784], units: 32, activation: 'relu'}),
    tf.layers.dense({units: 10, activation: 'softmax'}),
  ]
});

tfvis.show.layer({ name: 'Layer Inspection', tab: 'Layer' },
model.getLayer('first layer', 1));
```

The following screenshot shows the results:

Here, we can see the statistics of the internal values of the tensor, such as the min, the max, the number of elements, zeros, and NaNs. If it indicates that the parameter has completely random values during the training process, then the training process may fail. It is also able to show the distribution of the layer parameter. Clicking on **Show Values Distribution for:** will display a histogram of values. If you want to see the parameter distribution of any tensor, we can use the `tfvis.show.valueDistribution` method to do so:

```
const t1 = tf.randomNormal([100, 3]);

tfvis.show.valuesDistribution({name: 'Values Distribution', tab: 'Model Inspection'}, t1);
```

This results in the following output:

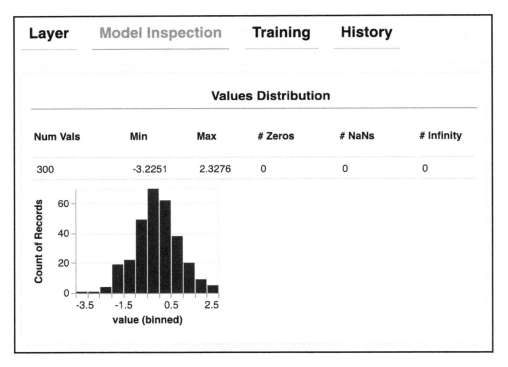

How the training makes progress is also a interesting topic. Knowing how the accuracy and loss values are changed impacts how we can validate the machine learning model. There are two ways we can look at our training progress:

- Callback style
- Static history style

When using the callback style, we pass the callback function that will be called during the training process so that we can hook any execution onto the training batch. `tfvis.show.fitCallbacks` modifies the callback functions so that they record the specified metrics:

```
const model = tf.sequential({
  layers: [
    tf.layers.dense({inputShape: [784], units: 32, activation: 'relu'}),
    tf.layers.dense({units: 10, activation: 'softmax'}),
  ]
});

model.compile({
  optimizer: 'sgd',
  loss: 'categoricalCrossentropy',
  metrics: ['accuracy']
});

const data = tf.randomNormal([100, 784]);
const labels = tf.randomUniform([100, 10]);

model.fit(data, labels, {
  epochs: 5,
  batchSize: 32,
  callbacks: tfvis.show.fitCallbacks({name: 'Training Inspection', tab:
'Training'},
    ['loss', 'acc']),
});
```

In the preceding code, we hooked the callback functions that record the loss values and the accuracy that's calculated in the training process. The events that were hooked by the callback were `onBatchEnd` and `onEpochEnd`. As their names suggest, they are called at the end of the batch and at the end of the epoch, respectively:

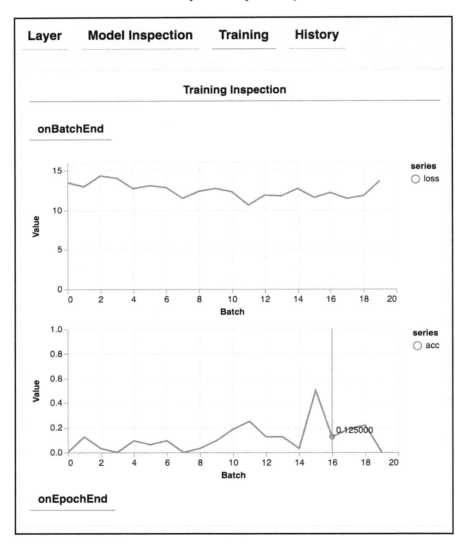

We can use the history data that's returned by the `fit` method of the model to see the effectiveness of the model. By using the `tfvis.show.history` method, we can show the same chart without hooking the callback function to the training process:

```
const history = await model.fit(data, labels, {
    epochs: 5,
    batchSize: 32,
});
tfvis.show.history({name: 'Training History', tab: 'History'}, history,
['loss', 'acc']);
```

Summary

In this chapter, we looked at several techniques we can use to improve the performance and stability of machine learning applications that are written in TensorFlow.js. Since TensorFlow.js is a framework that accelerates various kinds of runtime systems, such as WebGL, understanding its internal structure and implementation is the key to creating a performant application.

It is also important to profile our application's execution. Without complete knowledge of bottleneck and performance characteristics, we may end up with misplaced optimization. We can make use of the profiler that TensorFlow.js implements, as well as the Chrome profiler, to do this since the machine learning application in TensorFlow.js is just a web application. `tf-vis` shows us the other side of the application. The metrics that are obtained by `tf-vis` are more application-specific so that people who are familiar with machine learning can easily make use of it. In the next chapter, we will look at how Tensorflow.js can change the future of machine learning and various other applications.

Questions

1. How many backend implementations are supported by TensorFlow.js?
2. Which executes MNIST prediction the fastest: MobileNet, WebGL, or Node.js?
3. Write a benchmark that shows the poor performance of a WebGL backend compared to a vanilla CPU backend.
4. What compatibility can we use to reshape tensors? For example, we can reshape a tensor with the shape [2, 3] and make it [1, 2, 3], but we cannot make it [2, 2, 3]. Why?

5. What is the main disadvantage of using the asynchronous API to download data from a tensor?

6. How can we track training progress using `tf-vis`? What type of API can we use?

Further reading

- Node API: `https://js.tensorflow.org/api_node/1.2.7/`
- tfjs-vis: `https://js.tensorflow.org/api_vis/1.1.0/`

12
Future Work Around TensorFlow.js

Our discussion so far has been based on the functionalities and features available today. But while we were writing this book, TensorFlow 2.0 was released. Of course, many of the ideas from TensorFlow 2.0 have been implemented in TensorFlow.js too. In this last chapter of the book, we are going to introduce several on-going projects and future plans to make TensorFlow.js more accessible and useful to machine learning developers on the web platform.

The following topics will be covered in this chapter:

- Experimental backend implementations
  - WebGPU
  - WebAssembly
  - Mobile native applications with React Native
  - Native applications with Electron
- AutoML edge helper

Technical requirements

We will use the following tools in this chapter:

- TypeScript
- Parcel
- A web browser (Chrome is recommended)

Check out the following video to see the Code in Action:
http://bit.ly/331EZcL

Experimental backend implementations

We have introduced several backend implementations. They are Vanilla CPU, WebGL, and Node.js. These backends were provided from the very beginning of TensorFlow.js, but the community keeps developing new backend implementations to support many more use cases and platforms. Bear in mind that most of them are still experimental and they do not fully support all operations. Let's take a look at how and when to use these backends in our applications.

WebGPU – a new standard for accelerated graphics and computations

WebGPU is a new web standard for accelerated graphics processing and computation. It provides a brand-new JavaScript API that allows us to flexibly achieve higher-performance computing. Unlike WebGL, this does not just port across existing native APIs; instead, it is based on Vulkan, Metal, and so on. WebGPU was originally designed to replace the WebGL API but WebGL is much more popular than WebGPU nowadays; TensorFlow.js primarily supports WebGL. But considering the fact that more and more web browsers support WebGPU implementation, WebGPU is the major platform for hardware acceleration in web technologies.

The kernel function of the WebGPU backend is similar to WebGL functions. For example, the add kernel implementation is written as follows. This is the constructor of `WebGPUProgram`, which is a superclass consisting of all kernel classes:

```
constructor(op: string, aShape: number[], bShape: number[]) {
    this.outputShape = backend_util.assertAndGetBroadcastShape(aShape,
bShape);
  const size = util.sizeFromShape(this.outputShape);

    // We can configure how the data is distributed to the multiple
threads.
    this.dispatchLayout = flatDispatchLayout(this.outputShape);
    this.dispatch = computeDispatch(
        this.dispatchLayout, this.outputShape, this.workGroupSize,
        [this.workPerThread, 1, 1]);
  const type = getCoordsDataType(this.outputShape.length);

    // Shader code is much similar to WebGL one.
    this.userCode = `
      float binaryOperation(float a, float b) {
        ${op}
```

```
    }
    void main() {
      int index = int(gl_GlobalInvocationID.x);
      for(int i = 0; i < ${this.workPerThread}; i++) {
        int flatIndex = index * ${this.workPerThread} + i;
        if(flatIndex < ${size}) {
          ${type} coords = getCoordsFromFlatIndex(flatIndex);
          float a = getAAtOutCoords(coords);
          float b = getBAtOutCoords(coords);
          setOutput(flatIndex, binaryOperation(a, b));
        }
      }
    }
  `;
}
```

The following is the core of the implementation is almost the same as the WebGL kernel. In the WebGPU, we can control the size of the data passed to each thread. It is configured as `workPerThread` and embedded as a template variable. The tensor is flattened when passed to the thread. `getCoordsFromFlatIndex` is a helper method that gets the coordination of the given index in the flattened tensor. `gl_GlobalInvicationID` is an index given by the WebGPU API to identify the thread number. By using that, we can calculate the correct offset of each element as a whole.

Here is an overview of how the identifier is assigned to each GPU core. Each GPU core can execute the program in parallel and they have a multidimensional identifier like this. In that case, one specific GPU can be the identifier with an index such as (3, 3):

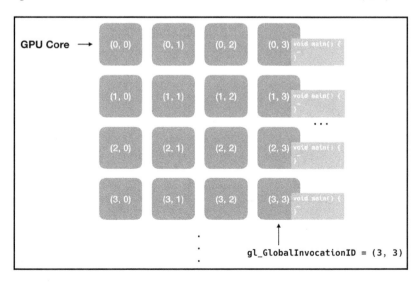

That identifier is passed to the program with the name gl_GlobalInvocationID so that the program knows which part is to be processed in the thread. workerPerThread is a parameter controlling the number of threads used by the kernel. We can control the parallelism by adjusting the parameter properly.

To test the WebGPU backend, an experimental package for the WebGPU backend is provided: @tensorflow/tfjs-backend-webgpu.

But it is not well integrated with the current TensorFlow.js APIs yet and is still unstable. Instead, the benchmark result is publicly available. We can see the result by running the benchmark application contained in the repository:

```
$ cd tfjs/tfjs-backend-webgpu
$ yarn
$ cd benchmarks

# See the benchmark application in the browser
$ open index.html
```

This results in the following output:

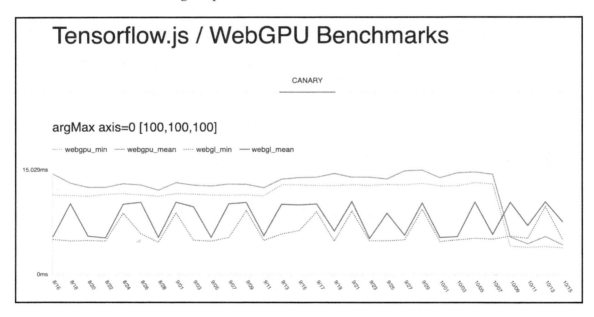

Bear in mind that the application does not run the WebGPU code on the local machine. It just downloads the benchmark result running in a specific environment day by day. That is the reason why the chart shows the past historical result of the benchmark measurement. The benchmark contains the result of several operators:

- argMax
- matMul
- add
- conv2d
- relu
- pad
- maxPool
- posenet

The result of argMax shows that it is much faster than the WebGL backend from October 9. But WebGPU does not always beat the WebGL backend. For instance, the benchmark result for the conv2d kernel shows a poor performance compared with the WebGL backend on average:

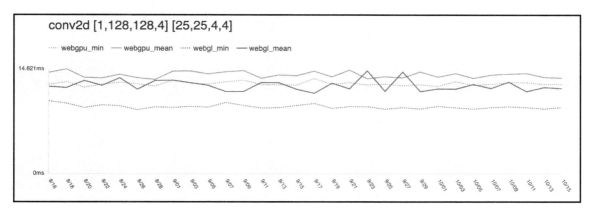

The cause is still not clear. It may be due to the halfway optimization of the WebGPU backend or the nature of the WebGPU API. Either way, it is important to use the appropriate backend implementation for our application.

WebAssembly – where the web meets the hardware instruction set

Another experimental backend for TensorFlow.js uses WebAssembly. **WebAssembly** is often abbreviated to **WASM**, so the file extension is `.wasm`. WebAssembly is a binary instruction set for a stack-based virtual machine implemented in the web browser. WebAssembly is designed to be portable among multiple target machines. It indicates that we can reuse the same WebAssembly code on various kinds of platforms as well as other higher-level languages.

The huge potential benefit of WebAssembly is efficiency and performance. WebAssembly aims to achieve native speed by running code with a common hardware capability that is available on a variety of architectures.

WebAssembly also achieves memory safety by providing a sandbox environment that is implemented in the JavaScript runtime. Enforcing the same security model with the web (for example, same-origin restriction) makes the WebAssembly environment safe. The memory field of WebAssembly is called **linear memory**. A linear memory is a contiguous memory field that is accessed by byte addressing. The page size of the memory is 64 KB. Every WebAssembly runtime has its linear memory isolated from other runtimes. Therefore, we can make sure we prevent constructs such as local variables and the execution stack from being accessed by other applications.

As the following diagram shows, the application is not able to touch the stack field, unlike other major programming languages such as C++, because it is completely separate from the application environment. We can guarantee the variables or classes inside the application are not modified by the WebAssembly program:

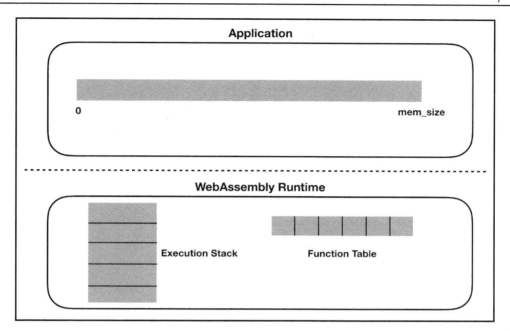

To use the WebAssembly backend of TensorFlow.js, it is necessary to install the **Emscripten SDK** in advance. Emscripten is a tool you can use to build the WebAssembly program. The backend kernels are compiled with the tool:

```
$ git clone https://github.com/emscripten-core/emsdk.git


$ cd emsdk
$ ./emsdk install 1.38.41
$ ./emsdk activate 1.38.41
```

We can build the npm package by running the yarn command:

```
$ cd tfjs/tfjs-backend-wasm
$ yarn build-npm
# You will see the package tensorflow-tfjs-backend-wasm-0.0.1.tgz
```

To include the package in the application, copy the package in the root directory and add the following dependency in the package.json of our application:

```
"dependencies": {
  // ...
  "tfjs-backend-wasm": "file:tensorflow-tfjs-backend-wasm-0.0.1.tgz",
  // ...
}
```

As the WebAssembly backend is not registered automatically, `tf.registerBacked` needs to be called beforehand:

```
import * as tf from '@tensorflow/tfjs';

// Get the backend implementation for WebAssembly
import * as BackendWasm from 'tfjs-backend-wasm';

window.onload = async (e) => {
  const element = document.getElementById('backend_name');
  // Register the backend with priority 3.
  tf.registerBackend('wasm', async () => {
    return new BackendWasm();
  }, 3 /*priority*/);
  // Specify the new backend in the application
  await tf.setBackend("wasm");
  const backendName = tf.getBackend();
  console.log(backendName);
  element.innerText = backendName;

  const t1 = tf.tensor([1,2,3]);
  t1.print();
  // Tensor
  //    [1, 2, 3]
}
```

Although it is a common workflow to register the WebAssembly backend, it may show several errors or exceptions. And keep in mind that the process itself will be changed. As we have shown in the WebGPU benchmark, we can't avoid performing the performance evaluation with our actual application.

React Native – moving forward to mobile-native applications

So far, we have introduced new backends using the standard API implemented in web browsers that are so powerful that we can make our application much more efficient and faster, but the application still runs in the web browser. It is difficult to create an application running outside the web browser by using these backends.

React Native is an open source framework that makes it easy to write an application on a mobile-native platform such as iOS or Android. It allows us to run our application on many native platforms once it is written. React Native wraps the existing native API and enables us to interact with the underlying system transparently.

Once we build our application with React Native, it becomes a cross-platform application:

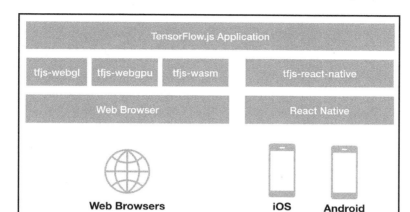

The React Native backend supports GPU acceleration by using the `expo-gl` library. It has competitive performance. Like the other cutting-edge backends, the React Native backend is the alpha release version. The API and its usage will be changed in the next version. In the following section, the API may require some knowledge or familiarity with React Native. Please refer to the official documentation of React Native if you find something unclear.

Creating a React Native app

To create a React Native app, it is common to use the React Native CLI or Expo tool. The React Native CLI is an initial official command-line tool for building a React Native app. But nowadays, using Expo is gaining popularity due to the ease with which you can start a project. Thus, using the Expo client is recommended to build a TensorFlow.js project too.

First, install the client tool in our environment. It takes a few minutes to download the packages:

```
$ npm install -g expo-cli
```

We can create the project with the `init` command. A `npm start` command will run the initial empty app. There are several options to be selected when bootstrapping the project. In this case, choose the minimal project with the TypeScript configuration:

```
$ expo init TensorFlowJSApp
$ cd TensorFlowJSApp
```

```
# Launch a server to provide the application bundle
$ yarn start
```

The command creates the initial project to run the minimal application in the first place for iOS and Android. The application bundle is distributed by the server launched on the machine. There is a dedicated native application to run the bundles in iOS and Android for debug purposes. We can download the Expo client for iOS from the App Store. The following applications are necessary to run a React Native app quickly:

- **Expo Client for iOS**: `https://apps.apple.com/us/app/expo-client/id982107779`.

- **Expo Client for Android**: `https://play.google.com/store/apps/details?id=host.exp.exponent`.

Installing the dependencies required for TensorFlow.js

To run TensorFlow.js with React Native, we need to install several dependent libraries. As they are distributed as `npm` packages, we can add them as follows. The `expo-gl` and `expo-gl-cpp` packages may not necessarily be required if we do not use GPU resources in the mobile device:

```
$ yarn add react-native-unimodules \
    expo-gl-cpp \
    expo-gl \
    async-storage
```

Writing an application

We can find the core of the application in the file named `App.tsx`. It has the main React component launched at the beginning of the application. Here is our full application code to calculate the addition of two tensors. The returned value from the `render()` method is JSX, which is a syntax extension of JavaScript. React Native recommends using JSX to render the UI because it enables us to focus on the components containing both markup and business logic:

```
import React from 'react';
import {Component} from 'react';
import { StyleSheet, Text, View } from 'react-native';

import * as tf from '@tensorflow/tfjs';
import * as tfjsNative from '@tensorflow/tfjs-react-native';
```

```
export default class TensorFlowJSApp extends Component {
  private aStr: string;
  private bStr: string;
  private cStr: string;
  constructor(props) {
    super(props);
    const a = tf.tensor([[1, 2], [3, 4]]);
    const b = tf.tensor([[1, 2], [3, 4]]);

    const c = a.add(b);

    this.aStr = a.toString();
    this.bStr = b.toString();
    this.cStr = c.toString();
  }

  // This method is called when the application renders this components.
  render() {
    return (
      <View style={styles.container}>
        <Text>Hello, TensorFlow.js! {'\n'}{'\n'}{this.aStr} +
{'\n'}{this.bStr} = {'\n'}{this.cStr}</Text>
      </View>
    );
  }
}

// It defines the stylesheet of the component.
const styles = StyleSheet.create({
  container: {
    flex: 1,
    backgroundColor: '#fff',
    alignItems: 'center',
    justifyContent: 'center',
  },
});
```

The application shows the result of a tensor calculation in the UI. To make it simple, the result is passed to the React component as a string.

Running the application

We can use the same method to run the application as we previously did. First, launch the server to distribute the bundled package:

```
$ cd TensorFlowJSApp
$ yarn start
```

We will see the server launch in the web browser since it opens the page to the application automatically. The following screenshot shows the page where we control the React Native application:

The bottom-left QR code is the URL to the endpoint from which to download the application bundle. If the Expo client app is already installed on the mobile device, scanning the QR code will download the app on the device. The Expo client app automatically downloads the app and launches the following scene on your device. This is a screen capture taken on my iPhone.

It shows TensorFlow.js calculation is working correctly:

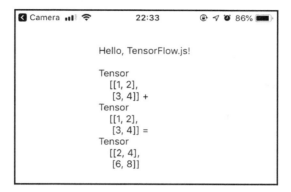

It is also possible to run the application on a simulator running on the local machine. Clicking the **Run on iOS simulator** button in the Expo server launches the iOS simulator. Make sure you install Xcode and the iOS simulator in advance:

If you have an Android simulator on the machine, the application can also be run on Android similarly, by clicking **Run on Android device/emulator**. Bear in mind that the React Native backend is an alpha release version, thus the API and the way to run the application will possibly change in future releases.

Electron – cross-platform desktop environment

While React Native is primarily used to run an application on mobile devices, Electron is a JavaScript platform used for desktop applications. The framework was originally invented by GitHub and is maintained by the open source community. It is designed to hide the features of the underlying platform in terms of the interface module. Once we build the application with Electron, it can be run on any platform that Electron supports.

Electron has its UI components as well as React Native. It gives us transparent access to manipulate the user interface without caring about the details of the platform. Users can get a similar experience across multiple platforms.

There are three files necessary to launch the Electron application:

- `package.json`: Declares the dependencies and build commands for TypeScript
- `index.html`: The front page of the application
- `main.ts`: The entry point where the application starts running

As Electron runs with Node.js, it is necessary to install the `tfjs-node` backend. This is the minimal list of dependencies the application should declare:

```
"devDependencies": {
  "@tensorflow/tfjs": "^1.2.11",
  "@tensorflow/tfjs-node": "^1.2.11",
  "electron": "^6.0.8"
}
```

Our sample application shows the addition of two tensors, as we do for React Native. The page layout can be described by HTML:

```
<!DOCTYPE html>
<html>
  <head>
    <meta charset="UTF-8">
    <title>Hello TensorFlow.js!</title>
  </head>
  <body>
    <h1>Hello TensorFlow.js!</h1>
    <span id='tensor-a'></span> + <br>
```

```
      <span id='tensor-b'></span> = <br>
      <span id='tensor-c'></span>
   </body>
</html>
```

`main.ts` controls the event happening in the Electron application. In this case, it loads the scripts, which should be run in advance, and the front page, `index.html`. `BrowserWindow` is a class representing the main window of the application. `preload` is a script running before the other script on the page. The core of the computation is executed in `preload.ts`:

```
import { app, BrowserWindow } from "electron";
import * as path from "path";

let mainWindow: Electron.BrowserWindow;

function createWindow() {
  mainWindow = new BrowserWindow({
    height: 600,
    width: 800,
    webPreferences: {
      preload: path.join(__dirname, "preload.js"),
    }
  });

  mainWindow.loadFile(path.join(__dirname, "../index.html"));

  mainWindow.on("closed", () => {
    mainWindow = null;
  });
}

// Once the initialization has been completed, the window
app.on("ready", createWindow);
```

This is `preload.ts`, which executes the tensor addition:

```
import * as tf from '@tensorflow/tfjs-node';

window.addEventListener("DOMContentLoaded", () => {
  const replaceText = (selector: string, text: string) => {
    const element = document.getElementById(selector);
    if (element) {
      element.innerText = text;
    }
  };

  const a = tf.tensor([[1, 2], [3, 4]]);
  const b = tf.tensor([[1, 2], [3, 4]]);
```

```
    const c = a.add(b);
    replaceText('tensor-a', a.toString());
    replaceText('tensor-b', b.toString());
    replaceText('tensor-c', c.toString());
});
```

To start the application, we can build the TypeScript and launch the entry point with the electron command:

```
$ tsc && electron ./dist/main.js
```

The application is shown with the following window. The tensor calculation is executed properly:

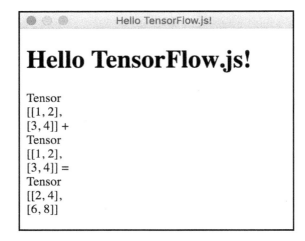

While the web browser is the primary universal platform we are discussing throughout this book, Electron is another important platform for hosting machine learning applications because of the ease with which a native application can be run.

AutoML edge helper

Automated machine learning (**AutoML**) has been getting hugely popular in recent years due to the ease and speed with which the machine learning technology can be applied to real services.

Cloud ML is a service to provide the functionality to train a machine learning model without much knowledge or experience in the machine learning field. All we need to have is the data and labels to be predicted. The system automatically finds the best model and tunes the hyperparameters. We can use the time saved, to build an adequately good model and apply it in our application.

`tfjs-automl` is a library to make the application easily integrate with the AutoML Vision Edge API. It allows us to import the model trained in the AutoML Vision Edge service. We can use the library using a `npm` package:

```
$ npm i @tensorflow/tfjs-automl
```

Alternatively, CDN can be used:

```
<script src="https://cdn.jsdelivr.net/npm/@tensorflow/tfjs-automl"></script>
```

The `tfjs-automl` library supports loading the following two types of model:

- Image classification
- Object detection

It is necessary to ensure that you load three files to make use of the model loaded from AutoML Edge:

- `model.json`: Model structure definition
- `dict.txt`: List of labels
- `*.bin`: Files containing weight parameters

Put these files in a path where our application is able to access them. The `loadImageClassification` method loads the model for the image classification task:

```
import * as automl from '@tensorflow/tfjs-automl';
const modelUrl = 'model.json'; // URL to the model.json file.
const model = await automl.loadImageClassification(modelUrl);
```

The loaded model is used normally, as we saw for the layer model previously. The training process tends to be tedious and time-consuming. Using the AutoML service allows us to offload all the heavy lifting in the machine learning application to the external service.

Summary

In the last part of the book, we covered several on-going projects in the community. These include several new backend implementations that provide us with a chance to use more cutting-edge hardware acceleration technology with TensorFlow.js. The fact that we do not modify the model code encourages us to try and compare several backend environments to find the best one for our application.

Additionally, we introduced a library to run the TensorFlow.js application in native environments (such as mobile- and desktop-based) to expose the application to more users on various kinds of platform. `tfjs-react-native` enables us to run it with React Native and TensorFlow.js can be run on Electron when we use the `tfjs-node` backend without any modifications. Try to port your application onto various kinds of platform. This will enable your application to move forward beyond the web platform to a higher one.

Bear in mind that the framework and libraries introduced in this chapter are experimental or alpha releases. The usage and API could be changed without any announcements in future releases.

Questions

1. Which backend implementations enable us to make use of GPU resources on the web platform?
2. Which web browser does not support the following new standards respectively?
    1. WebGPU
    2. WebAssembly
3. What is `gl_GlobalInvocationID` in the WebGPU context?
4. What's one benefit of using WebAssembly in our application?
5. Are the following platforms supported by React Native?
    1. Windows
    2. macOS
    3. tvOS
6. Can we make use of hardware acceleration such as the GPU in the Electron application?

Further Reading

- The WebGPU Draft: https://gpuweb.github.io/gpuweb/
- WebAssembly: https://webassembly.org
- Emscripten: https://emscripten.org/
- Expo iOS client: https://apps.apple.com/us/app/expo-client/id982107779
- Electron: https://electronjs.org/
- Electron Example: https://github.com/tensorflow/tfjs-examples/tree/master/electron
- AutoML Edge: https://cloud.google.com/vision/automl/docs/edge-quickstart

Other Books You May Enjoy

If you enjoyed this book, you may be interested in these other books by Packt:

Machine Learning for the Web
Andrea Isoni

ISBN: 978-1-78588-660-7

- Get familiar with the fundamental concepts and some of the jargons used in the machine learning community
- Use tools and techniques to mine data from websites
- Grasp the core concepts of Django framework
- Get to know the most useful clustering and classification techniques and implement them in Python
- Acquire all the necessary knowledge to build a web application with Django
- Successfully build and deploy a movie recommendation system application using the Django framework in Python

TensorFlow Machine Learning Cookbook, Second Edition

Nick McClure
ISBN: 978-1-78913-168-0

- Become familiar with the basic features of the TensorFlow library
- Get to know Linear Regression techniques with TensorFlow
- Learn SVMs with hands-on recipes
- Implement neural networks to improve predictive modeling
- Apply NLP and sentiment analysis to your data
- Master CNN and RNN through practical recipes
- Implement the gradient boosted random forest to predict housing prices
- Take TensorFlow into production

Leave a review - let other readers know what you think

Please share your thoughts on this book with others by leaving a review on the site that you bought it from. If you purchased the book from Amazon, please leave us an honest review on this book's Amazon page. This is vital so that other potential readers can see and use your unbiased opinion to make purchasing decisions, we can understand what our customers think about our products, and our authors can see your feedback on the title that they have worked with Packt to create. It will only take a few minutes of your time, but is valuable to other potential customers, our authors, and Packt. Thank you!

Index